THE AMERICAN SCHOOL SUPERINTENDENT

2010 Decennial Study

Theodore J. Kowalski, Robert S. McCord,
George J. Petersen, I. Phillip Young, and Noelle M. Ellerson

Published in partnership with the
American Association of School Administrators

ROWMAN & LITTLEFIELD EDUCATION
A division of
ROWMAN & LITTLEFIELD PUBLISHERS, INC.
Lanham • New York • Toronto • Plymouth, UK

Published in partnership with the American Association of School Administrators

Published by Rowman & Littlefield Education
A division of Rowman & Littlefield Publishers, Inc.
A wholly owned subsidiary of The Rowman & Littlefield Publishing Group, Inc.
4501 Forbes Boulevard, Suite 200, Lanham, Maryland 20706
http://www.rowmaneducation.com

Estover Road,
Plymouth PL6 7PY,
United Kingdom

British Library Cataloguing in Publication Information Available

Library of Congress Cataloging-in-Publication Data

The American school superintendent : 2010 decennial study / Theodore J. Kowalski . . . [et al.].
    p. cm.
  "Published in partnership with the American Association of School Administrators."
  Includes bibliographical references.
  ISBN 978-1-60709-996-3 (cloth : alk. paper)—ISBN 978-1-60709-997-0 (pbk. : alk. paper)—ISBN 978-1-60709-998-7 (electronic)
  1. School superintendents—United States. 2. Educational surveys—United States. I. Kowalski, Theodore J. II. American Association of School Administrators.
  LB2831.72.A44 2011
  371.2'011—dc22

                    2010029733

♾™ The paper used in this publication meets the minimum requirements of American National Standard for Information Sciences—Permanence of Paper for Printed Library Materials, ANSI/NISO Z39.48-1992. Printed in the United States of America

Contents

Figures

Tables

Foreword

Public education in America is constantly changing and evolving, the most recent tide of which emerged in the early 1980s and cemented its foothold with No Child Left Behind in 2002, the most recent reauthorization of the Elementary and Secondary Education Act of 1965. In the wake of this enduring attitude of change, innovation, and reform—both in academic practices and the students and staff who populate America's public schools—school administrators have offered a steady hand in navigating this sea of change. At the same time, the face of America's school superintendency is changing, as well, becoming more diverse and representative of the schools they lead.

Now, more than ever, the work portfolio of America's school superintendents is increasingly diverse: they are responsible for student progress and achievement while balancing the diversification of their student and staff populations, the explosion of technology and the digital divide, an expanded set of expectations and involvement from the federal level, the media, and board and community relations, all in the context of an increasingly globalized education system. The work is difficult, the hours are long, and the job comes with challenges and difficulties. Still, superintendents come back to work, reporting high levels of job satisfaction.

In the year prior to the survey and the year since the results were collected, America was in the throes of the most severe economic recession in history, an unmatched economic downturn outlasted by only one other: the Great Depression. School administrators across the country faced budgetary limitations and, at the same time, received unprecedented levels of federal funding for education. The funding relief was bundled with a unique set of policy implementation rules and regulations, compounding the already tough task of doing less with more. The federal push for innovation and reform is only now starting to fully play out, and the next 10 years will undoubtedly be marked not only by federal, state, and local fiscal recovery but also by the impact of growing federal influence on state and local decisions affecting education.

As the leaders and spokespeople of America's public schools, superintendents play a key role in local, state, and federal policy discussions and decisions, the very dialogues that ultimately impact and shape the future of public education. The weight of these voices and their collective experience are vital contributions to the debates that shape the face of America's public schools.

The 2010 decennial study was subject to change, as well. This edition marked the first time the survey was delivered, administered, and analyzed using an online survey tool. As the professional organization representing more than 13,000 school administrators across the country, the American Association of School Administrators has a keen interest in knowing their members, from their leadership characteristics and pathway to the superintendency to the challenges and opportunities they face in their daily work.

AASA thanks Theodore J. Kowalski, Robert S. McCord, George J. Petersen, I. Phillip Young, and Noelle M. Ellerson for their work in conducting this study. We all benefit from the time and effort these individuals devoted toward data collection and analysis.

This study of the American school superintendency was produced in the context of unprecedented economic hardship and ever-expanding interest in the future of public education. This unique coupling was a further catalyst for innovation and reform in education. Change is indeed inevitable and upon us, though far from final. America's superintendents will be valuable contributors and play a pivotal role in shaping the educational experience for the next generation of students. We hope that this profile of the profession is a resource to current, former, and future superintendents, those who prepare and support superintendents, and any participant involved in the dialogue for education reform, innovation, and change.

Daniel A. Domenech
Executive Director
American Association of School Administrators

Executive Summary

This research is an extension of national studies of school district superintendents that began in the 1920s. Sponsored by the American Association of School Administrators, the research was conducted in late 2009 and early 2010. Most data are reported in four district-enrollment categories—a practice used in preceding studies. By disaggregating data based on district enrollment, the reader is able to discern dissimilarities associated with the challenges faced by superintendents in very small to very large school systems. As findings in this and previous national studies establish, the job-related experiences of superintendents are not homogeneous.

The following findings provide a summary of the entire research study. They are not intended to provide a complete picture of the information that was developed.

Characteristics of Superintendents and Their Employing Districts

- The modal superintendent was a married, White male between the ages of 56 and 60.
- The percentage of female superintendents has increased substantially since 1992. In this study, nearly one in four respondents (24.1%) was a woman.
- In terms of political affiliation, superintendents remained a diverse group, with between 25% and 35% being registered *Democrats, Republicans,* or *Independents.* With respect to political philosophy, however, most (55.3%) considered themselves to be *moderates.* Of the remainder, twice as many (30%) were *conservative;* only 14% identified themselves as *liberals.*
- Only about half (51%) of the respondents said that they planned to still be a superintendent in 2015—a finding suggesting the probability of substantial turnover in the next few years.
- Only about 3% of the respondents in this study were employed in very large districts (i.e., 25,000 or more students), and about 9% were employed in very small districts (i.e., less than 300 students).
- Nearly half of the respondents were employed in low-diversity districts (i.e., fewer than 5% minority residents) and about 15% were employed in high-diversity districts (i.e., more than 51% minority residents).

Professional Experiences

- Most superintendents continued to follow the traditional career path en route to the superintendency via teacher and building-level principal positions.
- In contrast to previous studies, many entered the administrative ranks as an assistant principal rather than a principal.
- A high percentage of superintendents were employed in the position in less than one year after first applying for it.

- Superintendents reported that they were satisfied with their job, schools, programs, and employees in their current assignment.
- Most promising, superintendents indicated that they would follow the same career path if they had it to do over again.
- The level of job satisfaction expressed by superintendents remains very high. The vast majority are pleased with their career choice as evidenced by the fact that a high percentage would again seek to occupy the same position if given a chance to relive their careers.

Elements of Practice

- Distinct differences existed in elements of practice according to school system size with small school districts doing things differently from large school districts.
- With respect to effects on their personal practice, superintendents viewed school boards, other administrators in the district, and their compensation as assets; they viewed state departments of education, the court system, and the media as being neither assets nor liabilities.
- Superintendents viewed labor unions and formal employee associations as having had little influence on elements of their practice.
- Superintendents reported that the most important source for informing elements of their practice were peer superintendents, especially those in comparable school districts.
- Complementing elements of their practice, superintendents reported they are frequent readers of the professional literature and reported what they read to be informative. For example, most superintendents reported reading research frequently or occasionally, and over 90% found the research they read to be beneficial at least occasionally.

Superintendent and School Board Relations

- Compared to 2000, superintendents were almost twice as likely to have provided orientation for new board members.
- The vast majority of policy recommendations made by superintendents were approved by school boards—an outcome that also was reported in 2000.
- The amount of time superintendents spend communicating directly with school board members had increased since 2000.
- Respondents indicated that although their school boards emphasized each of the five major roles traditionally assumed by superintendents, the extent to which they did so varied considerably. The highest level of substantial emphasis was placed on being an *effective communicator*, followed by *manager, instructional leader, statesman/democratic leader*, and *applied social scientist*.
- Two-thirds of the superintendents received annual performance evaluations that included both formative and summative components. The most common criterion used to assess performance was the formal job description.
- Nearly three-fourths of the superintendents reported that their school boards had not been evaluated formally; of those that had been, the vast majority only conducted self-evaluations.
- Few school boards were all male (5.8%), and few were all female (4%). Just under one-fourth of the school boards (22.5%), however, had female majorities. Boards with female majorities were more common in large-enrollment districts than they were in small-enrollment districts.

Gender and Race/Ethnicity

- The percentage of female superintendents increased considerably since the 2000 study. The current representation, 24.1%, is the highest ever reported and substantially higher than the 13.2% reported in 2000.

- Female superintendents, on average, were older and had more teaching experience than their male peers. They were twice as likely to have had more than 20 years of teaching experience before becoming an administrator.
- While males and females both reported the same top three reasons for being selected to their current position (*personal characteristics*, *potential to be a change agent*, and *ability to be an instructional leader*), the most important among females was *to be an instructional leader*, whereas among males, it was *personal characteristics*.
- Superintendents often mentored colleagues aspiring to be administrators and especially those aspiring to be superintendents. About 83% of all respondents reported that they have mentored, and percentages for males and females serving in this role were essentially identical.
- Males, on average, became novice superintendents at an earlier age than did their female peers. More than half (56.3%) of males reached the position by the age of 45, and they were 4 times as likely as women to be a novice superintendent before the age of 36.
- Superintendents, regardless of race or gender, expressed a high level of job satisfaction: 97% of all respondents indicated that they were *very satisfied* or *moderately satisfied* with their position. Similarly, superintendents reported a high probability they would choose the same career path all over again if given the chance: 88.6% of the males and 87.7% of the females answered *definitely yes* or *probably yes*. Likewise, 86.3% of the minority group and 88.6% of the nonminority group answered *definitely yes* or *probably yes*.
- Minority group respondents were considerably more likely to view community diversity as an asset than were members of the nonminority group. Slightly more than half of the former (52.3%) indicated that community diversity was a *major* or *minor asset*, whereas slightly less than one-third of the nonminority group (31.4%) expressed the same opinions.
- Only slight differences existed between minority and nonminority respondents with respect to teaching experience. The modal response in both groups was 6 to 10 years.
- Nonminority group respondents more often entered the superintendency before the age of 46 than did their peers in the minority group.
- Nonminority group respondents were twice as likely as their peers in the minority group to have had more than 12 years of experience as a superintendent at the time of this study.
- Minority group respondents were more than twice as likely as their peers in the nonminority group to report that they had encountered discrimination in their pursuit of the superintendency.

Professional Preparation of Superintendents

- Just over three-fourths of the superintendents (78.7%) rated their preservice academic preparation as *good* or *excellent*.
- The vast majority of superintendents (94.7%) held a valid state license or endorsement for their position. Further, 85% had completed an accredited university program designed to prepare superintendents.
- Slightly less than half (45.3%) of all the responding superintendents possessed an earned doctoral degree. This percentage is identical to the finding reported in 2000. Thus, the trend toward an increasing percentage of superintendents having doctoral degrees reported between 1971 and 2000 was not sustained in this study. Superintendents in districts with 3,000 or more students, however, were much more likely to possess a doctorate than their peers in smaller districts. Just over 70% of the superintendents in these larger districts had a doctorate.
- Most superintendents (81.1%) rated the credibility of their former professors as *good* or *excellent*.
- The four academic courses rated as having the highest levels of importance were *school law*, *school finance*, *school public relations*, and *human resource management*.
- Superintendents were most likely to have attended continuing education provided by state superintendent associations, state government, and AASA.

- Most superintendents (83.3%) rated their continuing education experiences as *useful* or *very useful*.
- Potential continuing education topics identified as having the greatest value were *law/legal issues; finance personnel management; school reform/improvement, superintendent-board relations,* and *school-community relations.*
- The persons most influential in helping the respondents become superintendents were other superintendents. The next most influential persons were school board members and former professors.

Politics, Mandates, Standards, and Government Relations

- Superintendents saw the reform movement, including standards and assessment, as empowering increasing numbers of individuals; organized political action for matters related to curriculum, instruction, and reform, however, was reported generating comparatively less organized political action.
- Superintendents willingly worked with politically empowered individuals. They were less likely to consider coalitions of like-minded empowered individuals (e.g., unions) as an asset.
- Superintendents recognized that the intensity of political action was associated with district size (enrollment); though political action occurred across all districts, it was reported more often by superintendents of large districts.
- Superintendents considered community involvement and parent/family support as essential in relation to forging district missions and visions.
- Superintendents, regardless of the size of the student enrollment, viewed employee groups as assets for building a productive district culture.
- Superintendents generally did not view competition from charter and private schools as a liability for their districts.
- Superintendents, particularly in large districts, viewed diversity as an asset but, at the same time, acknowledged the negative impact of racial tensions.
- Superintendents perceived the loss of local autonomy caused by state and federal standards and assessments and court interventions to be more of a liability than an asset.
- Superintendents saw inadequate funding as a major problem.
- Superintendents viewed the legislative positions taken by AASA generally as representing a balanced political view and meeting their needs.

Acknowledgments

Many persons provided support and assistance to the authors of this study. They are acknowledged here for their contributions to the study. Persons who assisted with the development of the survey and participated in the pilot study also are identified and acknowledged in Chapter 2.

- Daniel Domenech, AASA Executive Director
- Ellen Schoetzau, AASA Associate Executive Director, Member Services
- Bruce Hunter, AASA Associate Executive Director, Advocacy, Policy and Communications
- Sharon Adams-Taylor, AASA Associate Executive Director, Children's Initiatives and Program Development
- Amy Vogt, AASA Director of Public and Media Relations
- Lori Vines, AASA Assistant Director for Membership and Affiliate Services
- Gayane Minasyan, AASA Website and Electronic Communications Manager
- Mary Ann Jobe, AASA Director of Leadership and Development (Persons Assisting with Production)
- Elizabeth A. Pearn, Publications Assistant, School of Education, University of Dayton
- Colleen A. Wildenhaus, Director of Publications, School of Education, University of Dayton
- Michael Amakyi, Doctoral Assistant, University of Dayton
- Lesley A. McCue, Doctoral Assistant, University of Dayton
- Karen Holsey Young, Science Department Chair, Fresno (CA) Unified School District (Persons Assisting with the Development and Validation of the Survey)
- Dr. John Box, Senior Vice-President-Education, JA Worldwide
- Dr. Kenneth Burnley, Director, Educational Leadership Center, University of Michigan
- Dr. David Dolph, Clinical Assistant Professor, University of Dayton
- Dr. Paul Dugan, Former Superintendent, Washoe County School District, Reno, Nevada
- Dr. Lew Finch, Former Superintendent, Cedar Rapids, Iowa
- Dr. Steve Grant, Former Superintendent, Tri-County North Local School District, Lewisburg, Ohio
- Dr. Timothy Ilg, Associate Professor, University of Dayton
- Dr. Paul Koehler, Former Superintendent, Peoria, Arizona
- Dr. Dennis Leone, Former Superintendent, Chillicothe City School District, Chillicothe, Ohio
- Dr. T. C. (Chris)Mattocks, Associate Professor, Bridgewater State College
- Dr. Daniel Raisch, Associate Dean and Associate Professor, University of Dayton
- Dr. Phillip Tieman, Administrator in Residence, University of Dayton
- Dr. Michael Virelli, Former Superintendent, Little Miami School District, Morrow, Ohio

1

Historical and Contemporary Perspectives

Since its founding, the American public education system has experienced multiple reform periods, each reflecting evolving needs, values, and political conditions. Current efforts to improve public elementary and secondary schools accelerated in the early 1980s after state policymakers began promulgating intensification mandates and accountability measures. By 1990, however, criticisms of their coercive approach had become pervasive, especially but not exclusively among teachers, administrators, and school board members. Disfavor was nested in empirical evidence, mainly student test data, revealing that the mandates had failed to produce the scale of improvement intended (Kowalski, Petersen, & Fusarelli, 2007). Yielding to public disfavor, policymakers in many states augmented their original coercive strategy by incorporating aspects of a popular private-sector concept known as directed autonomy (Weiler, 1990). Specifically, they (a) retained their earlier mandates, (b) set new broad improvement goals, (c) allowed local school officials discretion to determine how they would meet the goals, and (d) then held the local officials accountable for outcomes (Kowalski, Petersen, & Fusarelli, 2007). The evolution of school reform was subsequently shaped by the passage of the No Child Left Behind Act of 2001 (2002), which set even more performance standards for districts and schools.

By 2010, most superintendents and principals realized that their responsibilities in relation to school reform had expanded, requiring them to both design and carry out needed changes. Specifically, they had become responsible for determining *what* needed to be improved and for deciding *how* improvement initiatives would be carried out. Forging reforms at the local level, however, is clearly more difficult and risk-laden than just implementing state mandates because critical decisions, mired in uncertainty, must be made at a point where individual rights intersect directly with societal rights (Levin, 1987, 1999). On the one hand, parents seek to control the experiences, influences, and values expressed to their children in school at the same time that superintendents and school board members seek to determine the experiences, influences, and values society wants reproduced through a common public school curriculum (Gutmann, 1987). The resulting collision of professionalism and democracy is neither obscure nor inconsequential (Kowalski, 2009). Specifically in the case of superintendents, these administrators are expected to lead by relying on professional knowledge to make school-improvement recommendations, but they are expected to do so while remaining subservient to the will of the people (Wirt & Kirst, 2009).

Understandably, when the mission and vision of public education are altered, superintendents are affected, sometimes dramatically. This fact illuminates the importance and value of the national studies of the superintendency—research that dates back at least to 1920. To fully appreciate the complexity of this pivotal position and its evolution over more than 100 years, one must understand how roles and responsibilities have waxed and waned over time and how current social, educational, and professional issues affect their relevance in current practice.

Evolution of the Superintendency

Using a discursive analysis that relied heavily on rhetoric and writings from 1865 to 1965 (Brunner, Grogan, & Björk, 2002), historian Raymond Callahan (1962, 1966) concluded that four separate role conceptualizations of the school district superintendent—teacher-scholar, business manager, statesman, and applied social scientist—had emerged prior to 1970. Though each had been preeminent at a point in history, the emergence of new roles did not render previous ones irrelevant (Cuban, 1976). Consequently, the position of superintendent kept getting more demanding and complex, and that pattern persists to this day.

Nearly 2 decades after Callahan detailed the four conceptualizations, America transitioned from a manufacturing-base to an information-base. Reflecting on this societal change, Drucker (1999) claimed that all organizations had entered a new era—the Information Age. Analyzing how districts and schools were affected, Kowalski (2001, 2005, 2006) contended that a fifth distinct role conceptualization for superintendents had been institutionalized—the superintendent as effective communicator.

Superintendent as Teacher-Scholar

A conceptualization of superintendent as a teacher-scholar was dominant from approximately 1865 to 1910. During this period, the intent was to "have a person work full time supervising classroom instruction and assuring uniformity of curriculum" (Spring, 1990, p. 141). Persons selected for this position were typically males who were considered effective teachers. At the time, neither academic degrees nor courses in educational administration existed. Hence, superintendents essentially functioned as lead educators, subordinate to the board members but superior to principals, teachers, and pupils (Kowalski, 2006). In addition to supervising employees, they gave advice to the school board and completed written reports as required or directed (Gilland, 1935). Many local school boards actually were reluctant about hiring a superintendent, fearing that the person in the position would garner political power at their expense. When forced to employ a superintendent, boards, especially in larger districts, often resisted yielding authority over financial and personnel decisions (Carter & Cunningham, 1997).

Superintendents in large city districts were recognized as scholars because they frequently authored professional journal articles about philosophy, history, and pedagogy (Cuban, 1988). More than a few of them became state superintendents, professors, and even college presidents (Petersen & Barnett, 2005). The characterization of superintendent as teacher-scholar was summarized in an 1890 report on urban superintendents: "It must be made his recognized duty to train teachers and inspire them with high ideals; to revise the course of study when new light shows that improvement is possible; to see that pupils and teachers are supplied with needed appliances for the best possible work; to devise rational methods of promoting pupils" (Cuban, 1976, p. 16).

Superintendent as Business Manager

The conceptualization of superintendent as business manager emerged after 1910 and remained dominant for nearly 3 decades. Clearly, the Industrial Revolution and its tenets—classical theories and principles of scientific management—were instrumental in shaping the second role conceptualization. Specifically, many school boards in large city districts believed that innovations applied in burgeoning industries to produce technical efficiency could be equally effective if they were applied in public schools (Norton, Webb, Dlugosh, & Sybouts, 1996; Tyack, 1972). And as the new role gained acceptance, some school boards placed more emphasis on a superintendent's managerial skills than they did on his or her teaching skills.

Two groups of educators—professors and big-city superintendents—were instrumental in institutionalizing the business management conceptualization. Prior to 1910, there were no university courses in educational administration (Cubberley, 1924). After that point, however, a few courses were created at Teachers College, Columbia University, and professors at that and other institutions capitalized on the opportunity to develop a specialization that was separate from and superior to teaching (Callahan, 1962).

Why prominent superintendents supported the establishment of educational administration as a sub-specialization of the education profession has been debated by prominent scholars for some time. Callahan, for example, concluded the superintendents were essentially vulnerable "dupes" intent on appeasing school board members who valued efficiency. Other scholars, such as Burroughs (1974), Eaton (1990), and Tyack (1972) disagreed with Callahan's thesis of vulnerability. Rather than casting the superintendents as weak victims, they portrayed them as cunning, intelligent, political pragmatists who had responded to social realities. Thomas and Moran (1992) offered yet another conclusion. They classified these superintendents as opportunists, administrators who embraced industrial management in order to shed their persona as teachers and to expand and protect legitimate power. Motives aside, historians agree that the new role of superintendent as business manager produced what Schneider (1994) described as a control core culture—that is, an authoritative, impersonal, and task-oriented set of values and beliefs.

Superintendent as Statesman

Again, a social event, this time the Great Depression, gave rise to a new role conceptualization. The collapse of the stock market had eroded much of industrial management's glitter, and after 1930, citizens became more reluctant to accept the premise that superintendents should have more power at the expense of local citizen control (Kowalski, 2006; Kowalski, Petersen, & Fusarelli, in press). Several leading scholars at the time, such as George Sylvester Counts, relentlessly criticized the application of classical theories and scientific management in public schools, arguing that these ideas were incompatible with the core democratic values (Van Til, 1971). Collectively, concerns about centralization and managerial control gave rise to the conceptualization of the superintendent as statesman.

The statesman role was anchored in the concept of democratic administration, a concept championed by Ernest Melby, a former dean of education at Northwestern University and New York University (Callahan, 1966). Arguing that the community was public education's greatest resource, he urged administrators to "release the creative capacities of individuals" and "mobilize the educational resources of communities" (Melby, 1955, p. 250). As a statesman, a superintendent was expected to galvanize support for education (Howlett, 1993), a responsibility that had obvious political implications. Some authors, such as Björk and Gurley (2005), contend that statesmanship and democratic leadership were acceptable terms for political behavior.

After World War II, population growth, school consolidation, and research in the social sciences sparked new ideas about school governance and administration. Most notably, the concept of representative democracy was presented as a more effective alternative to democratic localism (a concept in which citizens actively engage in debate and attempt to influence policy based on individual rights). The proposed transition was based primarily on two contentions: public administration had become complex, and most citizens neither had the time nor expertise necessary to engage in policymaking (Katz, 1971; Levin, 1987).

Superintendent as Applied Social Scientist

By the mid-1950s, democratic administration was being disparaged as an overly idealistic and inattentive concept incapable of providing solutions to complex social and economic problems. Critics argued that superintendents embracing this role conceptualization were focused on political philosophy rather than on the emerging social sciences (Björk & Gurley, 2005). Concurrently, the nation was adjusting to post–World War II demographic changes, such as an increase in school-age children and the creation of new school districts in newly established suburbs. Collectively, these contextual variables spawned a fourth conceptualization, the superintendent as applied social scientist (Callahan, 1966).

The underlying intent of the fourth role was to develop superintendents who possessed "a greater sensitivity to large social problems through an interdisciplinary approach involving most of the social sciences" (Kellogg Foundation, 1961, p. 13). In sum, superintendents as applied social scientists were expected to solve education problems endemic in a multicultural, democratic society (Sergiovanni, Burlingame, Coombs, & Boyd, 1999) by relying on empiricism, predictability, and scientific certainty (Cooper & Boyd, 1987). As this new role gained acceptance, the professional preparation of superintendents became more extensive (Kowalski, 2009), less practice-based, and more theoretical (Fusarelli & Fusarelli, 2005). It was not uncommon in the 1960s and 1970s to require doctoral students in educational administration to complete a cognate in one of the behavioral sciences—such as psychology, economics, political science, or sociology (Kowalski, 2009). By the early 1960s, however, Callahan warned that the applied social scientist conceptualization could create superintendents who would be "high-level technicians, expert at keeping their organization going but not equipped to see or understand where they are going" (1966, p. 227).

Superintendent as Communicator

Historically, schools have had closed climates, an institutional characteristic that discouraged community interventions (Blase & Anderson, 1995) and encouraged teachers and administrators to work individually and in seclusion (Gideon, 2002). For the most part, superintendents were socialized to emulate business executives who had accepted the classical model of organizational communication as their norm. This paradigm encouraged them to emphasize their power and dominance (Burgoon & Hale, 1984) and to issue instructions and commands down a chain of command and only from them to the person or persons below (Luthans, 1981). As a result of accepting this behavior, many administrators learned to communicate impersonally and unilaterally (Achilles & Lintz, 1983).

Fifty years ago, popular books on administrative communication (e.g., Thayer, 1961) commonly identified only four communication functions: informing, instructing (or directing), evaluating, and influencing. Based on this narrow point of view, communication effectiveness usually was evaluated by the quality of messages managers composed and transmitted downward (Clampitt, 1991). Circa 1980, however, scholars (e.g., Guzley, 1992; Trombetta & Rogers, 1988) began to challenge the classical communication model, contending that the paradigm usually had negative effects on employee commitment, job satisfaction, and overall organizational effectiveness. Moreover, researchers found that poor communication was a pivotal factor determining perceptions of administrator effectiveness (Richmond, McCroskey, Davis, & Koontz, 1980; Snavely & Walters, 1983).

Today, a confluence of reform initiatives and the realities of the information-based society in which they are pursued have transformed normative communicative behavior for superintendents (Kowalski, 2001, 2005). Specifically, administrators now are expected to initiate and facilitate school improvement by collaborating with school employees, students, parents, and other stakeholders (Björk, 2001; Murphy, 1994). And in order to do this, they have to build and maintain positive relationships with a broad spectrum of stakeholder groups (Kowalski, Petersen, & Fusarelli, 2007). Thus, the classical model of communication has been replaced by the relational model of communication. According to Burgoon and Hale (1984) and Grunig (1989), relational communication is consistent (as opposed to situational), open, two-way, and symmetrical (i.e., intended to benefit all interactants). Further, it is intended to minimize formal authority and actual power differences (Burgoon & Hale, 1984) and to focus on both communicative behavior and mutual perceptions of communicative behavior (Littlejohn, 1992).

Though many administrators never study communication in the context of their professional responsibilities (Osterman, 1994), they clearly are judged on the basis of their communicative behavior. Studies centered on performance evaluation (e.g., Beverage, 2003; Peterson, 1999) and on administrator dismissals (Davis, 1998) reveal the penalties they incur if they are seen as incompetent and inconsistent communicators.

Synthesis of Role Conceptualizations

Since the late 1880s, five distinct role conceptualizations have developed and been described in the literature. As noted earlier, their importance has fluctuated depending on prevailing social conditions, but none has become irrelevant to modern practice. Thus, the contemporary superintendent is expected to wear five different hats, and she or he is expected to know when to transition among the roles. The need to function in all five roles is arguably greatest in small school systems, where superintendents have no professional support staff at the district level.

Conditions of Current Practice

As extant literature reveals, a great many issues and problems remain relevant to the position of district superintendent and to the administrators who occupy it. These concerns are dynamic, and they influence what federal, state, and local policymakers expect from superintendents. They are summarized here as social, education, and professional matters.

Social Issues

Social challenges are an amalgam of philosophical, demographic, economic, and fiscal issues that concurrently create demands for services from public schools and resistance to proposed changes. Protracted calls for school reform provide the quintessential example. Both the emergence of a global economy and America's transition to an information-based society spawned massive school-improvement efforts. They were nested primarily in the following convictions:

- The quality of public elementary and secondary education had declined markedly, thus jeopardizing the country's status as the world's dominant economic power (National Commission on Excellence in Education, 1983).
- The decline in school effectiveness was due primarily to unchallenged and lazy students and incompetent educators (Kirst, 1988).
- Educators, and especially superintendents, were not inclined to initiate major changes (DeYoung, 1986).

The first wave of school reform occurring during the 1980s essentially made students and educators do more of what they always had been doing. The results, at least those measured by state achievement tests, were modest at best (Hawley, 1988). Nevertheless, policymakers have not abandoned their fondness for political-coercive change strategies as evidenced by the No Child Left Behind Act of 2001 (2002). Instead, they have pursued mandates and school restructuring simultaneously (Kowalski, Petersen, & Fusarelli, 2007). The pursuit of restructuring is predicated on the belief that organizational characteristics of districts and schools, especially institutional culture, had to be reconfigured (Fullan, 1994). The quest for transforming schools shifted the burden for some reform decisions to the local level and had profound implications for both superintendents and principals (Leithwood, 1994). Rather than simply carrying out mandates, superintendents were expected to play pivotal leadership roles—most notably, determining the real needs of local schools and engaging a broad spectrum of stakeholders to determine how those needs would be met (Kowalski, 2006).

At the same time, however, superintendents and the districts in which they were employed were experiencing a rise in social problems that concurrently broadened demands for education services and made it more difficult to institutionalize changes. Mounting crime rates, acts of violence on school property, and escalating operating costs are examples. Changes in student needs and community complexity, though, were arguably the most pertinent problems. Across the country, the number of students living in poverty (Anyon, 2005), the number of immigrant students (Fix & Passel, 2003), and the number of students living without both parents (Kreider, 2008) were steadily increasing. And the population in many school districts became more diverse, resulting in the probability that any proposed change to improve schools would be opposed by one or more political factions (Wirt & Kirst, 2009).

In summary, social conditions over the past few decades have had discernible effects on most superintendents and most school districts. Many stakeholders are not highly satisfied with public schools, and even more are reluctant to put forth greater fiscal effort to support them.

Education Issues

The superintendency also is being affected by issues related to public elementary and secondary education and school governance. Perhaps, the most glaring matter in this category is the vast differences that exist across the nearly 14,000 local school systems providing direct services to local residents. As a consequence of their dissimilarities across and within states, these organizations have different needs, problems, resources, and philosophies. This variability affects both the type of person employed as superintendent and the performance expectations for those occupying the position. Consequently, generalizations about the superintendency and about superintendents can be deceptive.

Over time, another institutional issue receiving substantial attention from researchers has been superintendent and school board relationships. Interest in this topic is understandable given the fact that these associations affect both a superintendent's employment status and district effectiveness (Björk & Keedy, 2001; Petersen & Fusarelli, 2001). The nature of relationships developed between a superintendent and school board members often determines real and perceived administrative roles. In large measure, this reality explains why the work of superintendents, even in neighboring school districts, may vary considerably. In the 2000 AASA study (Glass, Björk, & Brunner, 2000), for example, superintendents were divided with respect to seeing themselves as a professional advisor (47.7%) or as a dominant decision maker (49.5%).

School reform is another decisive issue and has regenerated questions about the mission of public schools. From the point at which they were established, public elementary and secondary schools in this country received their designated purposes exclusively or primarily from state government (Coleman & Brockmeier, 1997). Until approximately 1950, their assigned purpose was reproductive in nature. Specifically, they were to prepare "numerate and literate citizens and workers by institutionalizing prevailing cultural norms, values, beliefs, and attitudes" (Kowalski, 2006, p. 311). Then, the mission was broadened to include readjustment. Expressly, schools were expected to amend pedagogy and curriculum as necessary but without altering traditional institutional structures. Circa 1980, the imposed mission was broadened again, this time by adding a reconstructive element. In particular, public schools were to reorganize as necessary to ensure that they met the emerging needs of society as well (Johnson, Collins, Dupuis, & Johnson, 1988). This most recent aspect of mission is visibly more complex than readjustment because it requires substantial changes to school climate (e.g., how schools are built, organized, and operate). Moreover, reproduction focusing on social conservation, continuity, and stability inherently conflicts with reconstruction focusing on proactive change. Because schools are expected to initiate institutional change while maintaining social stability, superintendents often feel "that regardless of what they do, they are wrong" (Kowalski, 2006, p. 311).

Even if social reproduction were not an issue, restructuring public schools would be a formidable task, primarily because school district stakeholders usually have dissimilar philosophies and political dispositions. As a result, any proposed change inevitably will be resisted by some stakeholders (Scoolis, 1998). Equally notable, conflict generated by school-improvement initiatives often reinforces educator beliefs that institutionalizing changes is an unattainable goal (Fullan, 2001). Yet, many authors (e.g., Bauman, 1996; Fullan, 2001; Sarason, 1996) stress that low-performing schools will not improve sufficiently unless they are restructured. Additionally, changes will not be institutionalized unless prevailing change-resistant school cultures are modified. In this vein, one of the greatest institutional issues facing current superintendents (and top executives across all types of organizations) is culture change (Schein, 1996).

In schools, culture not only shapes perspectives on student learning, but also it shapes decision-making norms, attitudes toward problem solving (e.g., the value of research), and relationships (Joyce & Murphy, 1990). If the underlying and shared assumptions in a district or school are negative (i.e., convictions incongruous with the professional knowledge base and counterproductive to school improvement), they will thwart school improvement. Moreover, they will be sustained unless educators come to see them as detrimental and understand why they are. As a change agent, the contemporary superintendent is expected to determine shared beliefs and their influence on school effectiveness. And if these beliefs are found to be negative, a superintendent needs to demonstrate why they are harmful and engage in cultural reconstruction (Fullan, 2001). These difficult assignments have elevated the critical nature of superintendent relationships, credibility, and trust—with school boards, district employees, and all other stakeholders (Kowalski, Petersen, & Fusarelli, 2007).

Professional Issues

Educators consider themselves professionals, and this certainly applies to superintendents, the members of this group who typically are the most highly educated and compensated. Professions are essentially "occupations with special power and prestige. Society grants these rewards because professions have special competence and esoteric bodies of knowledge linked to central needs and values of the social system" (Larson, 1977, p. x). True professions are characterized by (a) a knowledge base developed through research and shared experiences, (b) the licensing of practitioners based on a prolonged period of professional study prior to and during practice, (c) codes of ethics, and (d) practitioner autonomy (Kowalski, 2004, 2009). The scope of professional knowledge required for practice and the manner in which knowledge and skills are acquired have become increasingly important in a society where practitioners are expected to be near perfect in exercising authority. That is, society has come to expect that licensed practitioners will not err in making critical decisions (May, 2001).

Examining the contemporary superintendent through the lens of professionalism produces an array of actual and perceived problems. Three are addressed here because they are arguably among the most pervasive and crucial issues in this category.

Underrepresentation of Women and Persons of Color

In 1910, 8.9% of school superintendents were female, and over the remainder of that century, this statistic fluctuated hitting a historic low of 1.2% in 1982 (Blount, 1998) and a high of 13.2% in 2000 (Glass, Björk, & Brunner, 2000). Yet, toward the end of the 20th century, women comprised 65% of teachers, 43% of principals (Shakeshaft, 1999), 57% of central-office administrators, and 33% of the assistant and associate superintendents (Hodgkinson & Montenegro, 1999). Likewise, the representation of people of color in the superintendency remains problematic, especially when considered in relation to total population data and student enrollment data. In 1980, 2.1% of superintendents were in this demographic group (Cunningham & Hentges, 1982); since then, the figure increased to 3.9% in 1992 and to 5.1% in 2000 (Glass, Björk, & Brunner, 2000). Some analysts (e.g., Simmons, 2005) point out, however, that the rise in superintendents of color may be attributable to an increasing number of unattractive positions, such as those in troubled school districts.

Academic Preparation

There are approximately 600 institutions offering courses, degrees, or licensure programs for education administrators, though not all of them have superintendent preparation programs. Any generic reference to academic preparation, therefore, is ill-considered and unfair (Björk, Kowalski, & Young, 2005). The attention given to academic preparation by various commissions, associations, and journals has been substantial since 1980. A literature review produces a vast array of criticisms, including (a) low academic admission and completion standards (e.g., Clark, 1989; Guthrie & Sanders, 2001), (b) a general indifference toward instructional leadership (e.g., Björk, Kowalski, & Browne-Ferrigno, 2005; Grogan & Andrews, 2002; Murphy, 2002, 2007), (c) a disjunction between theory and practice (Björk, Kowalski, &

Young, 2005; Elmore, 2007; Hoy, 1996), (d) inattention to practice-based research (Foskett, Lumby, & Fidler, 2005; Heck & Hallinger, 2005; Kowalski, Place, Edmister, & Zigler, 2009), (e) an inadequate knowledge base (Cooper, Fusarelli, Jackson, & Poster, 2002), (f) a proclivity to treat superintendent preparation as an extension of principal preparation (Glass, Björk, & Brunner, 2000; Glass & Franceschini, 2007), and (g) considering a doctorate in educational administration as the equivalent of superintendent preparation (Grogan & Andrews, 2002).

Despite such concerns, the number of institutions, both traditional and nontraditional, preparing superintendents keeps growing. Many of the new providers previously had no mission in educational administration, and though some are portrayed as innovative, rigorous, and practice-based, facts suggest otherwise (Levine, 2005). The proliferation of academic programs is largely attributable to the absence of a national curriculum, a characteristic and requirement in virtually all other professions, and continuing efforts to deregulate state requirements for being superintendents (Kowalski, 2004).

State Licensing

Licensing criteria for most professions in the United States have been and remain highly uniform across states, supposedly because they are based on core aspects of a homogeneous curriculum that must be completed as a condition for entering practice (Connelly & Rosenberg, 2003). In education, however, licensing policy was often developed politically rather than professionally—that is, elected officials and not members of the profession determined licensing criteria. Consequently, when compared to other professions, the nexus between preparation and licensing is unique; specifically, licensing criteria have shaped preparation programs (Wise, 1992, 1994), whereas in other professions, the inverse has been true.

The issue of professionalism (and hence, licensing) has been especially contentious with respect to district superintendents. As early as 1910, elected officials in large cities were suspicious of school administrators who claimed to be professionals, fearing that this status would allow school officials to acquire political power (Callahan, 1962). Actually, tensions between democracy and professionalism go back to the formative years of this country. Conflict between these two concepts, though, has been especially obvious in public education, where schools have been governed under the concept of local control (Wirt & Kirst, 2009). Addressing the tug-of-war between democracy and professionalism, Sykes wrote,

> Democracy institutionalizes distrust. Professionalism relies on trust. Because we distrust our rulers, we have instituted a system of checks and balances to prevent any interest of office from amassing too much power. Because certain practices rest on expertise and knowledge not widely distributed in the populace, we trust professionals on their pledge to use such knowledge in the best interests of their clients. These two systems of preference formation, service delivery, and authority allocation appear fundamentally at odds with one another, and the great historical puzzle is how a strong form of professionalism flourished just in the world's greatest democracy. (1991, p. 137)

More recently, efforts to eliminate or attenuate licensing for superintendents have been reinvigorated by widespread dissatisfaction with public education and purported shortages of qualified practitioners. *Better Leaders for America's Schools: A Manifesto*, published by the Broad Foundation and Thomas B. Fordham Institute (2003), is a prime example of a concerted effort to de-professionalize the superintendency. Over the past 2 decades, many states have reconsidered licensing policy for administrators. In a 2003 study, Feistritzer reported that though 41 states still require preparation and licensing for superintendents, over half of them (54%) have provisions allowing waivers or emergency certificates to be issued. In addition, she found that 15 of the 41 states (37%) allow or sanction alternative routes to licensure (i.e., other than university-based study). In a study of three contiguous states requiring superintendent licensure, Kowalski (2008a) found substantially dissimilar requirements among the states.

Summary

In order to appreciate the complexity of the superintendency and persons occupying the position, one must know the past and present. This pivotal position of school superintendent has evolved over more than 100 years, and contemporary practice is affected by a range of issues, which take on varying levels of importance from state-to-state and district-to-district. The 10-year studies, sponsored solely by the American Association of School Administrators (AASA) since 1971, are framed by these realities and by the conviction that in order to appreciate research findings, one must have a reasonably accurate understanding of the position.

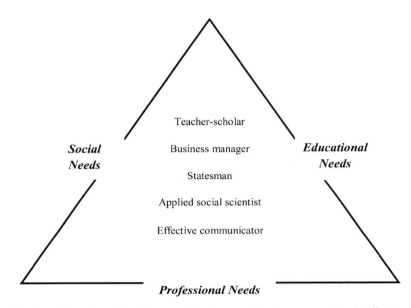

Figure 1.1   Superintendent Role Conceptualizations and Contemporary Needs Affecting Practice

2

Methodology

This study is an extension of research conducted approximately every 10 years that began in 1923. Earlier studies were sponsored by the Department of Superintendence, then a division of the National Education Association (NEA). Both the 1952 and 1960 studies were published jointly by the American Association of School Administrators (AASA) and the research division of NEA. Beginning in 1971 and continuing to this study, the sole sponsor has been AASA.

Reports of the previous studies have been published in various formats; however, the most recent have been released as a book. Contained in Table 2.1 is a list of all the decade studies, including the current study.

Although the content of these studies has varied, all the reports have defined the position, described the persons in the position, and analyzed the roles assumed by superintendents. Some aspects of the previous studies naturally emphasized contemporary issues and concerns. The following are examples of focused issues relative to certain time periods:

- The 1933 study, conducted during the height of the Great Depression, included a section on the role public schools would play in vitalizing economic and social growth.
- The 1952 study included data addressing similarities and differences between urban and rural superintendents.
- The 1960 study gave focused attention to superintendent preparation, then a pivotal topic generated by efforts to infuse theory and the behavioral sciences into school administration courses.
- The 1971 study included approximately one hundred questions about aspects of the position, the persons in the position, and the school districts employing them. This format has recurred in all subsequent studies.

Data Collection

Study Population

The defined population addressed in this study is all superintendents employed in local school districts providing direct education services to students within their assigned school district. Excluded are persons holding the title of superintendent but not meeting other criteria included in this definition (e.g., a superintendent of an educational service center or a state superintendent). At the time the research was conducted, the size of the defined population was estimated to be approximately 12,600.

Although all superintendents were eligible to complete the electronic survey developed for this study, a total of 1,867 opted to do so. As data in Table 2.2 verify, the respondents were employed in school districts across the United States, and thus, they provided a national perspective about the roles and responsibilities of contemporary district superintendents.

Table 2.1 Decade Studies on the Superintendency

Year	Title	Authors
1923	The Status of the Superintendent in 1923	Charles E. Chadsey
1933	Educational Leadership	Not listed
1952	The American School Superintendency (30th yearbook)	Not listed
1960	Profile of the School Superintendent, 1960	Not listed
1971	The American School Superintendent	Stephen J. Knezevich
1982	The American School Superintendency	Luvern L. Cunningham & Joseph Hentges
1992	The Study of the American School Superintendency	Thomas Glass
2000	The Study of the American School Superintendency	Thomas Glass, Lars Björk, & C. Cryss Brunner
2010	The American School Superintendent: 2010 Decennial Study	Theodore Kowalski, Robert McCord, George Petersen, I. Phillip Young, & Noelle Ellerson

Note: A study was not conducted circa 1940 due to World War II.

Data Sources

This study used a mixed method approach as sources for data for assessing the reactions of superintendents to their roles and to their responsibilities in current job assignments. One data source was archival and included research from past studies addressing the superintendency. These data were obtained from the professional literature, especially as reported by those taking part in past studies following the same research stream as this study (i.e., the studies listed in Table 2.1). The second data source was perceptions of standing superintendents. These self-reported perceptions of their current position were based on contextual perspectives that were purposefully aligned with past AASA-sponsored studies in this research stream.

Instrumentation

In this study, perceptions of standing superintendents were assessed relative to facets of their job assignment from multiple perspectives expressed via responses on an electronic survey. The survey instrument contains 88 items with varying formats. Some items are multiple choice (i.e., select a single response), while other items are multiple response (i.e., select all responses that apply).

Items comprising this survey met one of two criteria. They were included to provide a degree of continuity for data reported in past AASA-sponsored studies. Or they were included to address contemporary concerns of superintendents, especially as related to new legislation and to reform efforts in the public school setting.

After potential items were selected for inclusion in the initial survey instrument, content validity was assessed by a panel of experts. Panel members were invited to participate based on two qualifications: their past experiences as practicing superintendents in the public school setting and their current experiences as professors. Table 2.3 provides the names of the panel members and personal information pertinent to their qualifications.

The panel of experts was asked to review the proposed instrument relative to content associated with the roles and responsibilities of standing superintendents in the public school setting. Based on the recommendations of the panel of experts concerning the content of the proposed instrument, some items were deleted, some items were modified, and new items were included. After revising the survey instrument to comply with the panel's recommendations, a pilot test was performed with practicing school superintendents.

Table 2.2   Geographic Distribution of Responders by Location

Location	f	%
Alabama	19	1.03%
Alaska	12	0.65%
Arizona	36	1.96%
Arkansas	25	1.36%
California	76	4.13%
Colorado	32	1.74%
Connecticut	21	1.14%
District of Columbia	0	0.00%
Delaware	7	0.38%
Florida	7	0.38%
Georgia	33	1.80%
Hawaii	1	0.05%
Idaho	12	0.65%
Illinois	136	7.40%
Indiana	48	2.61%
Iowa	60	3.26%
Kansas	47	2.56%
Kentucky	22	1.20%
Louisiana	8	0.44%
Maine	8	0.44%
Maryland	7	0.38%
Massachusetts	39	2.12%
Michigan	111	6.04%
Minnesota	88	4.79%
Mississippi	8	0.44%
Missouri	71	3.86%
Montana	24	1.31%
Nebraska	57	3.10%
Nevada	5	0.27%
New Hampshire	9	0.49%
New Jersey	69	3.75%
New Mexico	11	0.60%
New York	98	5.33%
North Carolina	13	0.71%
North Dakota	12	0.65%
Ohio	106	5.77%
Oklahoma	54	2.94%
Oregon	22	1.20%
Pennsylvania	70	3.81%
Rhode Island	5	0.27%
South Carolina	10	0.54%
South Dakota	35	1.90%
Tennessee	11	0.60%
Texas	94	5.11%
Utah	9	0.49%
Vermont	8	0.44%
Virginia	26	1.41%
Washington	48	2.61%
West Virginia	6	0.33%
Wisconsin	85	4.62%
Wyoming	17	0.92%
Total	1838	100.00%

Table 2.3 Panel of Experts Addressing Content Validity

Panel member	Background
Kenneth Burnley	Dr. Burnley is currently a senior resident fellow and director of the Educational Leadership Center at the University of Michigan. He formerly was superintendent in Fairbanks, Alaska, Colorado Springs, Colorado, and CEO of the Detroit Public Schools. In 2008, he was named the AASA Superintendent-of-the-Year.
Timothy J. Ilg	Dr. Ilg is an associate professor in the Department of Educational Leadership at the University of Dayton in Dayton, Ohio. His research interests include distance learning and the impact of small high schools on urban children. He has 30 years' experience in public education, including 23 years in a large urban school district. Prior to his present position, he was superintendent of the Oakwood City Schools in Ohio. He currently assists the *Knowledge Works Foundation* in the creation of small urban high schools and Early College High Schools associated with local universities.
T. C. (Chris) Mattocks	Dr. Mattocks received his doctorate in educational leadership from Montana State University and prior to his present position as associate professor at Bridgewater State University, he spent 43 years in public elementary and secondary education. His most recent administrative position was as superintendent of the Bellingham, Massachusetts, school district from 2002 to 2008. He teaches courses in school law, finance, personnel administration, and the superintendency.
C. Daniel Raisch	Dr. Raisch is an associate professor and associate dean in the School of Education and Allied Professions at the University of Dayton where he has been on the faculty since 1991. He completed his Ph.D. at Miami University and his research interests include school finance, school law and educational leadership. He has published articles in the *Education Law Journal*, the *Journal of Research and Policy Studies*, *Encyclopedia of Administration, Education and Urban Society*, and *School Business Affairs*. He was a public school educator for 30 years; 25 as an administrator and 18 of which were as a superintendent.
Phillip Tieman	Dr. Tieman is the Administrator in Residence in the School of Education and Allied Professions at the University of Dayton where he has been on the faculty since 2001. He completed his Ph.D. at The Ohio State University and his teaching and research interests include educational leadership, the superintendency, community relations, school finance and business management, and administrative internship programs. He has published in *Key Legal Issues for Schools* and was a public school teacher and principal and served as a superintendent of schools for 33 years in Ohio, New Jersey, and New York.

Table 2.4 Pilot Study Participants

Person	*Current or most previous position*
Dr. John Box	Senior vice-president-education, JA Worldwide
Dr. Kenneth Burnley	Director, Educational Leadership Center, University of Michigan
Dr. David Dolph	Clinical assistant professor, University of Dayton
Dr. Paul Dugan	Former superintendent, Washoe County School District, Reno, Nevada
Dr. Lew Finch	Former superintendent, Cedar Rapids, Iowa
Dr. Steve Grant	Former superintendent, Tri-County North Local School District, Lewisburg, Ohio
Dr. Timothy Ilg	Associate professor, University of Dayton
Dr. Paul Koehler	Former superintendent, Peoria, Arizona
Dr. Dennis Leone	Former superintendent, Chillicothe City School District, Chillicothe, Ohio
Dr. T. C. (Chris) Mattocks	Associate professor, Bridgewater State College
Dr. Daniel Raisch	Associate dean and associate professor, University of Dayton
Dr. Phillip Tieman	Administrator in residence, University of Dayton
Dr. Michael Virelli	Former superintendent, Little Miami School District, Morrow, Ohio

Participants in the pilot study ($n = 13$) were asked to complete the proposed instrument and to make recommendations about format as well as content. Their names are listed in Table 2.4. Based on the reactions of pilot study participants, modifications were made again prior to administration with the defined population.

Procedure

In November 2009, AASA contacted all superintendents meeting the study population criteria and having an obtainable e-mail address. The communication, sent via e-mail, informed the superintendents about this study, requested their participation in it, and provided instructions regarding accessing the survey via the Internet. Several weeks later, AASA sent a follow-up e-mail requesting those who had not yet responded to do so. A third e-mail, sent in mid-December 2009, advised those who had not yet responded that they could submit the survey in hard copy via U.S. mail by downloading it and sending it to AASA. All analyzed surveys were completed between December 1, 2009, and January, 31, 2010.

Data Analyses

Completed surveys were analyzed by K12 Insight, a private research firm, in February 2010. Because the responses represent a working population reflecting the perceptions of standing superintendents, only frequencies and percentages for response items are reported throughout the ensuing chapters of this book. To align current reactions of superintendents with superintendents of the most recent past study of the superintendency (Glass, Björk, & Brunner, 2000), consideration of school size relative to student enrollments is reflected in most tables.

3

Characteristics of Superintendents and Their Employing Districts

Over time, researchers and practitioners have expressed considerable interest in the demographic profiles of superintendents. These reports are composed of data detailing characteristics of a defined human or organizational population. They are created and analyzed to enhance our understanding of a population's evolutionary nature and its stability in relation to dynamic social, economic, and political conditions.

This chapter's content is divided into two sections. The first addresses the demographic profile of superintendents in 2010; the second addresses the demographic profile of the school districts that employed them.

Personal Characteristics of Superintendents

After studying the first 100 years of the superintendency, Tyack and Hansot provided the following description of the persons in this important position: "there was remarkable similarity in the personal characteristics of these school leaders. The profession has been dominated by married, middle-aged, White males, who have a strong religious (usually Protestant) background" (1982, p. 118). Since 1980, however, there have been discernible changes in this profile, especially with respect to gender. The profile provided here includes gender, race/ethnicity, age, marital status, membership in professional organizations, career intentions, and political dispositions. Gender and race/ethnicity also are addressed in Chapter 7 where comparisons are made between and among subgroups.

Gender

Though females have never been a majority, their representation in the superintendency fluctuated considerably since the late 1800s. By 1910, for example, 8.9% of the superintendents were women (Blount, 1998). During the first half of the previous century, two factors increased access to the position for females. First, there were many small rural school districts and, thus, many more superintendents than there are today, and, women's presence as teachers in these districts assisted in their occasional transfers into administrative ranks (Shakeshaft, 1999). Second, the suffrage movement opened doors, allowing women to access public administrative positions (Brunner, 1999). Because males always have constituted a substantial majority in the position, a growing number of researchers (e.g., Brunner & Grogan, 2007; Grady, Ourada-Sieb, & Wesson, 1994; Grogan, 1996) over the past few decades have examined gender-related issues in the position. Virtually all of them have concluded the superintendency has been and remains a masculine role.

The lowest level of representation during the previous century was a mere 1.2% reported in 1982 (Glass, 1992). Arguably, many factors contributed to the declining numbers of female superintendents after 1950, including intolerable ones such as gender discrimination and stereotyping (Kowalski & Brunner, 2005). One other factor, however, was school district consolidation. After World War II, state policymakers focused more intently on adequacy and efficiency, and as a result, many small school systems, some employing female superintendents, were absorbed into larger systems (Kowalski, 2006; 2010). Since 1982, however, the percentage of female superintendents has been increasing incrementally. As examples, the percentage increased to 6.6% in 1992 and to 13.2% in 2000 (Glass, Björk, & Brunner, 2000). Interestingly, women are more prevalent as superintendents in large urban districts than they are in districts generally. The Council of the Great City Schools (2008–2009), a coalition of 66 of the nation's largest urban public school systems, reported that in 2008, 34% of its member superintendents were women, 20% were African American females, 12% were White females, and 2% were Hispanic females.

Among superintendents responding in this study, 24.1% were females as shown in Figure 3.1. This is a substantial increase over the past decade as demonstrated by a comparison of findings from recent AASA studies provided in Figure 3.2.

Race/Ethnicity

Historically, African Americans have constituted a substantial portion of persons of color in the superintendency. Prior to 1954, most of them were employed in rural, racially segregated school systems, predominately in southern states. But after the U.S. Supreme Court found the concept of separate but equal public schools to be unconstitutional, their numbers dropped considerably (Collier, 1987). In truth, even before this point in time, the representation of persons of color in the superintendency had been "shamefully small" (Kowalski, 2006, p. 321).

According to Simmons (2005), superintendents of color face several challenges beyond those facing all superintendents. One is accessing the superintendency, and another is the fact that they are often employed in problem-ridden, low-performing districts. Large urban districts are likely the only category of school systems where superintendents of color have constituted a majority. According to the Council of the Great City Schools (2008–2009), in 2008, 42% of the member superintendents identified themselves

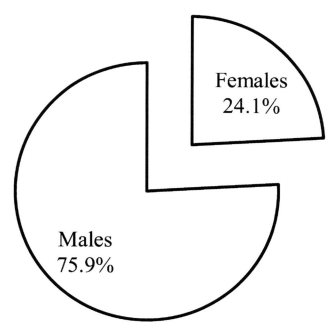

Figure 3.1   Percentage of Female and Male Superintendents in 2010

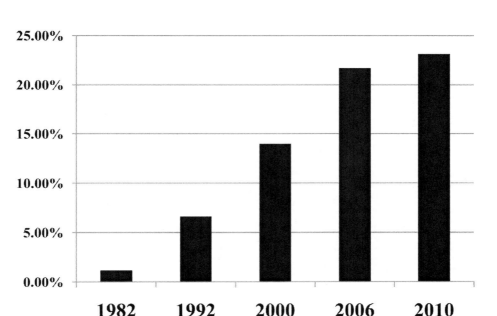

Figure 3.2   Percentages of Female Superintendents since 1982

as Black and another 10% as Hispanic. Figures reported by the council are higher than those reported in the 2000 AASA study; the latter study found that only 23% of the superintendents in districts with 25,000 or more students were persons of color (Glass, Björk, & Brunner, 2000).

In the 2000 AASA study (Glass, Björk, & Brunner, 2000), 5.1% of the respondents self-identified in some category other than *White (not Hispanic or Latino)*. Collectively, these respondents constituted the minority group in that research. In the 2006 mid-decade study, the minority group increased to 6.1% (Glass & Franceschini, 2007). In this study, it was 6%. Consequently, the percentage of non-White superintendents participating in this study was 0.9% higher than it was in the 2000 study but 0.1% lower than it was in the 2006 study. Race/ethnicity data for respondents in this study, based on categories designated in the United States census, are shown in Table 3.1.

The modest increase in the percentage of superintendents of color actually has been occurring over the past 30 years as confirmed by findings reported in 1980 (Cunningham & Hentges, 1982), 1990 (Jones & Montenegro, 1990), and 2000 (Glass, Björk, & Brunner, 2000). The trend is illustrated in Figure 3.3.

Age

Previous AASA studies indicate that between 1950 and 1991, the median age of superintendents hovered around 48 to 50. In 1992, the estimated median age increased to 52.5, the highest reported in any of the national studies up to that point (Glass, Björk, & Brunner, 2000). Median ages, however, were estimated and not actual. This was because data were collected in age range categories.

Findings in this study show notable differences between 2000 and 2010 with respect to age distributions. In 2000, only 9.8% of the superintendents were less than 46 years old; in 2010, 14.6% were in this category—a 50% increase in superintendents below age 46. At the other end of the spectrum, only 8% in 2000 were older than age 60; in 2010, 18.1% were in this age category—a 126% increase in superintendents above age 60. In this study, 25 respondents (1.3% of those completing the survey) did not answer the question pertaining to age. Figure 3.4 illustrates age grouping changes showing that the percentage of both younger and older superintendents has increased. Data for all age categories are shown in Table 3.2, disaggregated by district enrollment.

Table 3.1   Superintendent Profile: Race/Ethnicity

Response choices	District enrollment									
	Fewer than 300		300 to 2,999		3,000 to 24,999		25,000 or more		All	
	f	*%*	*f*	*%*	*f*	*%*	*f*	*%*	*f*	*%*
American Indian or Alaska Native	8	4.6	14	1.3	5	1.0	0	0.0	27	1.5
Asian	0	0.0	0	0.0	4	0.8	1	1.8	5	0.3
Black or African American	3	1.7	7	0.7	21	4.1	5	8.8	36	2.0
Hispanic or Latino	3	1.7	14	1.3	15	3.0	4	7.0	36	2.0
Native Hawaiian or other Pacific Islander	0	0.0	0	0.0	0	0.0	0	0.0	0	0.0
White (not Hispanic or Latino)	159	91.9	1022	96.3	464	91.2	47	82.50	1692	94.0
Other	0	0.0	4	0.4	0	0.0	0.0	0	4	0.2
Total	173	100.0	1061	100.0	509	100.0	57	100.0	1800	100.0

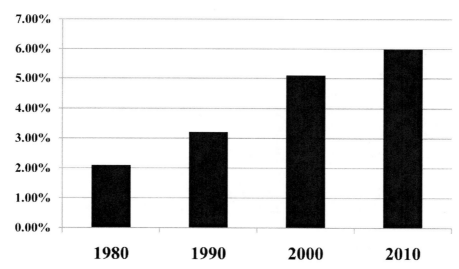

Figure 3.3   Superintendents of Color: 1980 to 2010

Marital Status

In the 2000 AASA study, marital status data were reported only in two categories: married and single. In this study, additional response choices were provided in an effort to produce more precise information. Results are shown in Table 3.3.

If categories in the 2010 study are collapsed by merging "married" and "legally separated" into one group (married) and by merging the remaining categories into a second group (single), a direct comparison of findings from 2000 and 2010 is possible. This interface reveals a 1.3% decline in married superintendents over the past decade; in 2000, 92.5% were married, and in 2010, 91.2% were married.

Membership in Professional Organizations

Respondents were asked to identify professional organizations in which they are current members. Percentages reported are based on the total number of superintendents who completed surveys. Respondents were able to identify more than one organization. The percentage of respondents who were AASA members, 76.4%, was nearly identical to findings reported in 1992 (76.6%) but slightly higher than the 75.9% reported in 2000 (Glass, Björk, & Brunner, 2000). All response data for organizational membership are contained in Table 3.4.

Expectedly, the highest levels of membership were in state superintendent organizations and AASA, both organizations that have a long history of serving the needs and interests of superintendents. Nearly half the respondents were members of the Association for Supervision and Curriculum Development.

Career Intentions

Career intentions have been viewed in two perspectives. The first focuses on an intent to remain in the position (superintendent) as opposed to moving to a different position in the education profession (e.g., teacher or professor) or outside the education profession (e.g., business executive). The second focuses on whether superintendents intend to remain in the superintendency and to change employers (e.g., becoming a superintendent in a larger school district) as opposed to remaining employed in the same district regardless of the position (Kowalski, 2006). Seminal research by Carlson (1969) described these two groups as *career-bound* and *place-bound* superintendents. The former are persons focused on career advancement, and they are willing to relocate in order to achieve their objectives; the latter are persons focused on remaining in a specific location or with a specific employer.

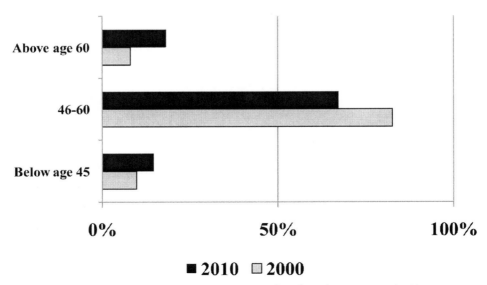

Figure 3.4   Age Categories: Comparison of Findings from 2000 and 2010

Table 3.2   Superintendent Profile: Age

Age	District enrollment									
	Fewer than 300		300 to 2,999		3,000 to 24,999		25,000 or more		All	
	f	%	f	%	f	%	f	%	f	%
<36	2	1.2	19	1.8	0	0.0	1	1.8	22	1.2
36–40	10	5.8	50	4.7	13	2.5	0	0.0	73	4.0
41–45	16	9.2	111	10.4	42	8.2	2	3.6	171	9.4
46–50	22	12.7	154	14.4	59	11.5	2	3.6	237	13.1
51–55	45	26.0	272	25.4	119	23.2	9	16.1	445	24.5
56–60	54	31.2	297	27.7	164	32.0	22	39.3	537	29.6
61–65	20	11.6	147	13.7	97	18.9	15	26.8	279	15.4
66>	4	2.3	22	2.1	18	3.5	5	8.9	49	2.7
Total	173	100.0	1072	100.0	512	100.0	56	100.0	1813	100.0

Table 3.3   Superintendent Profile: Marital Status

Response options	District enrollment									
	Fewer than 300		300 to 2,999		3,000 to 24,999		25,000 or more		All	
	f	%	f	%	f	%	f	%	f	%
Married	154	89.5	953	90.6	464	91.3	53	94.6	1624	90.8
Single	8	4.7	30	2.8	16	3.2	2	3.6	56	3.1
Divorced	7	4.1	56	5.3	23	4.5	1	1.8	87	4.9
Legally separated	1	0.6	5	0.5	0	0.0	0	0.0	6	0.4
Widowed	2	1.1	8	0.8	5	1.0	0	0.0	15	0.8
Total	1720	100.0	1052	100.0	508	100.0	56	100.0	1788	100.0

In this study, respondents were asked to identify where they intended to be professionally in 2015. Responses are contained in Table 3.5.

Combined, the first two response choices in Table 3.5 reveal that only 50.7% of the respondents intend to be superintendents in 2015. This finding foretells of a substantial number of career exits in the

Table 3.4   Superintendent Profile: Membership in Professional Organizations

Response choices	f	%
American Association of School Administrators	1426	76.4
Association of School Business Officials	167	8.9
Association for Supervision and Curriculum Development	890	47.4
National Association of Elementary School Principals	59	3.2
National Association of Secondary School Principals	110	5.9
State Superintendent Association	1661	89.0
Other associations	233	12.5
No memberships listed	23	1.2

Note: Respondents were able to select all response options that applied. Percentages reported are based on the number of superintendents who completed surveys.

next 5 years.* Among superintendents who intend to retire by 2015 ($n = 778$), 75.3% plan to continue working part-time post retirement. Though data in Table 3.5 provide no direct information about the extent to which the respondents were career-bound superintendents, the fact that less than 1 in 5 (18.8%) intend to be a superintendent in a different school system in 5 years is noteworthy. This finding suggests that the number of current superintendents who will seek to change employers in order to remain in the position (i.e., career-bound superintendents) is rather limited.

Political Dispositions

The nexus between school administration and politics has a long and interesting history. For much of the last century, authors often used terms such as *democratic leadership* and *statesmanship* when referring to political behavior advocated for and carried out by superintendents (Björk & Gurley, 2005). In reality, many superintendents must compete with other heads of public agencies to garner scarce resources for the schools and students they serve (Cooper, Fusarelli, & Randall, 2004). Moreover, ideological and moral differences among community factions require them to manage pervasive conflict (Keedy & Björk, 2002). In a democracy, policy and politics are squarely joined, and consequently, superintendent political proclivities remain relevant to understanding district administration.

In the 2000 AASA study (Glass, Björk, & Brunner, 2000), respondents were almost evenly divided with respect to political party preference, with approximately one-third Democrats, one-third Republicans, and one-third independents. This study included a slightly different question. Rather than being asked to identify party preference, respondents were asked to identify party affiliation. Only 91% of those taking the survey replied to this question. Results are presented in Table 3.6.

---

* Career exits are defined as leaving a specific position, in this case the superintendency, without an intention of returning to it. Conversely, turnovers are defined as a change of personnel in a given position regardless of the underlying reason for the change (Kowalski, 2008a).

Table 3.5 Superintendent Profile: Career Plan in 2015

Response options	f	%
Being retired but continuing to work part-time	586	32.0
Remaining in current position	584	31.9
Remaining a superintendent but in a different district	344	18.8
Being retired and not employed in any capacity	192	10.5
Being a college or university professor	56	3.1
Being a district administrator other than superintendent	25	1.4
Being a full-time employee outside of education	18	1.0
Being a full-time education consultant	17	0.9
Being a college or university administrator	6	0.3
Being an elementary or secondary school teacher	1	0.1
Total	1829	100.0

At first glance, comparisons to data reported in the 2000 study indicate a decline in the percentage of Republicans (33.5% in 2000 and 28.4% in 2010) and Independents (31.5% in 2000 and 24.6% in 2010) and an increase in the percentage of Democrats (35.0% in 2000 and 37.3% in 2010). However, the 2000 survey question and the 2010 survey question were dissimilar in two ways. First, the 2010 question asked for political party affiliation; the 2000 survey asked for political party preference. Second, the 2010 survey provided six response choices; the 2000 survey provided only three response choices (*Democrat, Independent,* and *Republican*). Among the 1,699 superintendents answering this question in 2010, a notable number (9.2%) selected *None*.

Only 93% of those completing the survey elected to answer the question pertaining to political philosophy. Results are contained in Table 3.7. Because the question and response options were virtually identical to those contained in the 2000 survey, a comparison of findings was made, and the results are contained in Table 3.8.

As data in Table 3.8 reveal, the percentage of superintendents identifying themselves as liberals increased slightly, and the percentages of superintendents identifying themselves as moderates and conservatives declined slightly. Nevertheless, the ranking of the three philosophy categories was unchanged; moderates continued to constitute the majority, and there were approximately twice as many conservatives as there were liberals. More data on political issues are contained in Chapter 9.

Characteristics of Employing Districts

The demographic profile of the typical school district has changed considerably over the past century. As examples, fewer taxpayers have children enrolled in the public schools, growing numbers of school-

Table 3.6   Superintendent Profile: Political Party Affiliation

| Response choices | District enrollment | | | | | | | | | |
| | Fewer than 300 | | 300 to 2,999 | | 3,000 to 24,999 | | 25,000 or more | | All | |
	f	%	f	%	f	%	f	%	f	%
Democrat	66	40.7	339	34.2	203	41.4	26	47.3	634	37.3
Republican	55	34.0	299	30.1	116	23.7	13	23.6	483	28.4
Independent	29	17.9	252	25.4	123	25.1	13	23.6	417	24.6
Libertarian	0	0.0	1	0.1	3	0.6	0	0.0	4	0.2
None	12	7.4	97	9.8	44	9.0	3	5.5	156	9.2
Other	0	0.0	4	0.4	1	0.2	0	0.0	5	0.3
Total	162	100.0	992	100.0	490	100.0	55	100.0	1699	100.0

aged children are being reared in poverty, and most communities have become increasingly diverse, ethnically, religiously, and culturally (Kowalski, 2008b). There also are far fewer school systems than in the past. In 1937, there were approximately 119,000 school districts in the United States. By 2001, the number fell to 14,859 (Snyder & Hoffman, 2003). Inconstant terminology and classifications, however, have made it difficult to identify the total number of school districts precisely.

In 2007, there were 17,775 local education agencies (LEAs); however, only 13,924 of them were responsible for educating students residing within their jurisdiction (Chen, 2009). Therefore, the latter number arguably provides the most accurate total. Most local school districts are independent legal entities (i.e., distinct corporations or quasi corporations under state law). Some, however, are dependent legal entities because they are part of or subordinate to other government agencies, such as a county or city.

There are substantially fewer superintendents than there are districts. In some states, one superintendent may be employed to administer multiple districts (Kowalski, 2006). At the time of this study, there were an estimated 12,600 district-level superintendents in the United States.

Enrollment

Historically, most data reported in the AASA decade studies have been disaggregated by district enrollment categories. In order to permit comparisons to previous studies, the same process and same enrollment categories were used in this study. Data for the distribution of employing school districts in 2010 are shown in Table 3.9. Note that 29 respondents did not answer the question regarding district enrollment.

Enrollment changes (i.e., increases or decreases in student enrollment) for the employing districts varied considerably with slightly more experiencing a loss of students than an increase of students. The percentages of districts experiencing declines, increases, or no appreciable changes are provided in Figure 3.5, and all responses for district enrollment change are contained in Table 3.10.

Table 3.7   Superintendent Profile: Political Philosophy

Response options	District enrollment									
	Fewer than 300		300 to 2,999		3,000 to 24,999		25,000 or more		All	
	f	%	f	%	f	%	f	%	f	%
Conservative	62	38.8	338	33.3	111	21.9	9	16.7	520	30.0
Liberal	20	12.5	139	13.7	86	17.0	8	14.8	253	14.6
Moderate	78	48.8	536	52.9	308	60.9	37	68.5	959	55.3
Other	0	0.0	1	0.1	1	0.2	0	0.0	2	0.1
Total	160	100.0	1014	100.0	506	100.0	54	100.0	1734	100.0

Community and District Racial/Ethnic Composition

The fact that America is becoming a more diverse nation with respect to race/ethnicity has been widely reported by demographers. The comparison of enrollments in public elementary schools since 1996 (Snyder, Dillow, & Hoffman, 2009) is provided below:

Category	1996	2006
White	64.2%	56.5%
Black	16.9%	17.1%
Hispanic	14.0%	20.5%
Asian/Pacific Islander	3.8%	4.7%
American Indian/Alaska Native	1.1%	1.2%

If enrollments in both public and private elementary schools are combined, the statistics are different. Below are the combined data for school year 2003–2004 reported by the U.S. Department of Education (n.d.):

- White, 59%
- African American, 17%
- Hispanic, 19%
- Asian/Pacific Islander, 4%
- American Indian/Alaskan Native, 1%

These data reveal two important facts about the demographics for elementary and secondary students in this country: the overall population has become more diverse since the mid-1990s; the student population in public schools alone is slightly more diverse than the combined student population of public and private schools.

Three aspects of racial/ethnic diversity in school districts were examined in this study. The first is the diversity of the total population residing within districts; findings are provided in Table 3.11. The second is diversity of the student population; findings are provided in Table 3.12. The third is the diversity of district employees; findings are provided in Table 3.13.

Overall, the districts had a higher percentage of minority students than they did minority employees. As examples, just over one-third (35.5%) reported having more than 15% minority students, but only 14.5% reported having more than 15% minority employees. Conversely, 47% reported having less than 6% minority students, but 71.4% reported having less than 6% minority employees.

Table 3.8   Superintendent Profile: Comparison of Political Philosophy in 2000 and 2010

Response options	2000 Study (n = 2201)		2010 Study (n = 1734)	
	f	%	f	%
Conservative	713	32.4	520	30.0
Liberal	243	11.0	253	14.6
Moderate	1245	56.6	959	55.3
Other	N/A	0.0	2	0.1
Total	2201	100.0	1734	100.0

Table 3.9   Distribution of Respondents by District Enrollment

Enrollment category	f	%
Fewer than 300 students	174	9.4
300 to 2,999 students	1082	58.9
3,000 to 24,999 students	524	28.5
25,000 or more students	58	3.2
Total	1838	100.0

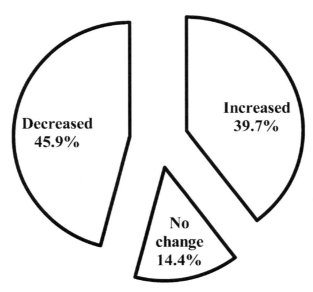

Figure 3.5   District Enrollment Changes

Table 3.10   Employing Districts' Profile: Enrollment Changes since October 1, 1999

| Response options | District enrollment | | | | | | | | | |
| | Fewer than 300 | | 300 to 2,999 | | 3,000 to 24,999 | | 25,000 or more | | All | |
	f	%	f	%	f	%	f	%	f	%
Increase of 25% or more	3	1.7	43	4.0	42	8.1	6	10.3	94	5.2
Increase of 20–24%	0	0.0	18	1.7	11	2.1	2	3.5	31	1.7
Increase of 15–19%	5	2.9	24	2.2	17	3.3	2	3.5	48	2.6
Increase of 10–14%	7	4.1	47	4.4	24	4.7	6	10.3	84	4.6
Increase of 5–9%	10	5.8	79	7.4	43	8.3	6	10.3	138	7.6
Increase of less than 5%	16	9.3	165	15.4	133	25.8	13	22.4	327	18.0
No change	26	15.0	158	14.7	70	13.6	8	13.8	262	14.4
Decrease of less than 5%	24	13.9	206	19.2	100	19.4	11	19.0	341	18.7
Decrease of 5–9%	28	16.2	133	12.4	43	8.3	1	1.7	205	11.3
Decrease of 10–14%	15	8.7	73	6.8	18	3.5	2	3.5	108	5.9
Decrease of 15–19%	11	6.4	51	4.8	9	1.7	1	1.7	72	4.0
Decrease of 10–24%	9	5.2	41	3.8	1	0.2	0	0.0	51	2.8
Decrease of 25% or more	19	11.0	35	3.5	5	1.0	0	0.0	59	3.2
Total	173	100.0	1073	100.0	516	100.0	58	100.0	1820	100.0

Summary

The purpose of this chapter is to provide foundational information about superintendents and the school districts employing them. Much more information about both topics is provided in the subsequent chapters. Though the modal superintendent remained a White male, the number of female superintendents has increased substantially, and the number of superintendents of color has increased slightly over the past decade. Compared to 2000, slight changes were noted with respect to marital status, political affiliation, and political philosophy. The modal age range has changed from 51 to 55 in 2000 to 56 to 60 in 2010. In 2010, 89% of the respondents were members of a state superintendent organization, and 76% were AASA members. The next highest organizational membership was reported for ASCD (47%).

Among respondents in this study, 68% were employed in districts with less than 3,000 students. In approximately 46% of these districts, enrollment had decreased in the past 5 years, and in approximately 40%, enrollment had increased during the same period. The remainder reported no appreciable enrollment change. Data also reveal that districts overall have more students from minority racial and ethnic groups than they do employees from minority racial and ethnic groups. Slightly over half the districts (53%) have enrollments in which 6% or more are from minority racial and ethnic groups.

Table 3.11   Employing Districts' Profile: Percentage of Racial/Ethnic Minorities in the Total Population

Response options	District enrollment									
	Fewer than 300		300 to 2,999		3,000 to 24,999		25,000 or more		All	
	f	%	f	%	f	%	f	%	f	%
5% or less	99	58.2	642	60.5	111	21.7	0	0.0	852	47.0
6 to 15%	21	12.4	158	14.9	134	26.2	12	21.4	325	17.5
16 to 25%	8	4.7	82	7.7	92	18.0	10	17.9	192	8.9
26 to 50%	25	14.7	81	7.6	99	19.3	20	35.7	225	12.1
51% or more	17	10.0	98	9.2	76	14.8	14	25.0	205	14.5
Total	170	100.0	1061	100.0	512	100.0	56	100.0	1799	100.0

Table 3.12   Employing Districts' Profile: Percentage of Racial/Ethnic Minority Students

Response options	District enrollment									
	Fewer than 300		300 to 2,999		3,000 to 24,999		25,000 or more		All	
	f	%	f	%	f	%	f	%	f	%
5% or less	101	58.1	641	59.7	109	21.4	1	1.8	852	47.0
6 to 15%	19	10.9	161	15.0	126	24.7	12	21.1	318	17.5
16 to 25%	9	5.2	71	6.6	76	14.9	6	10.5	162	8.9
26 to 50%	21	12.1	91	8.5	94	18.4	13	22.8	219	12.1
51% or more	24	13.8	109	10.2	105	20.6	25	43.9	263	14.5
Total	174	100.0	1073	100.0	510	100.0	57	100.0	1814	100.0

Table 3.13   Employing Districts' Profile: Percentage of Racial/Ethnic Minority Employees

Response options	District enrollment									
	Fewer than 300		300 to 2,999		3,000 to 24,999		25,000 or more		All	
	f	*%*	*f*	*%*	*f*	*%*	*f*	*%*	*f*	*%*
5% or less	134	77.0	866	80.4	292	56.1	14	24.6	1306	71.4
6 to 15%	16	9.2	104	9.7	123	23.7	14	24.6	257	14.1
16 to 25%	14	8.0	44	4.1	39	7.5	10	17.5	107	5.8
26 to 50%	9	5.2	39	3.6	53	10.2	14	24.6	115	6.3
51% or more	1	0.6	24	2.2	13	2.5	5	8.7	43	2.4
Total	174	100.0	1077	100.0	520	100.0	57	100.0	1828	100.0

4

Professional Experiences

The focus of this chapter is on the professional experiences of superintendents. Content is divided into three sections. The first examines data related to accessing a first superintendency, the second examines data while in the superintendency, and the third includes opinion data about experiences in the superintendency.

Accessing the Superintendency

Age at the Time of First Superintendency

In the 2000 study (Glass, Björk, & Brunner, 2000), results revealed that many superintendents (49%) obtained their first administrative position before age 30. In this study, the modal age for entering the position was 46 to 50 years old; approximately one-fourth of the superintendents entered the position in this age range. Only 13.3% of the respondents entered it before the age of 36.

Collectively, data in Table 4.1 reveal that the first assignment, as a superintendent, is likely to come at mid-career stages (i.e., chronological ages between 41 and 55 years). Findings indicate that individuals are more than twice as likely to become a superintendent before the age of 41 than after the age of 55. All response data for the age at first superintendency are in Table 4.1.

Level of First Teaching Position

The traditional career path for most superintendents involves moving through the organizational hierarchy of a public school district (Kowalski, 2006). That is, most superintendents have entered the education profession as teachers and then became building-level administrators (Glass, Björk, & Brunner, 2000). This particular career path leading to a superintendent's position was driven, no doubt, in the past by state certification requirements. Many states required prior teaching and principal-level experiences as prerequisites to superintendent licensing. Although this requirement has been waived by several states during the most recent decade, most of the superintendents taking part in this study have followed this typical career progression en route to the superintendency.

Analysis of teaching experiences was conducted using the results of several survey questions. One was the level of a respondent's first teaching experience. Outcomes are reported in Table 4.2. Just under half of the superintendents (45.2%) began teaching at a *high school*, and when the two secondary levels of schooling (*high school* and *middle school*) are combined, the data reveal that nearly two-thirds of the superintendents (65.4%) began teaching at the secondary school level.

Table 4.1 Age for First Superintendent Position

Response options	District enrollment									
	Fewer than 300		300 to 2,999		3,000 to 24,999		25,000 or more		All	
	f	*%*	*f*	*%*	*f*	*%*	*f*	*%*	*f*	*%*
Less than 36	26	15.1	151	14.0	56	10.9	8	14.0	241	13.3
36–40	26	15.1	180	16.7	87	17.0	8	14.0	301	16.6
41–45	33	19.2	223	20.7	92	18.0	8	14.0	356	19.6
46–50	48	27.9	258	24.0	127	24.8	13	22.8	446	24.5
51–55	25	14.5	193	17.9	100	19.5	13	22.8	331	18.2
56–60	12	7.0	60	5.6	43	8.4	6	10.5	121	6.7
61 or greater	2	1.2	11	1.0	7	1.4	1	1.8	21	1.2
Total	172	100.0	1076	100.0	512	100.0	57	100.0	1817	100.0

Table 4.2 First Teacher Position

Response options	District enrollment									
	Fewer than 300		300 to 2,999		3,000 to 24,999		25,000 or more		All	
	f	*%*	*f*	*%*	*f*	*%*	*f*	*%*	*f*	*%*
Special education	8	4.7	82	7.6	52	10.0	6	10.3	148	8.1
Elementary school	45	26.2	213	19.8	129	24.9	16	27.6	403	22.1
Middle school	29	16.9	209	19.4	121	23.3	9	15.5	368	20.2
High school	85	49.4	526	48.9	191	36.8	22	37.9	824	45.2
Counselor	1	0.6	16	1.5	3	0.6	0	0.0	20	1.1
Therapist	0	0.0	4	0.4	4	0.8	0	0.0	8	0.4
College teaching	2	1.2	5	0.5	7	1.3	2	3.4	16	0.9
No teaching	1	0.6	3	0.3	8	1.5	3	5.2	15	0.8
Other	1	0.6	18	1.7	4	0.8	0	0.0	23	1.3
Total	172	100.0	1076	100.0	519	100.0	58	100.0	1825	100.0

Amount of Teaching Experience

Respondents in this study were asked to identify the number of years they had been a teacher. The results are shown in Table 4.3. Less than 1% reported having no teaching experience; the modal experience range was 6 to 10 years. Equally noteworthy, only 7% reported having more than 21 years of teaching experience.

Interestingly, superintendents in school districts with 25,000 or more students had less teaching experience than peers in the other three district-enrollment categories; for example, only 3.8% of the superintendents in these very large districts had more than 15 years of teaching experience, whereas 27.7% of superintendents in districts with less than 300 students did so. One plausible explanation for this finding relates to career planning. Superintendents in larger school systems may have planned and pursued administrative careers earlier in life. Data regarding gender differences in teaching experience are reported in Chapter 7.

First Administrative Assignment

Both the 1992 and 2000 national studies found that superintendents entered administration in a variety of positions (Glass, Björk, & Brunner, 2000). That finding remained true in this study. As data in Table 4.4 reveal, the most common entry positions were *high school assistant principal* (19.1%), *district coordinator/director* (14.9%), *high school principal* (14.1%), *elementary school principal* (13.4%), and *junior high/middle school assistant principal* (11.9%).

Especially noteworthy, only 3.5% reported that they entered the superintendency without having served in some other administrative capacity. Respondents employed in districts with less than 300 pupils, however, were much more likely than peers in larger districts to have done so; 14.4% of superintendents in very small districts had no previous administrative experience prior to their current job. Also worth mentioning, superintendents in the larger district-enrollment categories (3,000 to 24,999 and 25,000 or more) were more likely than peers in the other two categories to have had their first adminis-

Table 4.3   Years of Teacher Experience

Response options	District enrollment									
	Fewer than 300		300 to 2,999		3,000 to 24,999		25,000 or more		All	
	f	*%*	*f*	*%*	*f*	*%*	*f*	*%*	*f*	*%*
No teaching	0	0.0	5	0.5	7	1.4	3	5.7	15	0.9
1-5	25	15.1	213	20.8	149	29.9	23	43.4	410	23.5
6-10	48	28.9	393	38.4	208	41.8	18	34.0	667	38.3
11-15	47	28.3	211	20.6	83	16.7	7	13.2	348	20.0
16-20	21	12.7	126	12.3	31	6.2	1	1.9	179	10.3
21-25	16	9.6	49	4.8	4	.8	0	0.0	69	4.0
26+	9	5.4	27	2.6	16	3.2	1	1.9	53	3.0
Total	166	100.0	1024	100.0	498	100.0	53	100.0	1741	100.0

trative experience in a district-level position. All response data concerning first administrative experience are in Table 4.4.

Range of Previous Administrative Positions

Commonly, superintendents have been found to have prior experience in several administrative positions (Glass, Björk, & Brunner, 2000). As data in Table 4.5 show, the most commonly held previous positions were (a) *high school principal*, (b) *district-level director/coordinator*, (c) *elementary school principal*, (d) *junior high or middle school principal*, and (e) *assistant/associate/deputy superintendent*.

Table 4.4   First Administrator Assignment

Response options	District enrollment									
	Fewer than 300		300 to 2,999		3,000 to 24,999		25,000 or more		All	
	f	*%*	*f*	*%*	*f*	*%*	*f*	*%*	*f*	*%*
Elementary assistant principal	12	6.9	65	6.0	45	8.6	9	15.5	131	7.2
Elementary principal	28	16.1	150	13.9	61	11.7	6	10.3	245	13.4
Dean of students	6	3.4	30	2.8	13	2.5	0	0.0	49	2.7
Junior/middle assistant principal	10	5.7	108	10.0	95	18.2	5	8.6	218	11.9
Junior/middle principal	9	5.2	56	5.2	25	4.8	1	1.7	91	5.0
High school assistant principal	13	7.5	218	20.2	109	20.9	9	15.5	349	19.1
High school principal	47	27.0	174	16.2	30	5.7	7	12.1	258	14.1
Athletic director	6	3.4	44	4.1	11	2.1	1	1.7	62	3.4
District director/ coordinator	12	6.9	143	13.3	104	19.9	13	22.4	272	14.9
Assistant/ associate/deputy superintendent	1	0.6	6	0.6	8	1.5	0	0.0	15	0.8
State education department	0	0.0	9	0.8	2	0.4	1	1.7	12	0.7
School business/chief financial officer	0	0.0	8	0.7	5	1.0	2	3.4	15	0.8
District treasurer	0	0.0	2	0.2	0	0.0	1	1.7	3	0.2
Superintendent	25	14.4	32	3.0	7	1.3	1	1.7	65	3.5
Other	5	2.9	32	3.0	7	1.3	2	3.4	46	2.5
Total	174	100.0	1077	100.0	522	100.0	58	100.0	1831	100.0

Table 4.5   Most Frequently Held Prior Administrator Positions for at Least One Year

Focal position	f	%
Elementary school assistant principal	177	9.7
Elementary school principal	732	40.0
Junior high or middle school assistant principal	355	19.4
Junior high or middle school principal	702	38.3
High school assistant principal	545	29.7
High school principal	872	47.6
District level director/coordinator	823	44.9
Assistant/associate/deputy superintendent	695	37.9

Note: Respondents were able to select all response options that applied.

Time from Application to Placement

This study assessed how long it took respondents to acquire their first superintendency once they began applying for the position. Responses to this query are reported in Table 4.6 and are broken down by size of the school district.

Two-thirds (67.2%) obtained their first position *less than 1 year* after first applying for a superintendency—and this statistic varied only slightly across district-enrollment categories. Superintendents in districts with less than 300 pupils, however, were the most likely to have entered the position in *less than 1 year* after first applying for a superintendency (78.2%)—a finding suggesting many superintendents in very small districts may have entered the position without having planned to do so (e.g., they are encouraged to apply because of a dearth of applicants). Overall, 5.8% of the respondents said they *never applied* for the position, meaning that they were hired without having to go through a formal selection process.

Findings in this study on time between first application and acquiring the position are dissimilar from those reported in 2000. In that study, 56.6% of all superintendents acquired the position in *less than 1 year*; 64.5% of those in districts with less than 300 pupils and 43% in districts with 25,000 or more pupils did so (Glass, Björk, & Brunner, 2000). In summary, the percentages of superintendents who acquired a first superintendency *less than 1 year* after beginning to apply increased overall and in every district-enrollment category since 2000. Diminishing applicant pools may be one plausible explanation for these findings.

Experiences as a Superintendent

This section examines information about experiences once a person has acquired the position. These data provide insights into issues such as mobility and motivation.

Table 4.6 Time of Application to Employment

Response options	District enrollment									
	Fewer than 300		300 to 2,999		3,000 to 24,999		25,000 or more		All	
	f	%	f	%	f	%	f	%	f	%
Less than 1 year	133	78.2	720	67.7	323	62.8	37	64.9	1213	67.2
1 year	14	8.2	109	10.2	57	11.1	9	15.8	189	10.5
2 years	10	5.9	95	8.9	55	10.7	3	5.3	163	9.0
3 years	3	1.8	42	3.9	18	3.5	2	3.5	65	3.6
4 years	1	0.6	14	1.3	15	2.9	1	1.8	31	1.7
5 + years	2	1.2	20	1.9	18	3.5	0	0.0	40	2.2
Never applied	7	4.1	64	6.0	28	5.4	5	8.8	104	5.8
Total	170	100.0	164	100.0	514	100.0	53	100.0	1805	100.0

Employment Immediately Prior to Current Position

School boards must decide before conducting a search for a new superintendent whether they will consider both internal candidates (i.e., persons who are already district employees) and external candidates (i.e., persons who are not already district employees). Historically, boards satisfied with the status quo have tended to at least consider if not give preference to internal candidates; internal promotions are thought to improve overall employee morale. Conversely, boards dissatisfied with the status quo may exclude internal candidates or at least give preference to external candidates (Kowalski, 2006). Consequently, researchers have often examined whether school boards have been employing internal or external candidates.

In this study, twice as many of the respondents were not already district employees when they were selected as superintendent (66.2% external and 33.8% internal). Superintendents in districts enrolling 25,000 or more students were more likely than peers in other district-enrollment categories to have been promoted internally. Conversely, superintendents in districts with less than 300 pupils were less likely to have been promoted internally than peers in the other categories. All response data concerning internal-external selection of superintendents are in Table 4.7.

Number of Prior Superintendencies

No doubt, prior experience as a superintendent has been a criterion for many school boards seeking to employ a new superintendent. In large measure, this is because past performance is often considered the best predictor of future performance (Heneman & Judge, 2006). Thus, larger districts or districts that can attract large applicant pools often seek candidates who already have proven to be successful superintendents.

Comparison between findings in the 2000 study and this study, however, suggest that it may be more difficult for school boards to attract experienced superintendents, possibly because mobility is declining. As examples, in 2000, 55.9% of the superintendents had only held the position in one school

Table 4.7   Internal/External Selection of Superintendents

Were you employed in the district when selected as superintendent?	District enrollment									
	Fewer than 300		300 to 2,999		3,000 to 24,999		25,000 or more		All	
	f	%	f	%	f	%	f	%	f	%
Yes	49	28.5	336	31.4	205	39.7	23	41.1	613	33.8
No	123	71.5	735	68.6	312	60.3	33	58.9	1203	66.2
Total	172	100.0	1071	100.0	517	100.0	58	100.0	1821	100.0

Table 4.8   Number of Districts Serving as a Superintendent

Response options	District enrollment									
	Fewer than 300		300 to 2,999		3,000 to 24,999		25,000 or more		All	
	f	%	f	%	f	%	f	%	f	%
1	108	62.1	661	61.4	286	55.1	29	50.0	1084	59.3
2	40	23.0	243	22.6	124	23.9	12	20.7	419	22.9
3	11	6.3	109	10.1	63	12.1	7	12.1	190	10.4
4	4	2.3	39	3.6	28	5.4	7	12.1	78	4.3
5	5	2.9	12	1.1	7	1.3	1	1.7	25	1.4
6	3	1.7	7	0.6	5	1.0	2	3.4	17	0.9
7 or more	3	1.7	6	0.6	6	1.2	0	0.0	15	0.8
Total	174	100.0	1077	100.0	519	100.0	58	100.0	1828	100.0

district, and 19.8% had served as superintendent in more than two districts (Glass, Björk, & Brunner, 2000). In this study, the former figure increased slightly and the latter figure decreased slightly. All response data concerning number of superintendencies are in Table 4.8.

Number of States in Which Respondents Were Employed as Superintendents

Two factors have made it attractive and easier for superintendents to work in multiple states during their careers: early retirement provisions in state pension funds and increased licensing reciprocity (Kowalski & Sweetland, 2002, 2005). Yet, 88.2% of the respondents in this study had been a superintendent in only *one* state. Only 2.3% reported having been a superintendent in more than *two* states.

Superintendents in districts with 25,000 or more students were slightly more likely than peers in the other district-enrollment categories to have been in the position in more than one state. All response data concerning this issue are in Table 4.9.

Years of Experience as a Superintendent

In the 2000 study, 6.9% of the superintendents were novices (i.e., they were in the first year of being a superintendent at the time of the research). That figure decreased slightly to 6% in this study. Interestingly, the percentages of novices in each of the four district-enrollment categories were nearly identical (a range of 5% to 6.9%).

Over half the superintendents participating in this study (54.3%) had between *2 and 8 years* of experience in the position, and one-fourth (24.8%) had *13 or more years* of experience in the position. Superintendents in districts with 25,000 or more students were about twice as likely as peers in other district-enrollment categories to have *13 or more years* of experience in the position. Response data for length of experience in the superintendency are in Table 4.10.

Currently Receiving a Pension

Circa 1970, many states promulgated early retirement provisions in pension funds for teachers and administrators based on the conviction that there was an oversupply of educators. By the mid-1980s, that conviction was reversed; however, state policymakers were reluctant to rescind early retirement options, fearing political repercussions (Kowalski & Sweetland, 2005). As applicant pools for superintendents declined, the demand for experienced practitioners increased, and many superintendents had opportunities to start drawing a pension while continuing to work—a situation commonly called "double dipping." This option could be pursued by simply gaining employment in a different state, but in a growing number of states, it also could be pursued by retiring and continuing to work in the same state—a provision commonly referred to as "retire-rehire" (Kowalski & Sweetland, 2002).

Despite growing opportunities to start drawing a pension while continuing to work as a superintendent, only one-fifth (20.6%) of the respondents in this study said they were doing this. District enrollment did not appear to have a discernible influence on this issue; however, superintendents in the largest districts (i.e., 25,000 or more pupils) were more likely than those in the smallest districts (i.e., less than 300 pupils) to be "double dipping." All response data concerning this issue are in Table 4.11.

Reason for Leaving Previous Superintendency

Superintendents who have held the position in more than one district were asked to identify the reason they left their most previous position. The modal response (30.3%) was to *assume a new challenge*. The

Table 4.9   Number of States Serving as a Superintendent

| Response options | District enrollment | | | | | | | | | |
| | Fewer than 300 | | 300 to 2,999 | | 3,000 to 24,999 | | 25,000 or more | | All | |
	f	*%*	*f*	*%*	*f*	*%*	*f*	*%*	*f*	*%*
1	157	90.8	974	90.9	432	83.4	43	74.1	1606	88.2
2	15	8.7	84	7.8	64	12.4	10	17.2	173	9.5
3	0	0.0	12	1.1	14	2.7	2	3.4	28	1.5
4 or more	1	0.6	2	0.2	8	1.5	3	5.2	14	0.8
Total	173	100.0	1072	100.0	518	100.0	58	100.0	1821	100.0

Table 4.10 Number of Years Serving as a Superintendent

Response options	District enrollment									
	Fewer than 300		300 to 2,999		3,000 to 24,999		25,000 or more		All	
	f	%	f	%	f	%	f	%	f	%
1	11	6.3	69	6.4	26	5.0	4	6.9	110	6.0
2–4	61	35.1	295	27.3	126	24.1	8	13.8	490	26.7
5–8	40	23.0	313	29.0	140	26.8	13	22.4	506	27.6
9–12	26	14.9	155	14.4	83	15.9	8	13.8	272	14.8
13 or more	36	20.7	247	22.9	147	28.2	25	43.1	455	24.8
Total	174	100.0	1079	100.0	522	100.0	58	100.0	1833	100.0

Table 4.11 Currently Receiving a Pension

Response options	District enrollment									
	Fewer than 300		300 to 2,999		3,000 to 24,999		25,000 or more		All	
	f	%	f	%	f	%	f	%	f	%
Yes/same system	27	16.7	116	11.1	52	10.2	5	8.9	200	11.3
Yes/different system	13	8.0	78	7.5	60	11.8	13	23.2	164	9.3
No pension	122	75.3	847	81.4	396	78.0	38	67.9	1403	79.4
Total	162	100.0	1041	100.0	508	100.0	56	100.0	1767	100.0

three next most common reasons were *school board conflict* (15.3%), *to supplement a pension* (13.7%), and *to seek employment in a higher performing school district* (11.4%). Very few superintendents said their contracts were *not renewed* (2.3%) or that they were otherwise *dismissed* (0.3%). Superintendents in districts with less than 300 pupils were much more likely than peers in the other district-enrollment categories to report *school board conflict* as the reason for leaving their previous superintendency. All response data concerning this issue are in Table 4.12.

Opinions about Success and Job Satisfaction

Well established in the social/psychological research (e.g., Michener, DeLamater, & Myers, 2004) is that individuals follow career paths where they enjoy success. Implied by the social/psychological research is that individuals choosing to be superintendents would continue to follow this career path if they perceive themselves to have been successful.

Table 4.12   Reasons for Leaving Prior Superintendency

| Response options | District enrollment | | | | | | | | | |
| | Fewer than 300 | | 300 to 2,999 | | 3,000 to 24,999 | | 25,000 or more | | All | |
	f	%	f	%	f	%	f	%	f	%
Non-renewed	2	3.1	8	1.9	7	2.9	0	0.0	17	2.3
Dismissed	0	0.0	1	0.2	1	0.4	0	0.0	2	0.3
School board conflict	19	29.2	63	15.0	31	13.0	2	6.9	115	15.3
Community conflict	0	0.0	6	1.4	4	1.7	1	3.4	11	1.5
Sought higher performing school district	2	3.1	45	10.7	36	15.1	3	10.3	86	11.4
Assume a new challenge	5	7.7	127	30.2	79	33.2	17	58.6	228	30.3
Increase compensation	5	7.7	39	9.3	20	8.4	1	3.4	65	8.6
Better schools for my children	6	9.2	40	9.5	15	6.3	1	3.4	62	8.2
Health reasons	0	0.0	2	0.5	0	0.0	0	0.0	2	0.3
Follow spouse	3	4.6	2	0.5	1	0.4	0	0.0	6	0.8
Better pension in another state	1	1.5	4	1.0	3	1.3	0	0.0	8	1.1
To supplement a pension	16	24.6	58	13.8	26	10.9	3	10.3	103	13.7
Other	6	9.2	26	6.2	15	6.3	1	3.4	48	6.4
Total	65	100.0	421	100.0	238	100.0	29	100.0	753	100.0

Self-Perception of Success as a Superintendent

Opinions of superintendents can be identified from alternate but related perspectives, including feelings of effectiveness related to their current position. In this study, respondents were asked to identify their level of success as a superintendent. Nearly all (97.2%) said they were *highly successful* (52.4%) or *moderately successful* (44.8%). District enrollment did not appear to influence these responses.

Findings in this study were quite similar to those reported in 1992 and 2000. In those studies, 96.9% and 95.1% of the respondents respectively said they were *very successful* or *successful*. All response data concerning self-perceptions of success are in Table 4.13.

Satisfaction with Job Facets

Although job satisfaction was viewed initially as a single overarching construct in the organizational literature (Lawler, 1994), more recently it has been deconstructed according to a facet perspective

Table 4.13   Self-Perception of Success as a Superintendent

Response options	District enrollment									
	Fewer than 300		300 to 2,999		3,000 to 24,999		25,000 or more		All	
	f	%	f	%	f	%	f	%	f	%
Highly successful	67	38.5	531	49.2	323	61.6	41	70.7	962	52.4
Moderately successful	97	55.7	523	48.4	189	36.1	14	24.1	823	44.8
Somewhat successful	6	3.4	10	0.9	4	0.8	0	0.0	20	1.1
Not at all successful	0	0.0	0	0.0	0	0.0	0	0.0	0	0.0
Uncertain	4	2.3	16	1.5	8	1.5	3	5.2	31	1.7
Total	174	100.0	1080	100.0	524	100.0	58	100.0	1836	100.0

(Scarpello, Huber, & Vandenberg, 1998). In this study, two facets of job satisfaction for superintendents along with their levels of stress to technology were assessed. These facets are satisfaction with their current assignment relative to district-level variables, satisfaction with their current compensation, and affective reactions to technology.

District-level variables are defined as a collective to include satisfaction with schools, programs, and employees. As shown in Table 4.14, 60.6% of the superintendents indicated that they are *very satisfied*, and an additional 35.4% indicated that they are *moderately satisfied*. The percentage of very satisfied responses increased with district enrollment; that is, superintendents in districts with 25,000 or more students were the most likely to be *very satisfied*, and peers in districts with less than 300 students were least likely to be *very satisfied*. Response data concerning this issue are in Table 4.14.

Like satisfaction with district-level variables, satisfaction with compensation is an important concern warranting the attention of researchers (Currall, Towler, Judge, & Kohn, 2005). Indeed, satisfaction with compensation is noted to be a primary predictor of job turnover as well as other undesirable organizational behaviors (for an extensive review, see Williams, McDaniel, & Nguyen, 2006). As a job facet, compensation includes two sources: salary and fringe benefits (Young, 2007).

Satisfaction of superintendents for their compensation (salary and fringe benefits) is reported in Table 4.15. Unlike satisfaction with district-level variables where the modal response was *very satisfied*, the modal response for satisfaction with compensation was *moderately satisfied* (52%). Only 34% reported that they were *very satisfied* with their compensation. Superintendents in districts with less than 300 pupils were somewhat less likely than peers in larger districts to be satisfied with their compensation (i.e., either *very satisfied* or *moderately satisfied*). Data concerning satisfaction with compensation are in Table 4.15.

Another facet of the job having potential affective implications for superintendents is technology. Since the 2000 study, technology has advanced at an exponential rate and has become a necessary component for the operation of public school districts. As such, technology can be an important source of stress or satisfaction.

Responses regarding stress associated with technology were mixed in this study. Slightly more than one-third (37.5%) said technology generated *no stress* for them. The remaining superintendents were divided indicating the level of stress was *considerable* (16%), *moderate* 27.9%), or *slight* (18.6%). Differences

Table 4.14   Satisfaction of Superintendents with District Schools, Programs, and Employees

Response options	District enrollment									
	Fewer than 300		300 to 2,999		3,000 to 24,999		25,000 or more		All	
	f	%	f	%	f	%	f	%	f	%
Very satisfied	93	54.1	616	57.2	356	68.2	42	73.7	1107	60.6
Moderately satisfied	69	40.1	412	38.3	154	29.5	13	22.8	648	35.4
Moderately dissatisfied	8	4.7	40	3.7	11	2.1	2	3.5	61	3.3
Very dissatisfied	2	1.2	9	0.8	1	0.2	0	0.0	12	0.7
Total	172	100.0	1077	100.0	522	100.0	57	100.0	1828	100.0

Table 4.15   Satisfaction of Superintendents with Their Compensation

Response options	District enrollment									
	Fewer than 300		300 to 2,999		3,000 to 24,999		25,000 or more		All	
	f	%	f	%	f	%	f	%	f	%
Very satisfied	43	25.0	348	32.3	209	40.3	27	47.4	627	34.3
Moderately satisfied	87	50.6	575	53.3	257	49.5	26	45.6	945	51.8
Moderately dissatisfied	37	21.5	125	11.6	45	8.7	2	3.5	209	11.4
Very dissatisfied	5	2.9	30	2.8	8	1.5	2	3.5	45	2.5
Total	172	100.0	1078	100.0	519	100.0	57	100.0	1826	100.0

in response percentages varied only slightly across the four district-enrollment categories. Response data for this issue are in Table 4.16.

Satisfaction with Career Choice

An old adage states "the proof of the pudding is in the eating." As applied to experiences of superintendents, this test concerns how satisfied they are with their current career choice and if they would choose again this career path as a superintendent. Consequently, responses to both perspectives were assessed in this chapter.

Data contained in Table 4.17 indicate that superintendents were satisfied with their career choice. Indeed, 69% reported being *very satisfied*, and another 27% reported being *moderately satisfied*. Again, only slight differences in response percentages were found across the four district-enrollment categories. Response data regarding satisfaction with career choice are in Table 4.17.

Job satisfaction research often seeks to determine if respondents would make the same career choice if given an opportunity to retrace their steps. In this study, just under two-thirds (63.2%) said they again would *definitely* opt to be a superintendent; an additional 25.1% said they would probably do so. Just under 5% said they *probably* or *definitely* would not make the same career choice. Of particular note, none of the respondents in districts with 25,000 or more pupils said they would not make the same career choice. All response data concerning this issue are in Table 4.18.

In the 2000 study, respondents were asked to identify levels of self-fulfillment. Although this question is not identical to those asked in this study, the results indicated that a high level of job satisfaction existed a decade ago as well. Glass, Björk, and Brunner (2000) reported that 94% of the superintendents said their level of self-fulfillment was either *moderate* or *considerable*.

Summary

This chapter explored data related to accessing and experiencing the superintendency. Some of the findings are nearly identical to those reported a decade ago, and some are notably dissimilar. As in the

Table 4.16   Stress of Superintendents Associated with Technology

Response options	*District enrollment*									
	Fewer than 300		*300 to 2,999*		*3,000 to 24,999*		*25,000 or more*		*All*	
	f	*%*	*f*	*%*	*f*	*%*	*f*	*%*	*f*	*%*
Yes considerable	22	12.7	174	16.1	87	16.9	9	15.8	292	16.0
Yes moderately	34	19.7	310	28.7	150	29.1	16	28.1	510	27.9
Yes slightly	42	24.3	202	18.7	84	16.3	11	19.3	339	18.6
No	75	43.4	395	36.5	195	37.8	21	36.8	686	37.5
Total	173	100.0	1081	100.0	516	100.0	57	100.0	1827	100.0

Table 4.17   Satisfaction with Career Choice

Response options	*District enrollment*									
	Fewer than 300		*300 to 2,999*		*3,000 to 24,999*		*25,000 or more*		*All*	
	f	*%*	*f*	*%*	*f*	*%*	*f*	*%*	*f*	*%*
Very satisfied	99	56.9	727	67.4	394	75.5	49	86.0	1269	69.3
Moderately satisfied	69	39.7	302	28.0	121	23.2	8	14.0	500	27.3
Moderately dissatisfied	6	3.4	39	3.6	7	1.3	0	0.0	52	2.8
Very dissatisfied	0	0.0	10	0.9	0	0.0	0	0.0	10	0.5
Total	174	100.0	1078	100.0	522	100.0	57	100.0	1831	100.0

Table 4.18   Would You Follow the Same Career Path?

Response options	District enrollment									
	Fewer than 300		300 to 2,999		3,000 to 24,999		25,000 or more		All	
	f	*%*	*f*	*%*	*f*	*%*	*f*	*%*	*f*	*%*
Definitely yes	102	60.0	647	60.8	345	67.6	44	75.9	1138	63.2
Probably yes	47	27.6	277	26.0	119	23.3	10	17.2	453	25.1
Unsure	10	5.9	79	7.4	31	6.1	4	6.9	124	6.9
Probably no	10	5.9	58	5.5	14	2.7	0	0.0	82	4.6
Definitely no	1	0.6	3	0.3	1	0.2	0	0.0	5	0.3
Total	170	100.0	1064	100.0	510	100.0	58	100.0	1802	100.0

past, for example, teaching was the entry point into the profession for most respondents; however, the percentage entering administration as a principal (not including assistant principal) was lower.

The following are among the most notable findings reported in this chapter:

- Most superintendents continued to follow the traditional career path en route to the superintendency via teacher and building-level principal positions.
- In contrast to previous studies, many entered the administrative ranks as an assistant principal rather than as a principal.
- A high percentage of superintendents were employed in the position in less than one year after first applying for it.
- Superintendents reported they were satisfied with their job, schools, programs, and employees in their current assignment.
- Most promising, superintendents indicated they would follow the same career path if they had it to do over again.
- The level of job satisfaction expressed by superintendents remains very high. The vast majority are pleased with their career choice as evidenced by the fact that a high percentage would again seek to occupy the same position if given a chance to relive their careers.

5

Elements of Practice

The roles of superintendents in the public school setting are numerous. As the chief executive officers, superintendents must be visionary leaders (Kowalski, 2006), financial planners (Owings & Kaplan, 2006), human resource managers (Young, 2008), and instructional experts (Cunningham & Cordeiro, 2006). These roles are commingled and are defined loosely to comprise the elements of practice for public school superintendents.

Without a doubt, superintendents must be visionary leaders (Kowalski, 2006) to chart the course of a public school district because schooling today is different from schooling in the past. With the passage of federal as well as state legislation, the emphasis has changed from a process perspective focusing only on procedures to an outcome perspective focusing largely on student achievement as assessed by standardized measures at the state level (Vang, 2008). To the extent that this change is met depends on the vision of a school superintendent.

Given the recent downturn of America's economy, superintendents must be astute financial planners. Budgets in most school districts have stagnated or have been reduced, while expectations for the schooling process have increased. As a result, standing superintendents must do more with fewer fiscal resources.

Within the operational budgets of school districts, the major expenditures are related to human resource activities (Webb & Norton, 2006). New instructional programs must be staffed, and existing instructional programs must be maintained. Of major concern from a human resource perspective for superintendents is equity for students, for employees, and for other stakeholders.

Never have outcomes associated with the schooling process received as much attention by the popular press as well as by important stakeholders than in recent times. With the advent of high stakes testing and with an emphasis on student achievement, instruction is at the forefront in all school districts (Sergiovanni, 2006). Certainly, the notion of accountability has been expanded over the last decade and is influenced by a variety of stakeholders.

Perceptions of Assets or Liabilities for Superintendents

As the chief executive officer of a public school district, superintendents wear many hats and interact with a variety of stakeholders. Interactions with stakeholders can vary in important ways, impacting superintendents' elements of practice when fulfilling position requirements. More specifically, stakeholders can be either an asset or a liability, and the extent to which they influence elements of practice for superintendents varies.

The intent of this portion of the research project was to determine respondents' perceptions of various groups and institutions as either assets or liabilities for superintendents. These responses should not be confused with those that pertain to assets and liabilities for school districts. Because differences in district size (enrollment) produce variations in contextual variables, data are reported in the four designated enrollment groups used in the 2000 study (Glass, Björk, & Brunner, 2000) and other chapters in this book.

School Boards

Because most superintendents are employed by school boards with only few being elected by popular vote of the public (Glass, Björk, & Brunner, 2000; Webb & Norton, 2006), their perceptions of board members are clearly important. Data in Table 5.1 indicate most respondents in this study viewed school board members as either a *major asset* (i.e., 56%) or a *minor asset* (i.e., 24%) in relation to them personally; less than 15% viewed the school board as a *minor* or *major liability*.

District-Level Administrators

Although school boards are responsible for policy decisions, superintendents depend on their executive cabinet members (e.g., assistant superintendents, directors) to help them carry out policy (Kowalski, 2011). Consequently, district-level administrators also can be an asset or liability for superintendents (Hoy & Miskel, 2008). Data assessed in this study indicate that most superintendents perceived their executive cabinet members as an asset. Just under two-thirds (62.4%) of them said that their district-level administrators were a *major asset*, and another 13.9% said they were a *minor asset*.

Though the responses to this question from superintendents in districts with less than three hundred pupils were quite dissimilar to responses of their peers, the differences are understandable. Most districts with fewer than 300 students are not likely to employ district-level administrators other than the superintendent (Webb & Norton, 2006). Response data for district-level support staff are in Table 5.2.

Building-Level Administrators

Because building-level administrators (e.g., principals, assistant principals) serve as stewards of the educational process at the school-building level (Cunningham & Cordeiro, 2006), they play a pivotal

Table 5.1   School Boards: Perceived Value to the Superintendent

Response options	District enrollment									
	Fewer than 300		300 to 2,999		3,000 to 24,999		25,000 or more		All	
	f	*%*	*f*	*%*	*f*	*%*	*f*	*%*	*f*	*%*
Major asset	80	46.0	620	57.4	300	57.4	33	56.9	1033	56.3
Minor asset	51	29.3	259	24.0	121	23.1	9	15.5	440	24.0
Neither an asset nor a liability	14	8.0	63	5.8	19	3.6	6	10.3	102	5.6
Minor liability	22	12.6	97	9.0	52	9.9	7	12.1	178	9.7
Major liability	7	4.0	41	3.8	31	5.9	3	5.2	82	4.5
Total	174	100.0	1080	100.0	523	100.0	58	100.0	1835	100.0

role relative to the instructional program. According to Sergiovanni, "it is clear that when schools are functioning especially well and school achievement is high, much of the credit typically belongs to the principal" (2006, p. 126). Consequently, building-level administrators can be either assets or liabilities for superintendents.

In this study, over 90% of the responding superintendents viewed building-level administrators as an asset, with 70% viewing them as a *major asset*. Only about 4% viewed these administrators as a *minor* or *major liability*. Superintendents in the largest districts (i.e., 25,000 or more pupils) were more likely to view building-level administrators as a *major asset* and approximately twice as likely to do so when compared to their peers in the smallest districts (i.e., less than 300 pupils). All response data pertaining to building-level administrators are in Table 5.3.

Table 5.2   District-Level Administrators: Perceived Value to the Superintendent

Response options	District enrollment									
	Fewer than 300		300 to 2,999		3,000 to 24,999		25,000 or more		All	
	f	*%*	*f*	*%*	*f*	*%*	*f*	*%*	*f*	*%*
Major asset	45	26.2	597	55.7	445	85.2	50	86.2	1137	62.4
Minor asset	16	9.3	169	15.8	63	12.1	6	10.3	254	13.9
Neither an asset nor a liability	109	63.4	285	26.6	7	1.3	0	0.0	401	22.0
Minor liability	2	1.2	17	1.6	7	1.3	2	3.4	28	1.5
Major liability	0	0.0	3	0.3	0	0.0	0	0.0	3	0.2
Total	172	100.0	1071	100.0	522	100.0	58	100.0	1823	100.0

Table 5.3   Building-Level Administrators: Perceived Value to the Superintendent

Response options	District enrollment									
	Fewer than 300		300 to 2,999		3,000 to 24,999		25,000 or more		All	
	f	*%*	*f*	*%*	*f*	*%*	*f*	*%*	*f*	*%*
Major asset	75	43.1	746	69.3	407	78.0	48	82.8	1276	69.7
Minor asset	36	20.7	251	23.3	95	18.2	7	12.1	389	21.2
Neither an asset nor a liability	54	31.0	37	3.4	8	1.5	1	1.7	100.0	5.5
Minor liability	9	5.2	40	3.7	12	2.3	2	3.4	63	3.4
Major liability	0	0.0	3	0.3	0	0.0	0	0.0	3	0.2
Total	174	100.0	1077	100.0	522	100.0	58	100.0	1831	100.0

Legal Interventions

Superintendents today, more than ever, are involved with the legal system given state and federal legislation and ensuing litigation (Gee & Daniel, 2009). The legal dimension of educational administration has long been recognized as evidenced by the fact that most states require both principals and superintendents to complete a course in school law.

Respondents in this study were asked whether they viewed legal interventions to be an asset or a liability for them personally. Just over half (55.1%) said the courts were neither. Among the remaining respondents, almost twice as many (28.8%) said they were a *minor* or *major liability* as those who said they were a *major* or *minor asset* (16.2%). Only slight variations in responses existed across the four district-size categories. Data regarding the influence of the courts are in Table 5.4.

Media

In most communities, local media cover public education continuously, and journalists' reports can be positive, neutral, or negative. Consequently, superintendents develop opinions that prompt them to view the media (including journalists) as an asset or liability (Kowalski, 2011). In this study, just over half the respondents (54.1%) viewed the media as a *major* or *minor asset*; another 25.6% said the media was *neither an asset nor a liability*. Superintendents employed in the largest districts (i.e., 25,000 or more pupils) were nearly three times as likely to view the media as a *minor* or *major liability* than were their peers in the smallest districts (i.e., less than 300 pupils). The difference between the two groups is logically explained by the fact that very large school districts receive substantially more media coverage and typically have to deal with more social, political, and economic problems. All response data pertaining to the media are in Table 5.5.

Community Involvement

The concept of local control for public schools in this country, a value rooted in liberty, establishes the right of citizens to pursue their interests through direct involvement with school boards and superintendents (Levin, 1987, 1999). Civic engagement, however, can be productive or destructive; consequently, superintendents do not always perceive community involvement as an asset for them personally (Kow-

Table 5.4 Legal Interventions: Perceived Value to the Superintendent

Response options	District enrollment									
	Fewer than 300		300 to 2,999		3,000 to 24,999		25,000 or more		All	
	f	%	f	%	f	%	f	%	f	%
Major asset	4	2.3	35	3.2	22	4.2	3	5.3	64	3.5
Minor asset	22	12.6	132	12.3	74	14.2	4	7.0	232	12.7
Neither an asset nor a liability	121	69.5	613	56.9	248	47.5	26	45.6	1008	55.1
Minor liability	24	13.8	241	22.4	131	25.1	17	29.8	413	22.6
Major liability	3	1.7	57	5.3	47	9.0	7	12.3	114	6.2
Total	174	100.0	1077	100.0	522	100.0	58	100.0	1831	100.0

alski, 2006). As an example, individuals or special-interest groups can support or challenge a superintendent's agenda or even the superintendent's job security. Table 5.6 contains data showing the extent to which respondents in this study view civic engagement to be an asset or liability.

These data indicate that over 85% of the superintendents viewed community involvement as an asset, with 43% saying it was a *major asset* and 42% saying it was a *minor asset*. Superintendents in the smallest districts (i.e., less than 300 pupils) were slightly less likely than their peers to view community involvement as a *major asset*. All response data for this issue are in Table 5.6.

Compensation and Fringe Benefits

As the chief executive officer of a school district, the compensation of superintendents attracts a great deal of interest and is used often as a barometer to gauge the efficiency of a public school district (Young,

Table 5.5   Media Coverage: Perceived Value to the Superintendent

Response options	District enrollment									
	Fewer than 300		300 to 2,999		3,000 to 24,999		25,000 or more		All	
	f	*%*	*f*	*%*	*f*	*%*	*f*	*%*	*f*	*%*
Major asset	20	11.5	157	14.6	81	15.5	9	15.5	267	14.6
Minor asset	52	29.9	443	41.1	207	39.7	21	36.2	723	39.5
Neither an asset nor a liability	82	47.1	284	26.4	92	17.6	10	17.2	468	25.6
Minor liability	16	9.2	155	14.4	102	19.5	12	20.7	285	15.6
Major liability	4	2.3	37	3.4	41	7.9	6	10.5	88	4.8
Total	174	100.0	1076	100.0	523	100.0	58	100.0	1831	100.0

Table 5.6   Community Involvement: Perceived Value to the Superintendent

Response options	District enrollment									
	Fewer than 300		300 to 2,999		3,000 to 24,999		25,000 or more		All	
	f	*%*	*f*	*%*	*f*	*%*	*f*	*%*	*f*	*%*
Major asset	60	34.9	428	39.7	256	49.0	37	63.8	781	42.7
Minor asset	77	44.8	470	43.6	205	39.3	17	29.3	769	42.0
Neither an asset nor a liability	13	7.6	105	9.7	36	6.9	4	6.9	158	8.6
Minor liability	19	11.0	69	6.4	26	5.0	0	0.0	114	6.2
Major liability	3	1.7	6	0.6	1	0.2	0	0.0	10	0.5
Total	172	100.0	1078	100.0	524	100.0	58	100.0	1832	100.0

2008). However, compensation received by superintendents has two components. "One is a base rate of pay, and it reflects direct compensation; the other involves the fringe benefit package, and it reflects indirect compensation" (Young, 2007, p. 126). Either or both sources of compensation can be perceived by superintendents to be a personal asset or liability.

Just over half the superintendents responding in this study (54%) perceived their salary to be either a *major* (19.1%) or *minor* (34.9%) *asset*. Superintendents in the two smaller district-enrollment categories (i.e., fewer than 300 pupils and 300 to 2,999 pupils) were slightly more likely than their peers in the two larger district-enrollment categories to view salary as either a *minor* or *major liability*. All response data for salary are in Table 5.7.

Unlike salary, information about fringe benefits is less reported, either in the public press or in the professional literature, because dissimilar configurations of benefit packages make it difficult to do so (Young, 1997). In this study, respondents produced a response pattern for their perceptions of fringe benefits as an asset or liability similar to the pattern they produced for salary. Just over half (52.9%) viewed their fringe benefits as either a *major* (17.7%) or *minor* (35.2%) *asset*. Superintendents in the largest school districts (i.e., 25,000 or more pupils) were less likely than their peers in the remaining three district-enrollment categories to view fringe benefits as a personal liability. All response data pertaining to fringe benefits are in Table 5.8.

State Departments of Education

With the passage of the No Child Left Behind Act of 2001 (2002) and with the advent of high stakes testing, state departments of education have assumed a larger role in the administration of public school districts (Vang, 2008). At minimum, state departments of education are responsible for developing statewide tests assessing student achievement and for issuing remedial guidelines relative to underperforming school districts (Goodman & Young, 2006). Although all state departments of education have enforcement responsibilities, they differ with respect to how they carry out this role and with respect to providing guidance and assistance to meet federal and state mandates (Kowalski, 2006). Consequently, state departments of education can be viewed as assets or liabilities for superintendents personally.

Superintendents were divided in their views about state departments of education. Whereas just over one-third (35.5%) viewed this agency as a *major or minor asset*, 43.6% viewed it as a *minor or*

Table 5.7   Current Salary: Perceived Value to the Superintendent

Response options	District enrollment									
	Fewer than 300		300 to 2,999		3,000 to 24,999		25,000 or more		All	
	f	*%*	*f*	*%*	*f*	*%*	*f*	*%*	*f*	*%*
Major asset	19	10.9	177	16.4	136	26.1	18	31.6	350	19.1
Minor asset	55	31.6	371	34.4	201	38.5	12	21.1	639	34.9
Neither an asset nor a liability	62	35.6	360	33.4	133	25.5	22	38.6	577	31.5
Minor liability	28	16.1	141	13.1	41	7.9	3	5.3	213	11.6
Major liability	10	5.7	31	2.9	12	2.3	2	3.5	55	3.0
Total	174	100.0	1080	100.0	523	100.0	57	100.0	1834	100.0

major liability, and 21.2% viewed it as *neither an asset nor a liability*. School district enrollment did not appear to have a discernible influence on the manner in which superintendents responded to this issue. Data regarding perceptions of the value of state departments of education for superintendents are in Table 5.9.

Level of Influence Exerted on Superintendents

In addition to assessing the perceived value of various groups and agencies, this study examined perceptions regarding levels of influence. Specifically, superintendents were asked to identify the extent to which selected groups, agencies, and information sources influenced elements of their practice.

Table 5.8   Fringe Benefits: Perceived Value to the Superintendent

Response options	District enrollment									
	Fewer than 300		300 to 2,999		3,000 to 24,999		25,000 or more		All	
	f	%	*f*	%	*f*	%	*f*	%	*f*	%
Major asset	21	12.1	154	14.3	135	25.9	15	25.9	325	17.7
Minor asset	50	28.7	393	36.5	187	35.8	15	25.9	645	35.2
Neither an asset nor a liability	67	38.5	371	34.4	141	27.0	25	43.1	604	33.0
Minor liability	27	15.5	130	12.1	48	9.2	2	3.4	207	11.3
Major liability	9	5.2	30	2.8	10	1.9	1	1.7	50	2.7
Total	174	100.0	1078	100.0	521	100.0	58	100.0	1831	100.0

Table 5.9   State Departments of Education: Perceived Value to the Superintendent

Response options	District enrollment									
	Fewer than 300		300 to 2,999		3,000 to 24,999		25,000 or more		All	
	f	%	*f*	%	*f*	%	*f*	%	*f*	%
Major asset	20	11.5	90	8.4	30	5.7	3	5.2	143	7.8
Minor asset	49	28.2	301	27.9	142	27.2	15	25.9	507	27.7
Neither an asset nor a liability	50	28.7	215	20.0	109	20.9	14	24.1	388	21.2
Minor liability	43	24.7	322	29.9	152	29.1	18	31.0	535	29.2
Major liability	12	6.9	153	14.2	91	17.4	8	13.8	264	14.4
Total	174	100.0	1081	100.0	524	100.0	58	100.0	1837	100.0

School Boards

Unsurprising is the extent of influence exerted by the school board on the elements of practice for superintendents. Among those responding, 69% perceived the level of school board influence to be *considerable* and 28% to be *moderate*. Superintendents in the smallest districts (i.e., less than 300 pupils), however, were slightly less likely than their peers to say that the school board had considerable influence on them. All response data concerning the level of board influence on the superintendent are in Table 5.10.

Other Administrators Employed by the School District

Both district-level and school-level administrators working in the same system have the potential to influence superintendents. The overwhelming majority of superintendents (91%) indicated that other administrators employed in the same school system had *considerable* (53.7%) or *moderate* (37.3%) *influence* with them. About one in five superintendents in districts with less than 300 pupils (21.2%) said that other administrators had *no influence* on them—and this outcome was much higher than the ones found in the other three district-enrollment categories. All response data concerning the influence of other administrators on the superintendent are in Table 5.11.

Teachers

Teachers are the largest employee group in a school district (Owings & Kaplan, 2006) and interface directly with students in the instructional program on a daily basis (Cunningham & Cordeiro, 2006; Sergiovanni, 2006). As such, their level of influence can be exerted either as individuals or collectively. Their individual influence on superintendents, however, may vary considerably depending on efforts to influence and a willingness to be influenced.

Findings related to individual teacher influence are similar to those reported for other administrators' influence. A large majority (84.4%) of the superintendents reported that teachers had either a *considerable* (30.2%) or *moderate* (54.2%) level of influence on them. Only 1% of the superintendents, regardless of district size, said teachers had *no influence* on them. All responses regarding the influence level of teachers individually are in Table 5.12

Table 5.10   Extent of School Board Influence on the Superintendent

Response options	District enrollment									
	Fewer than 300		300 to 2,999		3,000 to 24,999		25,000 or more		All	
	f	%	f	%	f	%	f	%	f	%
Considerable	102	58.6	739	68.5	381	72.9	41	70.7	1263	68.9
Moderate	65	37.4	94	27.3	128	24.5	16	27.6	503	27.7
Slight	7	4.0	43	4.0	13	2.5	1	1.7	64	3.5
None	0	0.0	3	0.3	1	0.2	0	0.0	4	0.2
Uncertain	0	0.0	0	0.0	0	0.0	0	0.0	0	0.0
Total	174	100.0	1079	100.0	523	100.0	58	100.0	1834	100.0

Table 5.11   Extent of Internal Administrator (Those Employed in the Same District) Influence on the Superintendent

| Response options | District enrollment | | | | | | | | | |
| | Fewer than 300 | | 300 to 2,999 | | 3,000 to 24,999 | | 25,000 or more | | All | |
	f	%	f	%	f	%	f	%	f	%
Considerable	35	20.6	584	54.0	332	63.4	34	58.6	985	53.7
Moderate	70	41.2	412	38.1	178	34.0	24	41.4	684	37.3
Slight	27	15.9	77	7.1	13	2.5	0	0.0	117	6.4
None	36	21.2	7	0.7	0.2	1	0	0.0	44	2.4
Uncertain	2	1.2	1	0.1	0	0.0	0	0.0	3	0.2
Total	170	100.0	1081	100.0	524	100.0	58	100.0	1833	100.0

Table 5.12   Extent of Teacher (Exclusive of Teacher Association/Union) Influence on the Superintendent

| Response options | District enrollment | | | | | | | | | |
| | Fewer than 300 | | 300 to 2,999 | | 3,000 to 24,999 | | 25,000 or more | | All | |
	f	%	f	%	f	%	f	%	f	%
Considerable	38	22.0	324	30.2	173	33.1	16	28.1	551	30.2
Moderate	98	56.7	564	52.6	290	55.5	38	66.7	990	54.2
Slight	33	19.1	172	16.0	55	10.5	3	5.3	263	14.4
None	4	2.3	10	0.9	4	0.8	0	0.0	18	1.0
Uncertain	0	0.0	3	0.3	1	0.2	0	0.0	4	0.2
Total	173	100.0	1073	100.0	523	100.0	57	100.0	1826	100.0

Employee Unions/Groups

Employee organizations in a school district can be either a union comprised of a bargaining unit having contractual/statutory rights or a professional in-house association having only an advisory status (Young, 2008). However, this study defined formal organizations involving representation of collective employee groups to include both types of representation and assessed perceptions of superintendents about the level of influence these formal organizations had on superintendents.

The findings indicate that employee groups had much less influence than did other administrators or teachers individually. Slightly less than half of the respondents (46.7%) said the influence of these groups was either *considerable* or *moderate*. Just over one in five (21.1%) said that these groups had *no influence*. Superintendents in districts with fewer than 300 pupils were over three times more likely than superintendents in districts with 25,000 or more pupils to indicate that employee unions or other formal groups had *no influence*. All response data for this issue are in Table 5.13.

Parents

Clearly, parents have been and continue to be an important source of potential influence on superintendents. As a collective, they have altered the schooling process at the local school-district level in meaningful ways to better serve their children. As examples, parents played a pivotal role in bringing to light problems that led to school desegregation based on race (see Title VII of the Civil Rights Act of 1964), creating provisions of equal opportunities based on gender (see U.S. Department of Labor), and expanding and improving programming for special needs students (see U.S. Department of Education).

Almost by definition, the influence of parents with superintendents is directed toward improving the schooling process for their children. The neediest students today have been defined by certain group characteristics such as (a) diversity, (b) English language learners, and (c) poverty (Berliner, 2006). Unlike special needs students, however, racially diverse students, English language learners, and students of poverty seldom have organized parent groups to represent them (Young, Reimer, & Young, 2010). Their cause often must be championed by parents working collaboratively with superintendents.

Although savvy superintendents are aware of the power parents can exert, the level of actual parental influence is not uniform across districts. A large majority of superintendents responding in this study (80.9%) said the level of parental influence with them was *considerable* (23.6%) or *moderate* (57.3%). Superintendents in districts with less than 300 pupils were more likely than their peers in the remaining three district-enrollment categories to say that parental influence with them was *slight*. All response data pertaining to parental influence on superintendents are in Table 5.14.

Students

Students also are a source of direct and indirect influence. Again, a large proportion of the superintendents responding in this study (77.4%) indicated that students had *considerable* (37.7%) or *moderate* (39.7%) influence on them. District enrollment did not appear to have a substantial effect on how superintendents responded to this issue. All response data concerning student influence on superintendents are in Table 5.15.

Table 5.13 Extent of Employee Union (or Other Formal Employee Organization) Influence on the Superintendent

| Response options | District enrollment | | | | | | | | | |
| | Fewer than 300 | | 300 to 2,999 | | 3,000 to 24,999 | | 25,000 or more | | All | |
	f	%	*f*	%	*f*	%	*f*	%	*f*	%
Considerable	6	3.5	103	9.6	68	13.0	9	15.8	186	10.2
Moderate	32	18.6	388	36.0	226	43.2	22	38.6	668	36.5
Slight	57	33.1	366	33.9	140	26.8	19	33.3	582	31.8
None	77	44.8	215	19.9	88	16.8	7	12.3	387	21.1
Uncertain	0	0.0	7	0.7	1	0.2	0	0.0	8	0.4
Total	172	100.0	1079	100.0	523	100.0	57	100.0	1831	100.0

Table 5.14   Extent of Parent Influence on the Superintendent

Response options	District enrollment									
	Fewer than 300		300 to 2,999		3,000 to 24,999		25,000 or more		All	
	f	%	f	%	f	%	f	%	f	%
Considerable	28	16.1	243	22.7	145	27.8	15	26.3	431	23.6
Moderate	100	57.5	614	57.3	296	56.7	35	61.4	1045	57.3
Slight	45	25.9	206	19.2	78	14.9	6	10.5	335	18.4
None	1	0.6	8	0.8	3	0.6	0	0.0	12	0.7
Uncertain	0	0.0	0	0.0	0	0.0	1	1.8	1	0.1
Total	174	100.0	1071	100.0	522	100.0	57	100.0	1824	100.0

Table 5.15   Extent of Student Influence on the Superintendent

Response options	District enrollment									
	Fewer than 300		300 to 2,999		3,000 to 24,999		25,000 or more		All	
	f	%	f	%	f	%	f	%	f	%
Considerable	57	33.0	415	38.5	199	38.0	19	32.8	690	37.7
Moderate	78	45.1	416	38.6	213	40.7	21	36.2	728	39.7
Slight	31	17.9	225	20.9	100.0	19.1	17	29.3	373	20.4
None	7	4.1	21	2.0	11	2.1	0	0.0	39	2.1
Uncertain	0	0.0	0	0.0	1	0.2	1	1.7	2	0.1
Total	173	100.0	1077	100.0	524	100.0	58	100.0	1832	100.0

Elected State and Local Officials

At the state and local levels, elected officials have the potential to influence superintendents. Just over half the respondents (53.4%) indicated that influence of state elected officials on them was *slight* (40.8%) or *none* (12.6%). Superintendents in districts with less than 300 pupils were more likely than their peers to say that state officials had no influence. All response data concerning the influence of state elected officials on superintendents are in Table 5.16.

The level of influence of local elected officials was found to be lower than the influence of state elected officials. Nearly three-fourths of the superintendents (72.5%) said that these officials had *slight* or *no influence* on them. Superintendents in districts with less than 300 pupils were far more likely than peers in the other three district-enrollment categories to indicate that local elected officials had *no influ-*

ence on them. In many very small districts located in rural areas, superintendents are less involved with local officials, and this fact likely explains this finding. All response data concerning the influence of local elected officials on superintendents are in Table 5.17

Business Elites

Business elites are defined in this study to include corporation executives and business owners. Among superintendents identifying this group's level of influence on their practice, 76% indicated that it was either a *slight influence* or that they had *no influence*. Nearly half of the respondents in districts with less than 300 pupils (47.7%) said that this group had *no influence* whereas only 5.2% of their peers in the larg-

Table 5.16 Extent of State Elected Officials' Influence on the Superintendent

Response options	District enrollment									
	Fewer than 300		300 to 2,999		3,000 to 24,999		25,000 or more		All	
	f	*%*	*f*	*%*	*f*	*%*	*f*	*%*	*f*	*%*
Considerable	16	9.3	161	14.9	58	11.1	11	19.0	246	13.4
Moderate	45	26.0	327	30.3	191	36.5	25	43.1	588	32.1
Slight	72	41.6	445	41.2	212	40.5	20	34.5	749	40.8
None	37	21.4	133	12.3	59	11.3	2	3.5	231	12.6
Uncertain	3	1.7	14	1.3	3	0.6	0	0.0	20	1.1
Total	173	100.0	1080	100.0	523	100.0	58	100.0	1834	100.0

Table 5.17 Extent of Local Elected Officials' Influence on the Superintendent

Response options	District enrollment									
	Fewer than 300		300 to 2,999		3,000 to 24,999		25,000 or more		All	
	f	*%*	*f*	*%*	*f*	*%*	*f*	*%*	*f*	*%*
Considerable	4	2.3	40	3.7	33	6.3	5	8.6	82	4.5
Moderate	25	14.5	213	19.9	141	27.1	22	37.9	401	22.0
Slight	63	36.4	494	46.1	246	47.2	26	44.8	829	45.4
None	78	45.1	314	29.3	98	18.8	4	6.9	494	27.1
Uncertain	3	1.7	11	1.0	3	0.6	1	1.7	18	1.0
Total	173	100.0	1081	100.0	524	100.0	58	100.0	1824	100.0

est district gave the same response. Differences between the smallest and the largest school districts on this matter are understandable given the nature of the communities in which these districts are situated. Corporation executives are more likely to be active politically in large school districts than they are in small school districts because most small school districts are located in rural areas.

Community Special Interest Groups

Like business elites, community special interest groups have the potential to influence superintendents. Response data concerning how respondents perceived the level of influence exerted by these groups are in Table 5.19. Superintendents in the largest districts were approximately twice as likely (44.9%) to report *considerable* or *moderate* levels as were their peers in the smallest districts (22.6%).

Table 5.18　Extent of Business Elites' (Corporation Executives, Business Owners) Influence on the Superintendent

Response options	District enrollment									
	Fewer than 300		300 to 2,999		3,000 to 24,999		25,000 or more		All	
	f	*%*	*f*	*%*	*f*	*%*	*f*	*%*	*f*	*%*
Considerable	3	1.7	22	2.1	16	3.1	4	6.9	45	2.5
Moderate	16	9.2	182	17.0	148	28.4	22	37.9	368	20.1
Slight	67	38.5	487	45.3	245	46.9	28	48.3	827	45.2
None	83	47.7	369	34.4	110	21.1	3	5.2	565	30.9
Uncertain	5	2.9	14	1.3	3	0.6	1	1.7	23	1.3
Total	174	100.0	1084	100.0	522	100.0	58	100.0	1828	100.0

Table 5.19　Extent of Community Special Interest Group Influence on the Superintendent

Response options	District enrollment									
	Fewer than 300		300 to 2,999		3,000 to 24,999		25,000 or more		All	
	f	*%*	*f*	*%*	*f*	*%*	*f*	*%*	*f*	*%*
Considerable	2	1.2	34	3.2	21	4.0	2	3.5	59	3.2
Moderate	37	21.4	273	25.3	186	35.7	24	41.4	520	28.4
Slight	74	42.8	545	50.6	256	49.1	30	51.7	905	49.5
None	57	33.0	216	20.0	56	10.8	2	3.5	331	18.1
Uncertain	3	1.7	10	0.9	2	0.4	0	0.0	15	0.8
Total	173	100.0	1078	100.0	521	100.0	58	100.0	1830	100.0

Potentially moderating the differences between small and large school districts for business elites as well as for special interest groups are other community factors. One likely factor is the media providing information about a local school district. Today, unlike the past, the media provide information about the schooling process and about schooling outcomes via report cards.

Media

Only 4.5% of the respondents said that the media exerted *considerable influence* on them (see Table 5.20). Conversely, over three times as many superintendents (16.9%) indicated that the media had *no influence* on them. Not unexpectedly, the lowest levels of influence for media were reported by superintendents in the smallest school districts (i.e., those with fewer than 300 students). All response data for this issue are reported in Table 5.20.

Peer Superintendents

As typical in professions, practitioners often turn to colleagues for advice and assistance. Superintendents appear to be no exception. Asked to identify the level of influence exerted by peer superintendents, slightly less than two-thirds (65.9%) said it was *considerable* or *moderate*. Superintendents in the smallest (i.e., less than 300 pupils) and largest (i.e., 25,000 or more pupils) districts reported slightly lower levels of peer influence than did superintendents in the remaining two district-enrollment categories. All response data for peer superintendent influence are in Table 5.21.

Research

As described in Chapter 1, the expectation for superintendents to rely on empirical data to solve problems and make important decisions emerged during the 1950s. More recently, federal and state laws have reinforced this anticipation. Respondents were asked to identify how often they read research related to their practice—an activity nested in their role as applied social scientists (Fusarelli & Fusarelli, 2005). Just over half of all superintendents (51%) said they read research *frequently*, and another 41.3% said they read it *occasionally*. Superintendents in the smallest districts (i.e., less than 300 pupils) were less likely to read research *frequently* than were peers in larger districts.

Table 5.20   Extent of Media Influence on the Superintendent

Response options	District enrollment									
	Fewer than 300		300 to 2,999		3,000 to 24,999		25,000 or more		All	
	f	%	f	%	f	%	f	%	f	%
Considerable	5	2.9	45	4.2	28	5.4	4	6.9	82	4.5
Moderate	29	16.7	283	26.2	177	34.0	16	27.6	505	27.6
Slight	82	47.1	571	52.9	229	44.0	34	58.6	916	50.0
None	57	32.8	170	15.8	79	15.2	3	5.2	309	16.9
Uncertain	1	0.6	10	0.9	7	1.4	1	1.7	19	1.0
Total	174	100.0	1079	100.0	520	100.0	58	100.0	1831	100.0

Respondents were then asked to identify the extent to which the research they read was beneficial. Just under two-thirds of all superintendents (64.6%) said it was *occasionally beneficial*, and another 28.1% said it was *always beneficial*. These findings are similar to those reported in 2000; in that study, 30.6% said it was *highly useful*, 45.2% said it was *usually useful*, and 23% said it was *occasionally useful*. In general, the findings regarding research indicate that this source of information had at least a moderate level of influence on superintendents. Response data for reading research and research importance are in Tables 5.22 and 5.23 respectively.

Influence of AASA

Respondents were asked to identify the extent to which they were influenced by AASA. Based on percentages of responses, most identified the level influence as being *slight* (46.8% of all respondents

Table 5.21 Extent of Peer Superintendents' (Superintendents from Other Districts) Influence on the Superintendent

Response options	District enrollment									
	Fewer than 300		300 to 2,999		3,000 to 24,999		25,000 or more		All	
	f	%	f	%	f	%	f	%	f	%
Considerable	40	23.0	261	24.3	109	20.9	11	19.0	421	23.0
Moderate	58	33.3	488	45.4	219	42.0	20	34.5	785	42.9
Slight	57	23.8	65	24.7	155	29.7	20	34.5	497	27.2
None	19	10.9	59	5.5	38	7.3	6	10.3	122	6.7
Uncertain	0	0.0	2	0.2	1	0.2	1	1.7	4	0.2
Total	174	100.0	1075	100.0	522	100.0	56	100.0	1829	100.0

Table 5.22 How Often Do You Read Research Relevant to the Superintendent's Position?

Response options	District enrollment									
	Fewer than 300		300 to 2,999		3,000 to 24,999		25,000 or more		All	
	f	%	f	%	f	%	f	%	f	%
Frequently	59	33.9	523	48.3	322	61.5	33	56.9	937	51.0
Occasionally	95	54.6	459	42.4	183	34.9	23	39.7	760	41.3
Rarely	20	11.5	93	8.6	19	3.6	2	3.4	134	7.3
Never	0	0.0	36	0.6	0	0.0	0	0.0	6	0.3
Did not answer	0	0.0	1	0.1	0	0.0	0	0.0	1	0.1
Total	174	100.0	1082	100.0	524	100.0	58	100.0	1838	100.0

regardless of district size). Superintendents in moderate size districts (i.e., with enrollments between 300 and 24,999) were slightly more likely than their peers in the smallest and largest districts to identify AASA's level of influence as *considerable* or *moderate*. All response data for level of AASA influence are in Table 5.24.

State Superintendent Associations

Respondents also were asked to identify the level of influence exerted by their respective state superintendent associations. Just over half of all superintendents (52.6%) identified the level as either being *considerable* or *moderate*. The higher level of influence reported for state superintendent associations compared to AASA is likely explained by the differences between federal and state control over public

Table 5.23   Value of Readings for Superintendents

Response options	District enrollment									
	Fewer than 300		300 to 2,999		3,000 to 24,999		25,000 or more		All	
	f	*%*	*f*	*%*	*f*	*%*	*f*	*%*	*f*	*%*
Always beneficial	46	26.6	275	25.5	178	34.0	16	27.6	515	28.1
Occasionally beneficial	107	61.8	720	66.7	320	61.2	37	63.8	1184	64.6
Rarely beneficial	17	9.8	68	6.3	21	4.0	5	8.6	111	6.1
Never beneficial	0	0.0	2	0.2	2	0.4	0	0.0	4	0.2
Have not read	3	1.7	14	1.3	2	0.4	0	0.0	19	1.0
Total	173	100.0	1079	100.0	523	100.0	58	100.0	1833	100.0

Table 5.24   Extent of AASA Influence on the Superintendent

Response options	District enrollment									
	Fewer than 300		300 to 2,999		3,000 to 24,999		25,000 or more		All	
	f	*%*	*f*	*%*	*f*	*%*	*f*	*%*	*f*	*%*
Considerable	9	5.2	44	4.1	26	5.0	1	1.8	80	4.4
Moderate	31	17.9	223	20.6	126	24.1	10	17.5	390	21.2
Slight	80	46.2	502	46.4	250	47.7	26	45.6	858	46.8
None	51	29.5	282	26.1	110	21.0	19	33.3	462	25.2
Uncertain	2	1.2	30	2.8	12	2.3	1	1.8	45	2.4
Total	173	100.0	1081	100.0	524	100.0	57	100.0	1835	100.0

education. Since public schools are an extension of state government, more laws, policies, and rules are promulgated at this level than at the federal level (Kowalski, 2006). Consequently, state superintendent associations are able to focus on specific state issues whereas AASA typically focuses on national issues. All response data for level of influence exerted by state superintendent associations are in Table 5.25.

Superintendent Status and Involvement

Two additional issues relate to the content in this chapter. The first is the perceived status superintendents have in their communities; the second is the involvement of superintendents in the local community and professional associations.

Perceived Status in the Local Community

Respondents were asked to identify their perceptions of the status accorded to superintendents in their communities. Nearly all (99%) answered that it was *very high* (49%) or *moderately high* (50%). Superintendents in the largest districts were considerably more likely than their peers to have answered that their status was *very high*. All response data for this issue are reported in Table 5.26.

Superintendent Involvement in the Local Community

The literature has traditionally identified community involvement as both a normative standard and a benefit for superintendents. Expectedly, a very high percentage of respondents in this study (78%) said their level of community involvement was either *considerable* or *moderate*. Superintendents in the largest school districts (i.e., 25,000 or more students) were nearly three times as likely to have reported *considerable* involvement as were their peers in the smallest school districts (i.e., less than 300 students). Nearly one-third of the superintendents in the smallest districts (32.8%) identified their level of community involvement as *limited* or *none* whereas only 6.9% of the superintendents in the largest enrollment districts reported *limited* involvement, and not a single respondent in this subgroup selected the *none* response option. All response data for levels of community involvement are in Table 5.27.

Table 5.25   Extent of State Superintendent Association Influence on the Superintendent

| Response options | District enrollment | | | | | | | | | |
| | Fewer than 300 | | 300 to 2,999 | | 3,000 to 24,999 | | 25,000 or more | | All | |
	f	*%*	*f*	*%*	*f*	*%*	*f*	*%*	*f*	*%*
Considerable	21	12.1	180	16.7	78	15.0	3	5.2	282	15.4
Moderate	51	29.3	409	37.9	200	38.4	22	37.9	682	37.2
Slight	76	43.7	347	32.2	182	34.9	22	37.9	627	34.2
None	25	14.4	132	12.2	57	10.9	11	19.0	225	12.3
Uncertain	1	0.6	11	1.0	4	0.8	0	0.0	16	0.9
Total	174	100.0	1079	100.0	521	100.0	58	100.0	1832	100.0

Table 5.26   Level of Status for Superintendents within the Community

Response options	District enrollment									
	Fewer than 300		300 to 2,999		3,000 to 24,999		25,000 or more		All	
	f	%	f	%	f	%	f	%	f	%
Very high	65	38.0	471	43.7	319	61.2	42	72.4	897	49.0
Moderately high	101	59.1	593	55.0	197	37.8	15	25.9	906	50.0
Moderately low	5	2.9	12	1.1	3	0.6	1	1.76	21	1.0
Very low	0	0.0	2	.02	2	0.4	0	0.1	4	0.0
Total	171	100.0	1078	100.0	521	100.0	58	100.0	1828	100.0

Table 5.27   Level of Involvement for Superintendents with the Community

Response options	District enrollment									
	Fewer than 300		300 to 2,999		3,000 to 24,999		25,000 or more		All	
	f	%	f	%	f	%	f	%	f	%
Considerable	34	19.5	382	35.3	265	50.6	32	55.2	713	39.0
Moderate	83	47.7	433	40.1	182	34.7	22	37.9	720	39.0
Limited	55	31.6	253	23.4	74	14.1	4	6.9	386	21.0
None	2	1.2	13	1.2	3	0.6	0	0	18	1.0
Total	174	100.0	1081	100.0	524	100.0	58	100.0	1827	100.0

As data in Tables 5.26 and 5.27 suggest, there appears to be an association between perceived status levels and perceived community involvement levels. Although these data are insensitive to a cause-effect relationship, it appears that a higher level of community involvement is likely to produce a higher level status.

Involvement in Professional Organizations

Elements of practice for superintendents may be influenced by professional associations as well as by the professional knowledge base. Thus, respondents were asked to identify their collective level of involvement in professional associations. A large percentage (83.9%) identified that level as being *considerable* or *moderate*. District size appeared to have little influence on levels of involvement; however, superintendents in districts with less than 300 pupils were slightly less involved than peers in the three other district-enrollment categories. All response data for involvement in professional organizations are reported in Table 5.28.

Table 5.28   Level of Involvement of Superintendents in Professional Associations (n = 1,817)

Response options	District enrollment									
	Fewer than 300		300 to 2,999		3,000 to 24,999		25,000 or more		All	
	f	%	f	%	f	%	f	%	f	%
Considerable	46	27.1	352	32.9	223	43.1	25	43.1	646	35.6
Moderate	88	51.8	534	49.9	232	44.8	23	39.7	877	48.3
Limited	34	20.0	178	16.6	60	11.6	9	15.5	281	15.5
None	2	1.2	7	0.7	3	0.6	1	1.7	13	0.7
Total	170	100.0	1071	100.0	518	100.0	58	100.0	1817	100.0

Summary

The content of this chapter addresses factors that affect superintendent practice. Specifically, data and findings relate to levels of influence exerted by individuals, groups, and organizations. Data disaggregated by district-size groups suggest several notable differences based on district enrollment. With few exceptions, superintendents employed in the smallest school districts (i.e., less than 300 pupils) differed from their peers in the largest districts (i.e., 25,000 or more pupils). Practice-based differences between superintendents in very large and very small districts have been found in numerous other studies (e.g., Blumberg, 1985; Glass, Björk, & Brunner, 2000; Kowalski, 1995).

The following are among the most salient findings reported in this chapter:

- With respect to effects on their personal practice, superintendents viewed school boards, other administrators in the district, and their compensation as *assets*; they viewed state departments of education, the court system, and the media as being *neither assets nor liabilities*.
- Superintendents viewed labor unions and formal employee associations as having had *little influence* on elements of their practice.
- Superintendents reported that the most important source for informing elements of their practice was *peer superintendents*, especially those in comparable school districts.
- Complementing elements of their practice, superintendents reported they are frequent readers of the professional literature and reported what they read to be informative. For example, most superintendents reported reading research *frequently* or *occasionally*, and over 90% found the research they read to be *beneficial* at least *occasionally*.

6

Superintendent Interactions with School Boards

Pivotal to the success of any school district is a positive relationship between school boards and their superintendents. School boards are legally extensions of state government, and they have a legislative responsibility to set policy and to ensure that state laws and regulations are followed. As top-level administrators, superintendents make policy recommendations, ensure policy enforcement, and provide leadership and management necessary for the day-to-day operation of districts and schools. Clearly, school boards and superintendents have dissimilar legitimate roles; pragmatically, however, the line separating policy development and administration is often indistinct and unobserved (Kowalski, 2006).

Three topics are addressed in this chapter. The first is issues affecting superintendent–school board relationships; the second is the employment and evaluation of superintendents; the third is information about the school boards employing respondents in this study.

Superintendent–School Board Relations

The relationships between superintendents and school boards have far-reaching leadership and policy implications that greatly affect the quality of school districts' educational programs (Conley, 2003; Smoley, 1999). Poor relationships, for example, can (a) weaken district stability and morale (Renchler, 1992), (b) increase conflict over district instructional goals and objectives (Morgan & Petersen, 2002; Petersen, 1999), (c) impede collaborative visioning and long-range planning (Kowalski, 2006), (d) negatively influence the superintendent's trustworthiness and credibility (Petersen & Short, 2002; Petersen & Williams, 2005), (e) deter school improvement efforts (Danzberger, Kirst, & Usdan, 1992), and (f) generate institutional instability (Carter & Cunningham, 1997; Renchler, 1992).

In an effort to determine the current quality of associations, superintendents were asked to identify the extent to which they maintained positive relationships with their school board members. Overall, 97% said that they maintained positive relationships with *all* (64%) or *most* (33%) board members. This outcome is similar to the one reported by Glass and Franceschini (2007) several years ago; they found that 93% of superintendents characterized their relationship with their respective boards as *good* or *very good*. A summary of the responses is provided in Table 6.1.

New Board Member Orientation

In general, school board members come to their positions with a limited understanding of their policy role or the role of the individual members as a governing body (Spillane & Regnier, 1998). Consequently, they are vulnerable to an array of external, social, economic, and political influences over which they have little or no control (Boyd, 1976). Thus, acclimation to their board-member role is pivotal, both in terms of understanding their prescribed responsibilities and in terms of understanding the importance of working with superintendents.

The orientation of new board members can be provided by various individuals and materials. Superintendents in this study were asked to identify the ones that were being used in their respective districts. The results are included in Table 6.2.

Table 6.1 Relationships with School Board Members

Response options	District enrollment									
	Fewer than 300		300 to 2,999		3,000 to 24,999		25,000 or more		All	
	f	%	f	%	f	%	f	%	f	%
Positive with all members	108	62.4	679	64.2	331	64.3	40	72.7	1158	64.3
Positive with a majority of members	57	33.0	358	33.9	169	32.8	13	23.7	597	33.2
Positive with only a few members	5	2.9	18	1.7	14	2.7	1	1.8	38	2.1
Not positive with any members	3	1.7	2	0.2	1	0.2	1	1.8	7	0.4
Total	173	100.0	1057	100.0	515	100.0	55	100.0	1800	100.0

Table 6.2 Who and/or What Provides Orientation for New School Board Members

Response options	District enrollment									
	Fewer than 300		300 to 2,999		3,000 to 24,999		25,000 or more		All	
	f	%	f	%	f	%	f	%	f	%
Superintendent	145	83.8	965	89.4	480	91.6	55	94.8	1645	89.7
State school board association	122	70.5	780	72.2	386	73.7	37	63.8	1325	72.2
Other board members	97	56.1	713	66.0	387	73.9	41	70.7	1238	67.5
Private consultants	15	8.7	93	8.6	86	16.4	13	22.4	207	11.3
Professors	0	0.0	11	1.0	8	1.5	0	0.0	19	1.0
Written materials	73	42.2	504	46.7	288	55.0	35	60.3	900	49.0
No orientation provided	7	4.0	17	1.6	5	1.0	1	1.7	30	1.6
Other	11	6.4	96	8.9	65	12.4	12	20.7	184	10.0

Note: Respondents were able to select all response options that applied.

The most frequently reported provider was the *superintendent*, followed by *state school board association*, *other board members*, and *written materials*. In their study conducted a decade ago, Glass, Björk, and Brunner (2000) reported that only 55% of superintendents and only 26% of state school board associations provided new school board members with an orientation. Thus, findings reported here represent substantial increases in both superintendent-provided and state school board association–provided orientation.

Board Approval of Superintendent Recommendations

Historically, superintendents have been cast as both professional educators and administrators. Their normative responsibility in the literature has been to make policy recommendations, especially on matters pertaining to curriculum, instruction, evaluation, and other aspects of the education process. In the context of increased and ever complex federal and state policies, board members may be depending heavily on their superintendent to translate and give localized meaning to state and federal laws, regulations, and goals.

Nowhere are the dynamics of superintendent–school board relations put to the test and played out in a more public arena than the board's acceptance or rejection of a superintendent's policy recommendations. This issue has two important dimensions: the extent to which superintendents provide policy recommendations and the extent to which school boards approve them. As data in Table 6.3 show, 92.8% of the respondents indicated that they made a recommendation on *all* or *most* issues presented to the school board for approval. This outcome indicates the normative responsibility to make recommendations to the board is still widely honored by superintendents.

The extent to which school boards approved superintendent recommendations was examined in relation to overall approval and approval for education-related and operations-related issues. With regard to the former, 97% of the respondents said that their recommendations were approved *at least 80% of the time* (see Table 6.4)—in the 2000 study, Glass, Björk, and Brunner found that 98% of superintendents said that their recommendations were approved *at least 80% of the time*.

Table 6.3 How Issues Are Presented to the School Board

Response options	District enrollment									
	Fewer than 300		300 to 2,999		3,000 to 24,999		25,000 or more		All	
	f	*%*	*f*	*%*	*f*	*%*	*f*	*%*	*f*	*%*
All issues are presented with a recommendation	51	29.3	315	29.2	224	42.9	21	36.2	611	33.3
Most issues are presented with a recommendation	102	58.6	691	64.1	266	51.0	31	53.5	1090	59.5
Some issues are presented with a recommendation	18	10.3	67	6.2	28	5.4	6	10.3	119	6.5
Few issues are presented with a recommendation	2	1.2	4	0.4	1	0.1	0	0.0	7	0.4
No issues are presented with a recommendation	1	0.6	1	0.1	3	0.6	0	0.0	5	0.3
Total	174	100.0	1078	100.0	522	100.0	58	100.0	1832	100.0

In the past, board support for a superintendent's recommendations has been found to vary according to the nature of the issue being addressed (Boyd, 1976). Broadly, recommendations can be categorized as education-related or operations-related; the former commonly pertain to matters of teaching, learning, and evaluation, and the latter commonly pertain to managerial functions, such as fiscal and facility controls. Although previous research has suggested that boards of education are more inclined to approve education-related recommendations (Petersen & Short, 2002), just over three-fourths of the respondents in this study indicated *no difference* in approval rates between the categories. These data are in Table 6.5.

Superintendent Influence on Boards

Because they are public officials, commonly elected to office, school board members are subjected to and influenced by a variety of political forces (Opfer, 2005). Consequently, determining who has influence with them has been and remains a cogent issue for those who study school district governance. In this study, superintendents were asked to identify the level of the influence of a variety of stakeholders, including themselves. Results clearly indicate that superintendents perceived themselves as having had the most influence with school boards. Table 6.6 provides data for superintendent influence disaggregated by district enrollment; Table 6.7 includes data regarding the perceived levels of influence attributed to other stakeholders. These responses show that other than superintendents, parents and other administrators employed in the district had the greatest levels of influence. Perhaps most notable are the differences between the responses for superintendent influence and the next highest category. Clearly, superintendents viewed themselves as having substantially more influence on school boards than any other individual or groups.

Communication with Board Members

The best intentions of superintendents and the value of their expertise can be diminished by poor communication. Recognizing this fact, effective superintendents constantly focus on how their communica-

Table 6.4 Frequency of Board Approval of Superintendent Recommendations

Response options	District enrollment									
	Fewer than 300		300 to 2,999		3,000 to 24,999		25,000 or more		All	
	f	*%*	*f*	*%*	*f*	*%*	*f*	*%*	*f*	*%*
90–100% of the time	146	84.4	982	91.8	477	91.9	49	84.5	1654	91.0
80–89% of the time	16	9.3	56	5.2	31	6.0	6	10.3	109	6.0
70–79% of the time	6	3.5	17	1.6	5	0.9	2	3.5	30	1.6
60–69% of the time	2	1.1	7	0.7	1	0.2	0	0.0	10	0.5
50–59% of the time	3	1.7	3	0.2	4	0.8	0	0.0	10	0.5
Less than 49% of the time	0	0.0	5	0.5	1	0.2	1	1.7	7	0.4
Total	173	100.0	1070	100.0	519	100.0	58	100.0	1820	100.0

Table 6.5   Board Approval of Superintendent Recommendations Based on the Nature of Issues

Response options	District enrollment									
	Fewer than 300		300 to 2,999		3,000 to 24,999		25,000 or more		All	
	f	%	f	%	f	%	f	%	f	%
Board has approved a higher percentage of recommendations for educational issues than other issues	54	31.2	222	20.6	121	23.2	14	24.6	411	22.5
Board has approved a lower percentage of recommendations for educational issues than other issues	2	1.2	10	0.9	4	0.7	1	1.7	17	0.9
There is no difference in the percentage of recommendations approved in the two categories	117	67.6	847	78.5	397	76.1	42	73.7	1403	76.6
Total	173	100.0	1079	100.0	522	100.0	57	100.0	1831	100.0

Table 6.6   Level of Superintendent Influence with the School Board

Response options	District enrollment									
	Fewer than 300		300 to 2,999		3,000 to 24,999		25,000 or more		All	
	f	%	f	%	f	%	f	%	f	%
Considerable	132	75.9	933	86.3	487	93.1	49	84.5	1601	87.2
Moderate	32	18.4	132	12.2	29	5.5	7	12.1	200	10.8
Slight	10	5.7	14	1.3	6	1.2	1	1.70	31	1.7
None	0	0.0	1	0.1	1	0.2	1	1.70	3	0.2
Uncertain	0	0.0	1	0.1	0	0.0	0	0.0	1	0.1
Total	174	100.0	1081	100.0	523	100.0	58	100.0	1836	100.0

Table 6.7   Levels of Influence Various Groups Have with the School Board

| Groups | District enrollment | | | | | | | | | |
| | Considerable | | Moderate | | Slight | | None | | Uncertain | |
	f	%	f	%	f	%	f	%	f	%
Parents in your district (n = 1829)	587	32.1	965	52.8	271	14.8	4	0.2	2	0.1
Administrators other than the superintendent (district & site level) (n = 1831)	559	30.5	925	50.5	285	15.6	61	3.3	1	0.1
Students in your district (n = 1832)	314	17.1	726	39.7	717	39.1	69	3.8	6	0.3
Teachers (not including the teachers' union) (n = 1833)	297	16.2	992	54.1	515	28.1	27	1.5	2	0.1
Employee unions/ organizations (n = 1834)	134	7.3	556	30.3	754	41.1	380	20.7	10	0.6
Community special interest groups in your district (n = 1830)	123	6.7	546	29.8	879	48.1	267	14.6	15	0.8
State school boards association (n = 1820)	129	7.1	521	28.6	851	46.8	302	16.6	17	0.9
Elected state officials (e.g., governor, state legislator) (n = 1831)	118	6.4	448	24.5	859	46.9	378	20.7	28	1.5
Media (all types, both press and electronic) (n = 1830)	102	5.6	506	27.7	904	49.4	304	16.6	14	0.7
Elected local officials (e.g., mayor, city council) (n = 1828)	100	5.5	358	19.6	864	47.2	484	26.5	22	1.2
Business elites (e.g., corp. presidents, small business owners) (n = 1825)	65	3.6	362	19.8	881	48.3	482	26.4	35	1.9
National school boards association (n = 1830)	16	0.9	147	8.0	708	38.7	908	49.6	51	2.8

tive behavior is being interpreted and is affecting relationships (Kowalski, Petersen, & Fusarelli, 2007). In this vein, respondents in this study were asked to specify the amount of time they spent weekly communicating directly with school board members. Approximately two-thirds of them indicated that they spend less than 6 hours per week in direct communication with board members. Moreover, superintendents employed in the smallest-enrollment districts (i.e., below 300 students) appeared to spend the least amount of time in direct communication with board members. Responses for this issue are included in Table 6.8.

Findings on direct communication with board members in this study differ from those reported by Glass, Björk, and Brunner in 2000. Whereas their study reported that 83% of superintendents, regardless of district size, spent less than 6 hours on this activity, this study found that only 63% reported this level of interaction. Three issues may explain the difference between findings in the two studies. First, the response scales in the 2000 and 2010 studies were not identical; the 2000 study provided several response options below 6 hours per week whereas 6 hours per week was the lowest response option in this study. Second, the current social and political climate may necessitate more direct communication between superintendents and board members. Third, both superintendents and board members have greater access to technology, which facilitates communication, than they did 10 years ago.

In an effort to gain insights about the use of technology to communicate with board members, respondents were asked to identify the extent to which they relied on technology to communicate with board members. Because the use of technology is often perceived to be affected by a person's age (i.e., younger persons are considered to use technology more often than older persons), data on this issue are reported by respondent age. The findings, found in Table 6.9, did not reveal a discernible pattern in technology use based on age.

Satisfaction with School Boards

Results of this investigation indicate that (91.3%) of superintendents were *very satisfied* or *moderately satisfied* with their school boards. Further, satisfaction levels were rather consistent regardless of school district enrollment. Responses regarding level of satisfaction with school boards are in Table 6.10.

Table 6.8   Hours per Week Spent Communicating Directly with Board Members

Response options	District enrollment									
	Fewer than 300		300 to 2,999		3,000 to 24,999		25,000 or more		All	
	f	*%*	*f*	*%*	*f*	*%*	*f*	*%*	*f*	*%*
Less than 6	130	76.9	715	67.6	255	49.8	27	48.2	1127	63.0
6 to 9	29	17.2	268	25.4	178	34.8	14	25.0	489	27.3
10 to 14	8	4.7	51	4.8	50	9.8	9	16.1	118	6.6
15 to 19	0	0.0	17	1.6	20	3.9	5	8.9	42	2.3
20 to 24	2	1.2	3	0.3	6	1.1	0	0.0	11	0.5
25 or more	0	0.0	3	0.3	3	0.6	1	1.8	7	0.3
Total	169	100.0	1057	100.0	512	100.0	56	100.0	1794	100.0

Table 6.9   Percentage of Direct Communication with Board Members Using Technology by Superintendent Age

Age	Percentage of communication using technology											
	Below 10%		11 to 20%		21 to 30%		31 to 40%		41 to 50%		Over 50%	
	f	%	*f*	%	*f*	%	*f*	%	*f*	%	*f*	%
<36	3	1.3	0	0.0	2	1.5	3	2.3	5	1.6	10	1.1
36 to 40	80	36.0	4	2.3	9	6.6	4	3.1	12	3.8	39	4.2
41 to 45	11	5.0	14	8.1	10	7.3	12	9.3	33	10.5	93	10.0
46 to 50	19	8.6	19	11.0	19	13.9	18	14.0	42	13.4	122	13.1
51 to 55	35	15.8	45	26.2	37	27.0	41	31.8	84	26.8	207	22.2
56 to 60	50	22.5	56	32.6	33	24.1	29	22.5	86	27.4	292	31.3
61 to 65	23	10.4	29	16.9	22	16.0	19	14.7	44	14.0	142	15.3
66+	1	0.4	5	2.9	5	3.6	3	2.3	8	2.5	26	2.8
Total	222	100.0	172	100.0	137	100.0	129	100.0	314	100.0	931	100.0

Table 6.10   Level of Superintendent Satisfaction with the School Board

Response options	District enrollment									
	Fewer than 300		300 to 2,999		3,000 to 24,999		25,000 or more		All	
	f	%	*f*	%	*f*	%	*f*	%	*f*	%
Very satisfied	100	57.5	653	60.7	315	60.6	31	54.4	1099	60.2
Moderately satisfied	60	34.5	331	30.8	157	30.2	19	33.3	567	31.1
Moderately dissatisfied	8	4.6	61	5.7	30	5.7	6	10.5	105	5.7
Very dissatisfied	6	3.4	30	2.8	18	3.5	1	1.8	55	3.0
Total	174	100.0	1075	100.0	520	100.0	57	100.0	1826	100.0

Superintendent Employment

Rapidly shifting social, political, and economic trends place a great demand on superintendents to be accountable for student achievement as well as human and material resources. As concerns about school effectiveness took center stage politically and as accountability became a priority for school boards, both the initial and continued employment of superintendents became more essential board responsibilities. Additional data related to the employment of superintendents is contained in Chapter 4 of this book.

Search Process

Today, there is no one selection process used universally to select and employ superintendents. Consequently, the superintendents were asked to identify the selection process that was deployed by the board to employ them. The most common response was that the school board acted independently. As one might expect, this option was most prevalent in the smallest enrollment category. The increased use of search consultants was associated with district enrollment; that is, the larger a school system, the more likely the board was to retain a search consultant. Data regarding this issue are in Table 6.11.

Reasons for Selection

Respondents were asked to identify the primary reason why they were selected for their current position. The most common response was *personal characteristics*, followed by the *potential to be a change agent* and *the ability to be an instructional leader*. Complete response data for this issue are in Table 6.12. In the 2000 study (Glass, Björk, & Brunner, 2000), 40% of the superintendents said the primary factor in their employment was *personal characteristics*, and an additional percentage (26%) said it was *to be a change agent* or an *instructional leader*. Thus, the results reported here are generally congruent with the 2000 study.

Primary Board Expectations of Their Superintendent

As described in Chapter 1, superintendents commonly are expected to assume five distinct roles: *instructional leader, manager, statesman/political leader, applied social scientist,* and *effective communica-*

Table 6.11 Search Process Used by the School Board to Hire the Superintendent

Response options	District enrollment									
	Fewer than 300		300 to 2,999		3,000 to 24,999		25,000 or more		All	
	f	*%*	*f*	*%*	*f*	*%*	*f*	*%*	*f*	*%*
School board acted independently (w/out consultants)	126	72.4	520	48.2	184	35.2	18	31.0	848	46.2
Private search firm involved	10	5.7	230	21.3	181	34.6	21	36.3	442	24.1
State school board association consultants involved	29	16.7	233	21.6	126	24.1	12	20.7	400	21.9
Other consultants involved	3	1.7	49	4.5	12	2.3	6	10.3	70	3.8
One or more professors involved	2	1.2	26	2.4	14	2.7	1	1.7	43	2.3
State superintendent's association consultants involved	4	2.3	22	2.0	6	1.1	0	0.0	32	1.7
Total	174	100.0	1080	100.0	523	100.0	58	100.0	1835	100.0

Table 6.12 Primary Reason Why the School Board Employed the Current Superintendent

| Response options | District enrollment | | | | | | | | | |
| | Fewer than 300 | | 300 to 2,999 | | 3,000 to 24,999 | | 25,000 or more | | All | |
	f	*%*	*f*	*%*	*f*	*%*	*f*	*%*	*f*	*%*
Personal characteristics	66	38.4	388	36.6	133	25.8	16	30.2	603	33.5
Potential to be change agent	41	23.8	242	22.8	150	29.1	15	28.3	448	24.9
Ability to be an instructional leader	17	9.9	191	18.0	139	27.0	12	22.6	359	20.0
Ability to communicate with stakeholders	7	4.1	72	6.8	39	7.5	7	13.2	125	6.9
Ability to manage fiscal resources	19	11.0	71	6.7	23	4.5	0	0.0	113	6.3
Uncertain	17	9.9	76	7.1	20	3.9	1	1.9	114	6.3
Ability to maintain status quo	4	2.3	16	1.5	8	1.6	1	1.9	29	1.6
Having leadership/managerial experience outside of education	1	0.6	5	0.5	3	0.6	1	1.9	10	0.5
Total	172	100.0	1061	100.0	515	100.0	53	100.0	1801	100.0

tor. Respondents were asked to identify the level of emphasis their school boards placed on each of them. The responses are totaled in Table 6.13. As these data show, the highest level of emphasis was placed on being an *effective communicator*, and the least amount of emphasis was placed on *applied social scientist*. Though the results regarding communication are not surprising in light of the realities of being a public administrator in an information-based society, the low level of emphasis placed on the scientific aspects of a superintendent's practice was less anticipated. The conceptualization of applied social scientist relates to using research and tacit knowledge to inform important decisions, and in the aftermath of the No Child Left Behind Act of 2001 (2002), tremendous emphasis has been placed on evidence-based practice and data-based decision making (Kowalski, 2009).

Length of Current Contract

State laws differ on the length of superintendent contracts, with some states mandating the number of years for an initial superintendent contract (Sharp & Walter, 2004). In this study, the most common contract length was *3 years*. Contracts of lesser duration were most common in smaller-enrollment districts. This is not unexpected since boards in larger and more urban districts are more likely to view multiyear contracts as necessary to attract and to retain high quality superintendents (Glass & Franceschini, 2007). Results on the length of superintendent contracts reported here mirror those reported in the 2000 study (Glass, Björk, & Brunner, 2000). That research reported that 45% of superintendents had a *3-year* contract, 18% had a *2-year* contract, and 13% had a *1-year* contract.

Merit/Performance Pay

A general acceptance of executive bonuses in the private sector as well as increasing demands for accountability have led to a strong public interest in pay-for-performance as part of the superinten-

Table 6.13   School Board Emphasis on Various Superintendent Roles

Superintendent roles	Level of emphasis							
	Substantial		Moderate		Low		None	
	f	*%*	*f*	*%*	*f*	*%*	*f*	*%*
Effective communicator (*n* = 1857)	1587	85.4	254	13.7	14	0.8	2	0.1
Manager (*n* = 1860)	1461	78.5	371	20.0	25	1.3	3	0.2
Instructional leader (*n* = 1860)	1119	60.1	641	34.5	89	4.8	11	0.6
Statesman, political leader (*n* = 1836)	1020	55.6	643	35.0	156	8.5	17	0.9
Applied social scientist (*n* = 1853)	298	16.0	758	40.9	646	34.9	151	8.2

Table 6.14   Length of Current Superintendent Contract

Response options	District enrollment									
	Fewer than 300		300 to 2,999		3,000 to 24,999		25,000 or more		All	
	f	*%*	*f*	*%*	*f*	*%*	*f*	*%*	*f*	*%*
1 year	54	31.2	122	11.4	19	3.7	1	1.8	196	10.8
2 years	42	24.3	248	23.1	64	12.3	6	10.7	360	19.8
3 years	57	33.0	431	40.1	268	51.6	24	42.9	780	42.8
4 years	6	3.5	88	8.2	83	16.0	18	32.1	195	10.7
5 or more years	8	4.6	170	15.8	80	15.4	7	12.5	265	14.5
Serving as an interim	3	1.7	10	0.9	3	0.6	0	0.0	16	0.9
Do not have a contract	3	1.7	5	0.5	2	0.4	0	0.0	10	0.5
Total	173	100.0	1074	100.0	519	100.0	56	100.0	1822	100.0

dent's compensation package. Although research has revealed that there are concerns about pay-for-performance provisions and the actual benefits of incremental bonuses (Johnson & Papay, 2010; Young, 2003), multistate investigations (e.g., Cox, 2006) have reported that pay-for-performance provisions are used for superintendents in several states for districts of all sizes.

In this study, the vast majority of respondents (85%) did not have a strict pay-for-performance provision in their contracts. In fact, 6% indicated that they had a pay provision based solely on personal performance, and 4% indicated they received compensation based both on personal and on district performance. Data for this issue are in Table 6.15.

Performance Evaluation

Most superintendents' evaluations are conducted through the use of checklists or rating scales focusing on traits, skills, knowledge, and style (Glass, Björk, & Brunner, 2000). Yet, to be effective and meaningful, performance evaluations should contain both formative as well as summative provisions, should be conducted properly, and should offer a means of professional development for sitting superintendents. As Kowalski (2006) pointed out, a well-structured evaluation plan for superintendents fortifies the division of roles and of responsibilities between superintendents and board members.

A well-structured evaluation process informs the superintendent about the school board's expectations and improves board-superintendent relations. In addition, a well-structured performance evaluation should identify strengths as well as areas of growth articulating clear methods and specific

Table 6.15   Provision for Merit or Performance Pay in Current Superintendent Contract

Response options	District enrollment									
	Fewer than 300		300 to 2,999		3,000 to 24,999		25,000 or more		All	
	f	%	f	%	f	%	f	%	f	%
No	165	95.4	930	87.1	403	77.5	42	72.4	1540	84.7
Yes, based solely on personal performance	4	2.2	49	4.6	43	8.3	5	8.6	101	5.5
Yes, based on both personal and district performance	2	1.2	37	3.5	34	6.5	4	6.9	77	4.2
Yes, based solely on district performance	0	0.0	17	1.6	18	3.5	3	5.2	38	2.1
Yes, based on both personal and district performance and other factors	1	0.6	26	2.4	20	3.8	3	5.2	50	2.8
Yes, based only on factors other than personal and district performance	1	0.6	8	0.7	0	0.0	0	0.0	9	0.5
Yes, other	0	0.0	1	0.1	2	0.4	1	1.7	4	0.2
Total	173	100.0	1068	100.0	520	100.0	58	100.0	1819	100.0

prescriptions to improve job performance where needed. Not to be overlooked, outcomes of performance reviews will determine whether or not a superintendent should be retained and whether or not any additional compensation should be awarded. In light of these important implications for superintendents relative to their performance evaluation, performance evaluations should be both timely and frequently administered.

Frequency of Evaluations

A large majority of respondents in this study (80%) reported that they were evaluated by the school board annually. Though midyear evaluations are suggested as a formative process to ensure that superintendents are making progress on annual goals and objectives (Glass & Franceschini, 2007), only 13% of the respondents said they were evaluated more than once each year. Results concerning evaluation frequency are in Table 6.16. The data are fairly consistent with the 2000 study (Glass, Björk, & Brunner, 2000) in which 80% of superintendents also reported being evaluated annually, with another 12% undergoing evaluation semiannually.

Types, Basis, and Input

Assessing and monitoring a superintendent's performance are among a school board's most important responsibilities; however, the manner in which they are addressed varies. Extant literature on performance evaluation emphasizes the need for both formative and summative evaluations. The former is intended to facilitate an employee's professional growth; the latter is intended to make judgments about adequate performance. Further, in the education profession, practitioners and scholars agree that fair and unbiased evaluations must be based on multiple data sources, and criteria should reflect the integration of the job definition and the professional expectations as cornerstones of the performance evaluation (DiPaola, 2007).

With respect to the type of evaluation conducted by the school board, two-thirds of the respondents in this study received *both summative and formative evaluations*. All responses for this issue are in Table 6.17

When asked about the factors that provide the basis for their performance evaluations, the most frequent factor was their *job description*, which was identified by nearly three-fourths of the respondents.

Table 6.16   How Frequently Does the School Board Formally Evaluate the Superintendent?

Response options	District enrollment									
	Fewer than 300		300 to 2,999		3,000 to 24,999		25,000 or more		All	
	f	*%*	*f*	*%*	*f*	*%*	*f*	*%*	*f*	*%*
At least twice a year	15	8.7	129	12.0	78	15.0	12	21.1	234	12.8
Once a year	137	79.2	862	80.2	418	80.2	38	66.7	1455	79.7
Every other year	7	4.0	31	2.9	4	0.8	4	7.0	46	2.5
Only prior to contract renewal	5	2.9	24	2.2	9	1.7	0	0.0	38	2.1
Never	9	5.2	29	2.7	12	2.3	3	5.2	53	2.9
Total	173	100.0	1075	100.0	521	100.0	57	100.0	1826	100.0

The next most commonly identified factor was *employment contract provisions*. All responses for this issue are in Table 6.18.

Input for a superintendent's performance evaluation can be obtained from various individuals, groups, and data sources. As expected, the most common source of input was the *school board*. The next most common response was superintendent *self-evaluation*. All responses for this issue are in Table 6.19.

Table 6.17   Type of Formal Superintendent Evaluation Conducted by the School Board

| Response options | District enrollment | | | | | | | | | |
| | Fewer than 300 | | 300 to 2,999 | | 3,000 to 24,999 | | 25,000 or more | | All | |
	f	%	f	%	f	%	f	%	f	%
Both summative and formative	105	60.3	699	65.5	350	68.1	41	70.7	1195	65.9
Only summative	38	21.9	240	22.5	114	22.2	8	13.8	400	22.1
Only formative	4	2.3	22	2.1	13	2.5	1	1.70	40	2.2
Not received any formal evaluation	27	15.5	106	9.9	37	7.2	8	13.8	178	9.8
Total	174	100.0	1067	100.0	514	100.0	58	100.0	1813	100.0

Table 6.18   Factors That Provide the Basis for the Superintendent's Formal Performance Evaluation

| Response options | District enrollment | | | | | | | | | |
| | Fewer than 300 | | 300 to 2,999 | | 3,000 to 24,999 | | 25,000 or more | | All | |
	f	%	f	%	f	%	f	%	f	%
Job description	124	73.8	786	74.4	351	68.4	31	54.4	1292	72.0
Employment contract provisions	71	42.3	470	44.5	230	44.8	27	47.4	798	44.5
National standards	11	6.5	149	14.1	95	18.5	6	10.5	261	14.5
Guidelines by state superintendent association	22	13.1	127	12.0	51	9.9	5	8.8	205	11.4
Guidelines by state school board association	55	32.7	323	30.6	153	29.8	9	15.8	540	30.1
Guidelines by consultants	2	1.2	22	2.1	24	4.7	4	7.0	52	2.9
Other	31	18.5	248	23.5	163	31.8	28	49.1	470	26.2

Note: Respondents were able to select all response options that applied.

Table 6.19   Who Provides Input for the Superintendent's Formal Performance Evaluations

Response options	District enrollment									
	Fewer than 300		300 to 2,999		3,000 to 24,999		25,000 or more		All	
	f	%	*f*	%	*f*	%	*f*	%	*f*	%
School board	168	98.8	1050	98.7	511	98.8	56	96.6	1785	98.6
Me (self-evaluation)	69	40.6	488	45.9	284	54.9	37	63.8	878	48.5
Other administrators in the district	14	8.2	188	17.7	104	20.1	14	24.1	320	17.6
Teachers	25	14.7	136	12.8	59	11.4	10	17.2	230	12.7
District employees not in professional categories	19	11.2	120	11.3	50	9.7	7	12.1	196	10.8
Parent and other community stakeholders	20	11.8	96	9.0	42	8.1	11	19.0	169	9.3
Student	8	4.7	29	2.7	13	2.5	4	6.9	54	2.9
Experts outside of the district	3	1.8	11	1.0	16	3.1	5	8.6	35	1.9

Note: Respondents were able to select all response options that applied.

In general, findings regarding the basis and types of formal evaluations would suggest that in a majority of cases, boards used specific and previously agreed upon criteria when conducting performance evaluations. It is also evident that in almost all cases, boards were responsible for providing formal input, and many considered the self-evaluation part of the process.

Results concerning the evaluation process differ from the 2000 study in that only 54% of superintendents participating in that research were formally evaluated, and another 32% indicated that their performance evaluation procedures contained both formal and informal aspects. While 72% (see Table 6.18) of superintendents in this study indicated that their *job description* was a basis for their performance evaluation, only 56% of superintendents in the 2000 study did so.

Overall Performance Rating

Slightly more than half (53%) of the respondents in this study indicated that they had received an overall performance evaluation of *excellent*. Approximately another one-third reported receiving an *above average* rating. Interestingly, the percentage of excellent ratings increased as enrollments got larger; that is, superintendents in the smallest districts (those with student populations of less than 300) were the least likely to have received this highest rating whereas their peers in the highest two enrollment groups were the most likely to have received it. Research on rural superintendents has shown that where job descriptions exist, they are difficult to fulfill and at times sufficiently ambiguous to allow for a variety of interpretations. Thus, the lower level of excellent ratings for superintendents in very small districts may be explained partially by the fact that they must directly and personally assume a very broad range of responsibilities (Canales, Tejeda-Delgado, & Slate, 2010). All data concerning overall ratings are in Table 6.20.

In the 2000 study (Glass, Björk, & Brunner, 2000), 69% of superintendents reported receiving an *excellent* rating. This decline in *excellent* ratings in this study may be attributed to several factors. Among them are the current political climate, an unyielding demand for greater accountability, and emphasis on student test scores as a measure of district (and, therefore, superintendent) success (Malen & Cochran, 2008). Another issue may be the current financial situation facing many districts. Inadequate funding, declining enrollment, and shifting demographics take their respective toll on superintendents' ability to concentrate on the results-based goals of current reform mandates. All of these issues influence the perceived success of superintendents (Fusarelli & Cooper, 2009).

School Board Characteristics

In an effort to enhance knowledge about relationships, demographic data about school boards also were collected from the respondents. Additional profile information about the districts employing respondents in this study are in Chapter 3.

School Board Size

The vast majority of school boards (91%) had between *5 and 9 members*. The modal size was *7 members*. School boards with less than 7 members were less prevalent in school districts with 25,000 or more pupils than they were in smaller districts. Findings on the size of school boards in this study are similar to those reported by Glass, Björk, and Brunner in 2000. They found, for example, that 80% of the superintendents were employed in districts that had between *5 and 8 members*. All response data regarding school board size are in Table 6.21.

Average Length of Board Member Service

Instability on school boards is an issue that has repeatedly been linked to efforts to improve schools at the local level. For example, turnover on boards makes it difficult to promulgate and sustain strategic plans

Table 6.20 Performance Rating the Superintendent Received in His or Her Most Recent Performance Evaluation

Response options	District enrollment									
	Fewer than 300		300 to 2,999		3,000 to 24,999		25,000 or more		All	
	f	*%*	*f*	*%*	*f*	*%*	*f*	*%*	*f*	*%*
Excellent	69	39.7	540	50.0	327	62.4	36	62.1	972	52.9
Above average	69	39.7	364	33.7	123	23.5	10	17.2	566	31.0
Average	10	5.7	49	4.5	26	5.0	3	5.2	88	4.8
Below average	3	1.7	7	0.6	1	0.2	0	0.0	11	0.6
Poor	0	0.0	2	0.2	1	0.2	0	0.0	3	0.1
Not applicable, not evaluated	23	13.2	118	11.0	46	8.7	9	15.5	196	10.6
Total	174	100.0	1080	100.0	524	100.0	58	100.0	1836	100.0

and policy for necessary changes (Kowalski, 2006). In this study, modal average for board member service was *4 to 6 years* (48.5%). Slight variations in percentages existed among the four district-enrollment categories; interestingly, the largest districts (i.e., 25,000 or more pupils) had a higher percentage for the *10 or more years* response than did the other three district-enrollment categories. All response data concerning length of board member service are contained in Table 6.22.

Board Member Gender

Sixty-four percent of the respondents in this study were employed in districts in which females comprised between *26% and 75%* of all board members; just 5.8% were employed in districts having all male school boards. Female majorities on school boards were more common in the largest districts than they were in the smallest districts. All data regarding gender and school boards are in Table 6.23.

Table 6.21   Number of Members on the School Board

Response option	*District enrollment*									
	Fewer than 300		*300 to 2,999*		*3,000 to 24,999*		*25,000 or more*		*All*	
	f	*%*	*f*	*%*	*f*	*%*	*f*	*%*	*f*	*%*
3	6	3.4	3	0.3	0	0.0	0	0.0	9	0.5
5	73	42.0	406	37.7	189	36.2	17	29.3	685	37.4
7	67	38.5	472	43.9	220	42.2	23	39.7	782	42.7
9	7	4.0	95	8.8	81	15.5	12	20.7	195	10.7
Other	21	12.1	100	9.3	32	6.1	6	10.3	159	8.7
Total	174	100.0	1076	100.0	522	100.0	58	100.0	1830	100.0

Table 6.22   Average Length of Current School Board Member Service

Response options	*District enrollment*									
	Fewer than 300		*300 to 2,999*		*3,000 to 24,999*		*25,000 or more*		*All*	
	f	*%*	*f*	*%*	*f*	*%*	*f*	*%*	*f*	*%*
1–3 years	35	20.2	150	13.9	58	11.1	13	22.4	256	14.0
4–6 years	81	46.8	532	49.4	255	48.9	18	31.0	886	48.5
7–9 years	43	24.9	312	29.1	158	30.3	16	27.6	529	28.9
10 or more years	14	8.1	82	7.6	50	9.7	11	19.0	157	8.6
Total	173	100.0	1076	100.0	521	100.0	58	100.0	1828	100.0

Table 6.23   Percentage of Females on the School Board

Response options	District enrollment									
	Fewer than 300		300 to 2,999		3,000 to 24,999		25,000 or more		All	
	f	%	f	%	f	%	f	%	f	%
0%	10	5.8	73	6.9	20	3.9	0	0.0	103	5.8
Less than 25%	44	25.6	303	28.8	104	20.4	9	15.8	460	25.7
26 to 50%	77	44.8	476	45.2	245	48.0	27	47.4	825	46.0
51 to 75%	29	16.9	169	16.1	109	21.4	18	31.6	325	18.1
76 to 100%	12	6.9	32	3.0	32	6.3	3	5.2	79	4.4
Total	172	100.0	1053	100.0	510	100.0	57	100.0	1792	100.0

Table 6.24   Is the School Board Evaluated Formally?

Response options	All	
	f	%
No	1338	71.3
Yes, by board members' self-evaluations	497	26.5
Yes, externally (e.g., by a consultant, state department of education)	29	1.6
Yes, by an evaluation committee	12	0.6
Total	1876	100.0

Evaluation of School Boards

Although school boards play a significant role in determining the quality of the education provided, they typically have not been required to undergo formal evaluations. This condition is largely premised on the assumption most of them are evaluated by stakeholders via democratic elections (Glass & Franceschini, 2007). Results here show that nearly three-fourths of the school boards were never evaluated formally, and among those that were, most relied solely on self-evaluations. Data regarding this issue are in Table 6.24.

Summary

Content in this chapter describes and enriches understanding of the intricate relationships between superintendents and their school boards. The following are the most noteworthy findings reported in this chapter:

- Compared to 2000, superintendents were almost twice as likely to have provided orientation for new board members.

- The vast majority of policy recommendations made by superintendents were approved by school boards—an outcome that also was reported in 2000.
- The amount of time superintendents spend communicating directly with school board members had increased since 2000.
- Respondents indicated that although their school boards emphasized each of the five major roles traditionally assumed by superintendents, the extent to which they did so varied considerably. The highest level of substantial emphasis was placed on being an *effective communicator*, followed by *manager, instructional leader, statesman/democratic leader*, and *applied social scientist*.
- Two-thirds of the superintendents received annual performance evaluations that included both formative and summative components. The most common criterion used to assess performance was the formal job description.
- Nearly three-fourths of the superintendents reported that their school boards had not been evaluated formally; of those that had been, the vast majority only conducted self-evaluations.
- Few school boards were all male (5.8%), and few were all female (4%). Just under one-fourth of the school boards (22.5%), however, had female majorities. Boards with female majorities were more common in large-enrollment districts than they were in small-enrollment districts.

7

Gender and Race/Ethnicity

As noted in Chapter 3 of this study, the percentages of females and persons of color in the superintendency have increased over the past decade. Nevertheless, both groups continue to be underrepresented because their presence in the position does not reflect the diversity of both the total national population and the total student population in public schools. Because White males always have constituted the vast majority of superintendents, the experiences of women and persons of color received limited attention, especially before the 1980s (Shakeshaft, 1989). Acknowledging this fact, scholars have attempted to study females and persons of color who hold this important position, both to understand the uniqueness of their practice and to provide role models for aspiring administrators (Kowalski & Brunner, 2005).

Extant literature reveals a history of both gender-related (e.g., Brunner, 2003; Brunner & Grogan, 2007; Grogan, 1996, 2008; Loder, 2005; Shakeshaft, 1989) and race-related (e.g., Kalbus, 2000; Ortiz, 1982; Ortiz & Ortiz, 1995; Simmons, 2005) barriers to administrative positions. As a result, forward-thinking members of the education profession are seeking ways to improve academic preparation and superintendent selection to eliminate obstacles that have previously discouraged women and racial/ethnic minorities from pursuing careers as district and school administrators.

Two factors frame concerns about the underrepresentation of women and people of color in the superintendency: the presence of women in the education profession and the nation's changing demographic profile. In 2004, for example, 72% of all full-time public school teachers were females, and from 1993 to 2004, the percentage of female public elementary school principals increased from 41% to 56%, and the percentage of female secondary school principals increased from 14% to 26% (Strizek, Pittsonberger, Riordan, Lyter, & Orlofsky, 2006). Further, anecdotal information from school administration professors indicates that a large majority of their students are female, and state agencies report that a considerable number of women possess certificates or licenses to serve as superintendents (Dana & Bourisaw, 2006).

The demographic profile of public elementary and secondary school students has changed substantially since 1972. According to Planty and others (2008), the percentage of students classified as members of a racial/ethnic minority group increased from 22% in 1972 to 31% in 1986 and to 43% in 2006. Moreover, the percentage of White students declined from 78% to 57% between 1972 and 2006 (Planty et al., 2008, p. 10). In 2004, 83% of all full-time public school teachers were non-Hispanic Whites (Strizek et al., 2006).

Even though the percentage of female superintendents has increased substantially over the last 2 decades, at the current rate of change, it will take more than 3 additional decades before the percentage of female superintendents approaches parity with the percentage of male superintendents (Derrington & Sharratt, 2009). Arguably, the underrepresentation of racial/ethnic minorities is even more disconcerting, especially when one considers the rapid changes in student demographics.

The content of this chapter is divided broadly into two parts: gender and race/ethnicity. With respect to race/ethnicity, data are analyzed by comparing two groups. The *nonminority* group was composed of all respondents who identified themselves as *White*. The *minority* group was composed of all respondents who identified themselves as *American Indian* or *Alaska Native; Asian; Black* or *African American; Hispanic* or *Latino;* and *Native Hawaiian, Other Pacific Islander,* and *Other*.

Gender

Among the superintendents completing the survey for this study ($n = 1,867$), 95% answered the gender-identification question. Among these respondents, nearly one in four (24.1%) was a woman—a figure that is almost double that in the 2000 study (13.2%) and nearly four times the figure reported in 1992 (6.6%; Glass, Björk, & Brunner, 2000). A breakdown of gender data by district enrollment is shown in Table 7.1. The percentage of female respondents varied considerably across the enrollment categories, with women least likely to be employed in the largest and smallest enrollment districts. Just over two-thirds (64.3%) of female respondents were employed in districts with fewer than 3,000 students, a finding slightly lower than the 68.3% reported in 2000 (Glass, Björk, & Brunner, 2000).

School District and Community Data

As shown in Table 7.2, nearly half the female superintendents (48.7%) identified the location of their employing district as *rural;* in the 2000 study, the figure was 48.5% (Glass, Björk, & Brunner, 2000). *Rural* was the only district location category in which the percentages of male and female superintendents were nearly identical.

Table 7.3 includes data showing percentages of male and female superintendents by levels of community diversity. As these data reveal, percentages of females and males across the community diversity categories were similar. The greatest differences were at the extremes (i.e., in the lowest and highest diversity categories); the percentage of females was slightly lower in the former and slightly higher in the latter.

Table 7.4 includes data showing the percentages of male and female superintendents by levels of student diversity. Again, the percentages of females and males across the student diversity categories were similar, and the greatest differences were at the extremes (lowest and highest diversity categories); the percentage of females was slightly lower in the former and slightly higher in the latter.

Data showing the percentages of males and females by levels of diversity among school district employees are in Table 7.5. Although the distribution of females was not particularly dissimilar to the distribution of male superintendents across the response categories, the fact that only about 14% of the districts had more than 15% minority employees is certainly notable.

Table 7.1 Gender and District Enrollment

District enrollment	Male		Female		All	
	f	%	*f*	%	*f*	%
Fewer than 300	118	8.8	50	11.7	168	9.5
300 to 2,999	823	61.4	224	52.6	1047	59.3
3,000 to 24,999	356	26.6	141	33.1	497	28.1
25,000 or more	43	3.2	11	2.6	54	3.1
Total	1340	100.0	426	100.0	1766	100.0

Table 7.6 includes responses comparing male and female opinions about the value of diversity. From a percentage perspective, the distribution of female opinions was not particularly dissimilar to the distribution of male opinions.

Personal Characteristics

Three personal characteristics were analyzed in relation to gender: marital status, age, and highest level of academic attainment. Data regarding the marital status of male and female superintendents are in Table 7.7. In the 2000 study, data were reported in only two categories: *married* and *single*, and 76.9% of females responded that they were married (Glass, Björk, & Brunner, 2000). In this study, the figure increased slightly to 81.8%.

As reported in the 2000 study, female superintendents, on average, were older than their male peers. That outcome held true in this study. Only 21.5% of females were below the age of 51, whereas 30.9% of males were in this category. Data comparing males and females by age groups are in Table 7.8.

Historically, female superintendents typically have had more formal education and professional experience than their male peers (Kowalski, 2006). In both the 2000 study and this study, a higher

Table 7.2 Gender and District Geographic Descriptor

Descriptor	Male		Female		All	
	f	*%*	*f*	*%*	*f*	*%*
Urban	73	5.4	28	6.5	101	5.7
Suburban	279	20.6	90	21.0	369	20.7
Small town/city	271	20.1	97	22.6	368	20.7
Rural	711	52.6	209	48.7	920	51.7
Other	17	1.3	5	1.2	22	1.2
Total	1351	100.0	429	100.0	1780	100.0

Table 7.3 Gender and the Level of Diversity in the District's Total Population

Percentage of district minority residents	Male		Female		All	
	f	*%*	*f*	*%*	*f*	*%*
5% or less	660	49.6	180	43.2	840	48.1
6 to 15%	238	17.9	77	18.5	315	18.0
16 to 25%	136	10.2	44	10.5	180	10.3
26 to 50%	161	12.1	58	13.9	219	12.5
51% or more	136	10.2	58	13.9	194	11.1
Total	1331	100.0	417	100.0	1748	100.0

Table 7.4   Gender and the Level of Diversity in the District's Student Population

Percentage of minority students	Male		Female		All	
	f	%	f	%	f	%
5% or less	648	48.5	190	44.7	838	47.6
6 to 15%	231	17.3	77	18.1	308	17.5
16 to 25%	120	9.0	31	7.3	151	8.5
26 to 50%	166	12.4	48	11.3	214	12.2
51% or more	171	12.8	79	18.6	250	14.2
Total	1336	100.0	425	100.0	1761	100.0

Table 7.5   Gender and the Level of Diversity in the District's Employee Population

Percentage of minority employees	Male		Female		All	
	f	%	f	%	f	%
5% or less	980	72.6	297	69.7	1277	71.9
6 to 15%	192	14.2	56	13.1	248	14.0
16 to 25%	77	5.7	25	5.9	102	5.7
26 to 50%	70	5.2	39	9.2	109	6.1
51% or more	31	2.3	9	2.1	40	2.3
Total	1350	100.0	426	100.0	1776	100.0

Table 7.6   Gender and Perception of the Value of Community Diversity

Perception of community diversity	Male		Female		All	
	f	%	f	%	f	%
Major asset	230	17.1	83	19.3	313	17.6
Minor asset	205	15.2	51	11.9	256	14.4
Neither asset nor liability	762	56.5	238	55.3	1000	56.2
Minor liability	130	9.6	49	11.4	179	10.1
Major liability	21	1.6	9	2.1	30	1.7
Total	1348	100.0	430	100.0	1778	100.0

percentage of female superintendents held doctorates. In 2000, 56.8% of females and 43.7% of males held a doctorate (Glass, Björk, & Brunner, 2000). In this study, both figures declined slightly to 52.1% for females and 42.1% for males.

Roles and Involvement

Respondents were asked to identify the primary reason why they were selected for their current position. Results comparing females and males are in Table 7.9. In both groups, the three most frequent responses were (a) *personal characteristics*, (b) *potential to be a change agent*, and (c) *ability to be an instructional leader*. However, the order of the reasons differed between women and men. Among the former, the most frequently identified reason was the *ability to be an instructional leader*. Among the latter, the most

Table 7.7 Gender and Marital Status

Marital status	Male		Female		All	
	f	%	f	%	f	%
Married	1250	93.6	345	81.8	1595	90.8
Single	26	2.0	28	6.6	54	3.1
Divorced	49	3.7	37	8.8	86	4.9
Legally separated	6	0.4	2	0.5	8	0.4
Widowed	4	0.3	10	2.3	14	0.8
Total	1335	100.0	422	100.0	1757	100.0

Table 7.8 Gender and Age

Age	Male		Female		All	
	f	%	f	%	f	%
Less than 36	22	1.6	1	0.2	23	1.3
36–40	65	4.8	11	2.6	76	4.3
41–45	141	10.5	32	7.5	173	9.8
46–50	188	14.0	48	11.2	236	13.3
51–55	312	23.2	125	29.2	437	24.6
56–60	383	28.5	136	31.8	519	29.3
61–65	197	14.6	64	15.0	261	14.7
66+	37	2.8	11	2.5	48	2.7
Total	1345	100.0	428	100.0	1773	100.0

frequently identified reason was *personal characteristics*. These findings are congruent with data reported in the 2000 study (Glass, Björk, & Brunner, 2000).

As detailed in Chapter 1, five distinct role characterizations evolved for superintendents during the past century. The first four—*instructional leader, manager, statesman/political leader,* and *applied social scientist*—were identified in the 1960s by Callahan (1966). The fifth role, *effective communicator,* was formalized more recently by Kowalski (2001, 2005). Respondents were asked to identify the level of emphasis their school boards placed on each of these roles. Data comparing male and female responses are in Table 7.10. The following summary of differences for *substantial influence* responses between the two groups is especially insightful:

- *Instructional leader.* Women were much more likely than men to respond that their school boards placed *substantial* emphasis on this role (74.6% of women and 55.2% of men).
- *Manager.* There was virtually no difference between the two groups with respect to their boards placing *substantial* emphasis on this role (79.3% of women and 78.1% of men).
- *Statesman/political leader.* Men were moderately more likely than women to respond that their school boards placed *substantial* emphasis on this role (49.3% of women and 57.1% of men).
- *Applied social scientist.* There was virtually no difference between the two groups with respect to their boards placing *substantial* emphasis on this role (17.3% of women and 15.4% of men). Compared to the other role conceptualizations, however, the overall percent reporting *substantial* emphasis was very low—much lower than the other four roles.
- *Effective communicator.* Women were moderately more likely than men to respond that their school boards placed *substantial* emphasis on this role (89% of women and 83.9% of men). Among the five role conceptualizations, this one had the highest percentages of *substantial* emphasis responses.

Superintendents commonly are expected to be involved in their local community. Respondents were asked to identify the extent to which they were involved. Responses are shown in Table 7.11. Two points are notable. First, about 22% of both men and women reported having less than a *moderate* level of involvement. Second, gender differences in community involvement were minimal.

Table 7.9   Gender and Primary Reason for Being Selected as Superintendent

Primary reason for being selected	*Male*		*Female*		*All*	
	f	*%*	*f*	*%*	*f*	*%*
Personal characteristics (e.g., honesty, tact)	489	36.7	93	22.1	582	33.2
Potential to be a change agent	321	24.1	119	28.3	440	25.1
Ability to maintain the status quo	22	1.7	6	1.4	28	1.6
Ability to be an instructional leader	209	15.7	138	32.9	347	19.8
Ability to manage fiscal resources	95	7.1	13	3.1	108	6.2
Having leadership/managerial experience outside of education	10	0.8	0	0.0	10	0.6
Ability to communicate with stakeholders	92	6.9	31	7.4	123	7.0
Uncertain	94	7.0	20	4.8	114	6.5
Total	1332	100.0	420	100.0	1752	100.0

Table 7.10 Gender and Level of School Board Emphasis on Superintendent Role Conceptualizations

Role/level of emphasis	Male		Female		All	
	f	%	f	%	f	%
Instructional leader (n = 1784)						
Substantial	748	55.2	320	74.6	1068	59.9
Moderate	524	38.7	94	21.9	618	34.6
Low	74	5.4	14	3.3	88	4.9
None	9	0.7	1	0.2	10	0.6
Total	1355	100.0	429	100.0	1784	100.0
Manager (n = 1784)						
Substantial	1057	78.1	341	79.3	1398	78.4
Moderate	278	20.5	81	18.8	359	20.1
Low	18	1.3	6	1.4	24	1.3
None	1	0.1	2	0.5	3	0.2
Total	1354	100.0	430	100.0	1784	100.0
Statesman/political leader(n = 1762)						
Substantial	764	57.1	209	49.3	973	55.2
Moderate	458	34.2	163	38.5	621	35.2
Low	105	7.9	46	10.8	151	8.6
None	11	0.8	6	1.4	17	1.0
Total	1338	100.0	424	100.0	1762	100.0
Applied social scientist (n = 1777)						
Substantial	207	15.4	74	17.3	281	15.8
Moderate	556	41.2	171	40.0	727	40.9
Low	482	35.7	142	33.2	624	35.1
None	104	7.7	41	9.5	145	8.2
Total	1349	100.0	428	100.0	1777	100.0
Effective communicator (n = 1782)						
Substantial	1136	83.9	381	89.0	1517	85.1
Moderate	209	15.4	40	9.4	249	14.0
Low	8	0.6	6	1.4	14	0.8
None	1	0.1	1	0.2	2	0.1
Total	1354	100.0	428	100.0	1782	100.0

Superintendents often mentor colleagues aspiring to be administrators, especially those aspiring to be superintendents. As data in Table 7.12 reveal, about 83% of all respondents reported that they have mentored, and percentages for male and female responses were nearly identical.

Career History and Development

The most common entry position for females in the education profession was an *elementary school teacher* (34.6%); the most common entry position for males was a *high school teacher* (50.5%). Response data for initial positions in education are in Table 7.13.

Table 7.11 Gender and Level of Community Involvement

Level of involvement	Male		Female		All	
	f	%	f	%	f	%
Considerable	529	39.0	165	38.2	694	38.8
Moderate	537	39.5	170	39.3	707	39.5
Limited	277	20.4	94	21.8	371	20.7
None	15	1.1	3	0.7	18	1.0
Total	1358	100.0	432	100.0	1790	100.0

Table 7.12 Gender and Mentoring Prospective Administrators

Having served as a mentor	Male		Female		All	
	f	%	f	%	f	%
Yes	1108	82.0	366	84.9	1474	82.7
No	244	18.0	65	15.1	309	17.3
Total	1352	100.0	431	100.0	1783	100.0

Females, on average, reported having been in the classroom longer than their male counterparts. Approximately two-thirds of males had 10 years or less of teaching experience before their first administrative position, compared to just under half of the females. Further, female superintendents were twice as likely as male superintendents to have had more than 20 years of classroom experience before becoming an administrator. Data comparing the teaching experience of women and men are in Table 7.14.

Table 7.15 includes data regarding the variety of positions held by the respondents at some point in their careers. The three most commonly held positions reported by females were *district level director/coordinator/supervisor* (66.5%), *elementary school teacher* (52.8%), and *elementary school principal* (52.8%). The three most commonly held positions reported by males were *high school teacher* (67.6%), *high school principal* (54.5%), and *junior high/middle school teacher* (53.5%).

Data regarding entry level administrative positions for women and men are in Table 7.16. The most common entry position for women was a *district level director/coordinator* (28.4%), whereas the most common entry position for men was a *high school assistant principal* (21.7%). But as the data show, superintendents entered administration in a wide variety of positions.

Males, on average, became novice superintendents at an earlier age than did their female peers. More than half (56.3%) of them reached the position by the age of 45, whereas slightly less than one-third (30.6%) of the females had done so. Moreover, men were four times as likely as women to enter the position before the age of 36; 16.4% of men and only 4.4% of women reported doing so. Table 7.17 contains response data regarding respondent age at the time of first being appointed a superintendent.

Though females generally had more teaching experience over the course of their careers, males, on average, had more experience as superintendents. Approximately 30% of the male respondents and 43%

Table 7.13   Gender and First Teaching Position

First teaching position	Male		Female		All	
	f	%	f	%	f	%
Special education teacher	77	5.7	65	15.2	142	8.0
Elementary school teacher	238	17.6	148	34.6	386	21.7
Middle school teacher	293	21.7	70	16.4	363	20.4
High school teacher	684	50.5	124	28.9	808	45.3
Counselor	16	1.2	4	0.9	20	1.1
Therapist (e.g., speech and language)	4	0.3	5	1.2	9	0.5
College teacher	14	1.0	2	0.5	16	0.9
No teaching experience	14	1.0	1	0.2	15	0.8
Others	14	1.0	9	2.1	23	1.3
Total	1354	100.0	428	100.0	1782	100.0

Table 7.14   Gender and Teaching Experience

Years of teaching experience	Male		Female		All	
	f	%	f	%	f	%
0	13	1.0	2	0.5	15	0.9
1-5	350	27.0	52	12.8	402	23.6
6-10	508	39.2	146	36.0	654	38.4
11-15	251	19.3	95	23.4	346	20.3
16-20	109	8.4	60	14.8	169	9.9
21-25	33	2.5	34	8.4	67	3.9
26+	34	2.6	17	4.1	51	3.0
Total	1298	100.0	406	100.0	1704	100.0

of the female respondents had less than 5 years of experience in the position. Response data for experience as a superintendent are detailed in Table 7.18.

A substantial percentage of both females (76.9%) and males (78.1%) were employed as superintendents in 1 year or less after making their first-ever application for the position. These figures are slightly

Table 7.15   Gender and Positions Held Previously for at Least One Year

Previous positions	Male (n = 1356)		Female (n = 430)	
	f	%	f	%
Elementary classroom teacher	367	27.1	227	52.8
Elementary assistant principal	110	8.1	66	15.3
Elementary principal	483	35.6	227	52.8
Junior high/middle school teacher	726	53.5	218	50.7
Junior high/middle school assistant principal	270	19.9	79	18.4
Junior high/middle school principal	558	41.2	128	29.8
High school teacher	916	67.6	202	47.0
High school assistant principal	454	33.5	77	17.9
High school principal	739	54.5	111	25.8
School counselor	80	5.9	42	9.8
District level director/coordinator/supervisor	514	37.9	286	66.5
Assistant/associate/deputy superintendent	460	33.9	215	50.0
College or university professor	205	15.1	107	24.9
College administrator (e.g., department chair or dean)	17	1.3	5	1.2
Other	110	8.1	49	11.4

Note: Respondents were able to select all response options that applied; percentages are based on the frequency of responses for each possible answer divided by the number in each group responding to the survey question relevant to these data.

higher than those reported for the same time period in both the 1992 and 2000 studies (Glass, Björk, & Brunner, 2000). Table 7.19 includes all responses for this issue.

More than two-thirds of both females (67.2%) and males (69.0%) reported that they were *very satisfied* with their position as superintendent. Overall, 97% of all respondents indicated that they were *very satisfied* or *moderately satisfied*. These findings are similar to those reported in both the 1992 and 2000 studies (Glass, Björk, & Brunner, 2000). Data concerning job satisfaction are in Table 7.20.

A high level of job satisfaction also was apparent in responses regarding possible remorse over career choice. When respondents were asked if they would choose to be a superintendent if given an opportunity to refashion their careers, 88.6% of the males and 87.7% of the females answered *definitely yes* or *probably yes*. Response data comparing males and females are in Table 7.21.

As data in Table 7.22 show, the percentage of women indicating that they had encountered discrimination in their quest to be a superintendent was more than three times the percentage of men expressing the same experience. When asked to identify factors that restricted women from becoming superinten-

Table 7.16   Gender and First Administrative Position

First administrative position	Male		Female		All	
	f	*%*	*f*	*%*	*f*	*%*
Elementary school assistant principal	79	5.8	50	11.7	129	7.2
Elementary school principal	159	11.7	78	18.2	237	13.3
Dean of students	41	3.0	8	1.9	49	2.7
Junior high or middle school assistant principal	170	12.5	41	9.6	211	11.8
Junior high or middle school principal	70	5.2	19	4.4	89	5.0
High school assistant principal	295	21.7	44	10.3	339	19.0
High school principal	231	17.0	24	5.6	255	14.3
Athletic director	59	4.3	3	0.7	62	3.5
District level director/coordinator	142	10.5	122	28.4	264	14.8
Assistant/associate/deputy superintendent	8	0.6	6	1.4	14	0.8
State education department administrator	7	0.5	5	1.2	12	0.7
School business official or chief financial officer	14	1.0	1	0.2	15	0.8
School district treasurer	1	0.1	2	0.5	3	0.2
Superintendent of schools	48	3.6	15	3.4	63	3.5
Other	34	2.5	11	2.5	45	2.5
Total	1358	100.0	429	100.0	1787	100.0

dents, males were almost twice as likely to select the response option *No factors perceived to be restrictive.* Data for all responses regarding perceived restrictions are in Table 7.23.

Professional Preparation

Overall, respondents' opinions about their professional preparation were quite positive, and as shown in Table 7.24, female and male superintendents expressed virtually identical opinions. Ratings of academic preparation were even more positive in 2010 than they were in 2000. In 2010, 76.7% of females and 77.9% of males rated their preparation as *excellent* or *good*, compared to 71% of females and 73.7% of males in 2000 (Glass, Björk, & Brunner, 2000).

Males and females also exhibited limited differences in their opinions about the nature of academic courses and the credibility of school administration professors. Data regarding the former are in Table 7.25, and data regarding the latter are in Table 7.26.

Table 7.17   Gender and Age as a Novice Superintendent

Age as a novice superintendent	Male		Female		All	
	f	*%*	*f*	*%*	*f*	*%*
Less than 36	221	16.4	19	4.4	240	13.6
36–40	261	19.4	39	9.1	300	16.9
41–45	276	20.5	73	17.1	349	19.7
46–50	311	23.1	122	28.6	433	24.4
51–55	204	15.2	113	26.5	317	17.9
56–60	63	4.7	51	12.0	114	6.4
61 or more	10	0.7	10	2.3	20	1.1
Total	1346	100.0	427	100.0	1773	100.0

Table 7.18   Gender and Experience as a Superintendent

Years as a superintendent	Male		Female		All	
	f	*%*	*f*	*%*	*f*	*%*
1	77	5.7	30	7.0	107	6.0
2–4	328	24.2	156	36.2	484	27.1
5–8	356	26.2	135	31.3	491	27.5
9–12	205	15.1	64	14.8	269	15.0
13 or more	391	28.8	46	10.7	437	24.4
Total	1357	100.0	431	100.0	1788	100.0

Reading Research

Almost all respondents, 95.1% of females and 91.4% of males, reported that they read research *frequently* or *occasionally*. Equally notable, 92.6% of them said that the research they read was *almost always* or *occasionally* useful. Females were slightly more inclined to express these opinions about usefulness than were males. Data regarding responses about research are in Tables 7.27 and 7.28.

Professional Organization Involvement

Respondents were asked to identify their level of involvement in professional organizations. Tabulations are shown in Table 7.29. As these data reveal, differences between the male and female respondents were minimal. Women reported being slightly more involved in organizations than men. The percentages of

Table 7.19   Gender and Time Elapsed between First Applying for and Being Employed in the Superintendency

Years between initial application and employment	Male		Female		All	
	f	*%*	*f*	*%*	*f*	*%*
Less than 1	906	67.7	287	67.3	1193	67.6
1	139	10.4	41	9.6	180	10.2
2	121	9.0	37	8.7	158	8.9
3	49	3.7	13	3.1	62	3.5
4	25	1.9	6	1.4	31	1.8
5	34	2.5	6	1.4	40	2.3
Never applied	64	4.8	36	8.5	100	5.7
Total	1338	100.0	426	100.0	1764	100.0

Table 7.20   Gender and Level of Satisfaction Related to Being a Superintendent

Level of satisfaction	Male		Female		All	
	f	*%*	*f*	*%*	*f*	*%*
Very satisfied	936	69.0	289	67.2	1225	68.6
Moderately satisfied	373	27.5	126	29.3	499	27.9
Moderately dissatisfied	39	2.9	12	2.8	51	2.9
Very dissatisfied	8	0.6	3	0.7	11	0.6
Total	1356	100.0	430	100.0	1786	100.0

Table 7.21   Gender and Inclination to Re-select Being a Superintendent

Would again be a superintendent	Male		Female		All	
	f	*%*	*f*	*%*	*f*	*%*
Definitely yes	835	62.7	267	62.8	1102	62.7
Probably yes	345	25.9	106	24.9	451	25.6
Unsure	91	6.8	28	6.6	119	6.8
Probably not	59	4.4	22	5.2	81	4.6
Definitely not	3	0.2	2	0.5	5	0.3
Total	1333	100.0	425	100.0	1758	100.0

Table 7.22 Gender and Encountering Discrimination

Encountered discrimination	Male		Female		All	
	f	%	f	%	f	%
Yes	179	13.2	196	45.4	375	21.0
No	1128	83.2	210	48.6	1338	74.8
Uncertain	49	3.6	26	6.0	75	4.2
Total	1356	100.0	432	100.0	1788	100.0

Table 7.23 Gender and Perceptions of Factors Restricting Access to the Superintendency for Women

Factors restricting access for women	Male (n = 1316)		Female (n = 430)	
	f	%	f	%
Absence of mentors who are district or school administrators	189	14.4	118	27.4
Absence of mentors who are professors of school administration	71	5.4	49	11.4
Family concerns, restrictions, obligations	358	27.2	190	44.2
Gender discrimination (i.e., treatment of a person based on gender rather than individual merit)	194	14.8	205	47.7
Limited role models (female superintendents)	245	18.7	127	29.5
No factors perceived to be restrictive	771	58.7	132	30.7
Other	46	3.5	29	6.7

Note: Respondents were able to select all response options that applied; percentages are based on the frequency of responses for each possible answer divided by the number in each group responding to the survey question relevant to these data.

Table 7.24 Gender and Evaluation of Academic Preparation to be a Superintendent

Rating of academic preparation	Male		Female		All	
	f	%	f	%	f	%
Excellent	313	23.5	119	28.0	432	24.6
Good	726	54.4	207	48.7	933	53.0
Fair	234	17.6	79	18.6	313	17.8
Poor	51	3.8	12	2.8	63	3.6
None*	10	0.7	8	1.9	18	1.0
Total	1334	100.0	425	100.0	1759	100.0

*Did not complete a professional preparation program.

Table 7.25   Gender and Opinions of Courses in Administrator Preparation Program

Opinion of courses	Male		Female		All	
	f	*%*	*f*	*%*	*f*	*%*
They were sufficiently theoretical and sufficiently practice-based.	562	41.5	176	40.7	738	41.3
They were sufficiently theoretical but insufficiently practice-based.	675	49.9	216	50.0	891	49.9
They were sufficiently practice based but insufficiently theoretical.	38	2.8	10	2.3	48	2.7
They were insufficiently theoretical and insufficiently practice-based.	71	5.2	27	6.3	98	5.5
None*	7	0.5	3	0.7	10	0.6
Total	1353	100.0	432	100.0	1785	100.0

*Did not complete a professional preparation program.

Table 7.26   Gender and Opinions of Professor Credibility

Credibility rating	Male		Female		All	
	f	*%*	*f*	*%*	*f*	*%*
Excellent	452	33.4	140	32.7	592	33.2
Good	639	47.2	203	47.5	842	47.3
Fair	219	16.2	69	16.1	288	16.2
Poor	35	2.6	12	2.8	47	2.6
Not applicable*	8	0.6	4	0.9	12	0.7
Total	1353	100.0	428	100.0	1781	100.0

*Did not complete a professional preparation program.

Table 7.27   Gender and How Often Superintendents Read Research

How often research is read	Male		Female		All	
	f	*%*	*f*	*%*	*f*	*%*
Frequently	623	45.8	284	65.9	907	50.7
Occasionally	620	45.6	126	29.2	746	41.7
Rarely	112	8.3	19	4.4	131	7.3
Never	4	0.3	2	0.5	6	0.3
Total	1359	100.0	431	100.0	1790	100.0

male and female membership in the *American Association of School Administrators* (AASA) were virtually identical; with respect to membership in *state superintendent associations*, the percentage of male members (92.8%) was slightly higher than the percentage of female members (88%). Women, however, had a higher percentage of membership in the *Association for Supervision and Curriculum Development* (66.1% compared to 43.9% for men). Data regarding membership in specific professional organizations are in Table 7.30.

Perceptions of Self-Efficacy

No respondent in this study indicated that he or she was *not at all successful* as a superintendent. Just over half of both male and female respondents considered themselves *highly successful*. Response data comparing males and females on the issue of success in the superintendency are in Table 7.31. This issue was also addressed in general terms in Chapter 4 of this study.

Future Plans

Respondents were asked to identify their intended career status in 2015. Just over half the males (53%) and slightly less than half of the females (45.1%) indicated that they would *still be a superintendent*, ei-

Table 7.28   Gender and Value Given to Research

Extent to which research has been beneficial	Male		Female		All	
	f	%	*f*	%	*f*	%
Almost always	329	24.3	170	39.4	499	27.9
Occasionally	915	67.5	240	55.7	1155	64.7
Rarely	92	6.8	15	3.5	107	6.0
Never	4	0.3	0	0.0	4	0.2
Have not read research	15	1.1	6	1.4	21	1.2
Total	1355	100.0	431	100.0	1786	100.0

Table 7.29   Gender and Level of Involvement in Professional Organizations

Level of involvement	Male		Female		All	
	f	%	*f*	%	*f*	%
Considerable	472	35.1	162	37.7	634	35.8
Moderate	643	47.9	211	49.0	854	48.2
Limited	217	16.2	55	12.8	272	15.3
None	11	0.8	2	0.5	13	0.7
Total	1343	100.0	430	100.0	1773	100.0

ther working for the same or another employer. These findings are lower than those reported in 2000, where 59.9% of the men and 62.5% of the women said they would still be superintendents 5 years into the future (Glass, Björk, & Brunner, 2000). All data for the responses to the career intention question are found in Table 7.32.

Race/Ethnicity

Of the 1,867 respondents participating in this study, 1,800 (96.4%) answered the race-identity question. Among them, 94% identified themselves *White (not Hispanic or Latino)*; the remaining 6% constituted the

Table 7.30   Gender and Membership in Professional Organizations

Organization	Male (n = 1349)		Female (n = 425)	
	f	*%*	*f*	*%*
American Association of School Administrators (AASA)	1056	78.6	332	78.1
Association of School Business Officials (ASBO)	131	9.8	36	8.5
Association for Supervision and Curriculum Development (ASCD)	589	43.9	281	66.1
National Association of Elementary School Principal (NAESP)	36	2.7	21	4.9
National Association of Secondary School Principals (NASSP)	78	5.8	29	6.8
State superintendent association	1246	92.8	374	88.0
Other	153	11.4	72	16.9

Note: Respondents were able to select all response options that applied; percentages are based on the frequency of responses for each possible answer divided by the number in each group responding to the survey question relevant to these data.

Table 7.31   Gender and Self-Perception of Effectiveness as a Superintendent

Self-perception	Male		Female		All	
	f	*%*	*f*	*%*	*f*	*%*
Highly successful	691	50.9	235	54.5	926	51.8
Moderately successful	629	46.3	181	42.0	810	45.3
Only somewhat successful	18	1.3	4	0.9	22	1.2
Not at all successful	0	0.0	0	0.0	0	0.0
Uncertain	20	1.5	11	2.6	31	1.7
Total	1358	100.0	431	100.0	1789	100.0

Table 7.32   Gender and Career Plan for 2015

Career plan	Male		Female		All	
	f	%	f	%	f	%
Remaining in my current position	453	33.4	117	27.3	570	32.0
Remaining a superintendent but in a different district	265	19.6	76	17.8	341	19.1
Being a district or school administrator other than a superintendent	16	1.2	9	2.1	25	1.4
Being a college or university professor	38	2.8	16	3.7	54	3.0
Being a college or university administrator	4	0.3	2	0.5	6	0.3
Being an elementary or secondary school teacher	1	0.1	0	0.0	1	0.1
Being a full-time education consultant	9	0.7	7	1.6	16	0.9
Being a full-time employee in a field outside education	15	1.1	2	0.5	17	1.0
Being retired but continuing to work in some capacity on a part-time basis	407	30.1	160	37.4	567	31.8
Being retired but not employed in any capacity	146	10.8	39	9.1	185	10.4
Total	1354	100.0	428	100.0	1782	100.0

Minority category reported in this chapter. In 2000, Glass, Björk, and Brunner reported that 5.1% of the superintendents participating in their study were in the *Minority* category. Consequently, the percentage of minority respondents in this study is almost 1% higher than it was in 2000.

Data in this section of the chapter are reported in three categories: *Minority*, *Nonminority*, and *All*. Table 7.33 shows the distribution of respondents in the *Minority* group by actual responses on the survey.

Community and District Data

Respondents in the *Minority* group were employed in districts in all geographic locations and school district size categories. Nearly half worked in *rural* school systems with one in five working in an *urban* district. These findings are similar to those reported in 2000. In that study, 45.8% of the minority group members were employed in rural districts, and 23.7% were employed in urban districts (Glass, Björk, & Brunner, 2000). Data for the location of the employing school system in 2010 are in Table 7.34, and data for the size (enrollment) of the employing school districts in 2010 are in Table 7.35.

More than half (55.6%) the minority group superintendents were employed in school districts in which the percentage of residents of color exceeded 50%, whereas only 3.7% were employed in districts in which the percentage of residents of color was 5% or less. Data comparing the diversity of employing school districts by respondent race/ethnicity are in Table 7.36.

Nearly two-thirds (61.7%) of minority group respondents were employed in school districts in which the percentage of students of color exceeded 50%, whereas only 4.7% of them were employed in districts in which the percentage of students of color was 5% or less. Data comparing the student populations of employing school districts for minority and nonminority respondents are in Table 7.37.

Table 7.33   Distribution of Minority Group Members by Race/Ethnicity Categories and District Enrollment

| Race/ethnicity | District Enrollment | | | | | | | | | |
| | Fewer than 300 | | 300 to 2,999 | | 3,000 to 24,999 | | 25,000 or more | | All | |
	f	%	f	%	f	%	f	%	f	%
American Indian or Alaska Native	8	4.7	14	1.3	5	1.0	0	0.0	27	1.5
Asian	0	0.0	0	0.0	4	0.8	1	1.7	5	0.3
Black or African American	3	1.7	7	0.7	21	4.1	5	8.8	36	2.0
Hispanic or Latino	3	1.7	14	1.3	15	2.9	4	7.0	36	2.0
Native Hawaiian or other Pacific Islander	0	0.0	0	0.0	0	0.0	0	0.0	0	0.0
White (not Hispanic or Latino)	159	91.9	1022	96.3	464	91.2	47	82.5	1692	94.0
Other	0	0.0	4	0.4	0	0.0	0	0.0	4	0.2
Total	173	100.0	1061	100.0	509	100.0	57	100.0	1800	100.0

Table 7.34   Race/Ethnicity and District Geographic Descriptor

| Descriptor | Minority | | Nonminority | | All | |
	f	%	f	%	f	%
Urban	22	20.2	84	4.9	106	5.8
Suburban	15	13.8	363	21.2	378	20.8
Small town/city	21	19.3	359	21.0	380	20.9
Rural	49	44.9	883	51.7	932	51.2
Other	2	1.8	21	1.2	23	1.3
Total	109	100.0	1710	100.0	1819	100.0

Three out of four White superintendents (74.8%) were employed in districts that had fewer than 5% minority employees, whereas only 1.2% of them were employed in districts that had more than 50% minority employees. Data comparing district employee race/ethnicity for minority and nonminority respondents are in Table 7.38.

Minority group respondents were considerably more likely to view community diversity as an asset than were other respondents. Slightly more than half of them (52.3%) indicated that community diversity was a *major* or *minor asset*, whereas slightly less than one-third of the *Nonminority* group (31.4%) expressed the same opinions. Data comparing opinions of *Minority* and *Nonminority* respondents on this issue are in Table 7.39.

Table 7.35   Race/Ethnicity and District Enrollment

District enrollment	Minority		Nonminority		All	
	f	%	f	%	f	%
Fewer than 300	14	13.0	159	9.4	173	9.6
300 to 2,999	39	36.1	1022	60.4	1061	58.9
3,000 to 24,999	45	41.6	464	27.4	509	28.3
25,000 or more	10	9.3	47	2.8	57	3.2
Total	108	100.0	1692	100.0	1800	100.0

Table 7.36   Race/Ethnicity and the Level of Diversity in the District's Total Population

Percentage of district minority residents	Minority		Nonminority		All	
	f	%	f	%	f	%
5% or less	4	3.7	841	50.2	845	47.4
6 to 15%	9	8.3	316	18.9	325	18.2
16 to 25%	15	13.9	173	10.3	188	10.5
26 to 50%	20	18.5	204	12.2	224	12.6
51% or more	60	55.6	142	8.4	202	11.3
Total	108	100.0	1676	100.0	1784	100.0

Table 7.37   Race/Ethnicity and the Level of Diversity in the District's Student Population

Percentage of minority students	Minority		Nonminority		All	
	f	%	f	%	f	%
5% or less	5	4.7	840	49.6	845	47.0
6 to 15%	7	6.5	308	18.2	315	17.5
16 to 25%	7	6.5	155	9.2	162	9.0
26 to 50%	22	20.6	196	11.6	218	12.1
51% or more	66	61.7	193	11.4	259	14.4
Total	107	100.0	1692	100.0	1799	100.0

Table 7.38   Race/Ethnicity and the Level of Diversity in the District's Employee Population

Percentage of minority employees	Minority		Nonminority		All	
	f	%	f	%	f	%
5% or less	24	22.0	1275	74.8	1299	71.6
6 to 15%	20	18.3	235	13.8	255	14.1
16 to 25%	20	18.3	86	5.0	106	5.8
26 to 50%	24	22.0	88	5.2	112	6.2
51% or more	21	19.4	21	1.2	42	2.3
Total	109	100.0	1705	100.0	1814	100.0

Table 7.39   Race/Ethnicity and Perception of the Value of Community Diversity

Perception of community diversity	Minority		Non-minority		All	
	f	%	f	%	f	%
Major asset	39	35.8	283	16.6	322	17.7
Minor asset	18	16.5	252	14.8	270	14.9
Neither an asset nor a liability	37	33.9	972	56.9	1009	55.6
Minor liability	12	11.0	172	10.1	184	10.1
Major liability	3	2.8	28	1.6	31	1.7
Total	109	100.0	1707	100.0	1816	100.0

Personal Characteristics

Table 7.40 contains data comparing the age of *Minority* and *Nonminority* superintendents. The figures for the two groups are not strikingly dissimilar; however, a slightly higher percentage of White superintendents were over the age of 55 (47.9% compared to 42.6% in the *Minority* group). Age data for both respondent groups are in Table 7.40.

In 1992, 92.6% of superintendents of color were married (Glass, 1992), and that figure dropped to 87.7% in 2000 (Glass, Björk, & Brunner, 2000). In this study, the figure declined again to 82.3%. Moreover, the percentage of married *Minority* superintendents in this study was lower than the percentage of married White superintendents (91.2%). Marital status data for both respondent groups are in Table 7.41.

Roles and Involvement

In response to a question about the reason they were selected for their current positions, the three most common responses (in order of frequency) for *Minority* superintendents were: (a) *potential to be a change agent*, (b) *ability to be an instructional leader*, and (c) *personal characteristics*. These are the same three most common responses reported for the *Minority* group in the 2000 study (Glass, Björk, & Brunner, 2000). Conversely, the three most common responses for White superintendents were (a) *personal characteristics*, (b) *potential to be a change agent*, and (c) *ability to be an instructional leader*. Again, these are the same three most common responses for the *Nonminority* group reported in 2000; in that study, however, the second most common and third most common reasons were reversed. Data comparing the responses of *Minority* and *Nonminority* respondents on this issue are in Table 7.42.

With respect to board expectations based on role conceptualization (explained previously in Chapter 1 and in the section on gender in this chapter), differences between the *Minority* group and *Nonminority* group were minimal. The percentage of responses indicating *substantial emphasis* in the former, however, was slightly or moderately higher for all five roles. Table 7.43 contains the response data for this question.

Table 7.40   Race/Ethnicity and Age

Age	Minority		Non-minority		All	
	f	*%*	*f*	*%*	*f*	*%*
Less than 36	0	0.0	21	1.2	21	1.2
36-40	6	5.5	70	4.1	76	4.2
41-45	10	9.3	160	9.4	170	9.4
46-50	14	13.0	222	13.1	236	13.0
51-55	32	29.6	413	24.3	445	24.5
56-60	30	27.8	508	29.8	538	29.8
61-65	13	12.0	262	15.4	275	15.2
66+	3	2.8	46	2.7	49	2.7
Total	108	100.0	1702	100.0	1810	100.0

Table 7.41   Race/Ethnicity and Marital Status

Marital status	Minority		Non-minority		All	
	f	*%*	*f*	*%*	*f*	*%*
Married	88	82.3	1537	91.2	1625	90.7
Single	6	5.6	52	3.1	58	3.2
Divorced	12	11.2	74	4.4	86	4.8
Legally separated	0	0.0	8	0.5	8	0.4
Widowed	1	0.9	14	0.8	15	0.9
Total	107	100.0	1685	100.0	1792	100.0

On the issue of community involvement, the percentage of *Minority* superintendents responding that their involvement was *considerable* or *moderate* (81.7%) was slightly higher than the percentage for the same responses in the *Nonminority* group (77.8%). The comparison of responses for this question is in Table 7.44.

Career History and Development

Only slight differences existed between *Minority* and *Nonminority* respondents with respect to teaching experience. The modal response in both groups was 6 to 10 years. Data for responses to this question are in Table 7.45.

Respondents in the *Minority* group entered administration in a wide array of positions. The most common, identified by 22%, was as a *district level director or coordinator*. All data comparing responses for first administrative position are in Table 7.46.

Nonminority group respondents more often became a superintendent before the age of 46. Half of them (50.4%) did so compared to a little more than one-third (35.8%) of the *Minority* group respondents. Complete response data comparing entry age between the two groups are in Table 7.47.

Based on percentages, White respondents were twice as likely as superintendents of color to have more than 12 years of experience in the position. Response data comparing the two groups with respect to experience in the superintendency are in Table 7.48.

With respect to the time between first-ever application for a superintendency and acquiring the position, only minor differences were found between the two race/ethnicity groups. A comparison of response data is in Table 7.49.

Asked if they had encountered discrimination in their pursuit of the superintendency, *Minority* group respondents were more than twice as likely to have answered *yes* (44.9% compared to 19.1% of White respondents). Response data comparing the two groups are in Table 7.50.

Respondents also were asked to identify factors they perceived as restricting access to the superintendency for people of color. Those in the *Nonminority* group were much more likely to respond *none,*

Table 7.42 Race/Ethnicity and Primary Reason for Being Selected as Superintendent

Primary reason	Minority		Nonminority		All	
	f	*%*	*f*	*%*	*f*	*%*
Personal characteristics (e.g., honesty, tact)	20	18.9	578	34.3	598	33.4
Potential to be a change agent	43	40.6	405	24.1	448	25.0
Ability to maintain the status quo	2	1.9	26	1.5	28	1.6
Ability to be an instructional leader	22	20.7	332	19.7	354	19.8
Ability to manage fiscal resources	6	5.6	109	6.5	115	6.5
Having leadership/managerial experience outside of education	1	0.9	10	0.6	11	0.6
Ability to communicate with stakeholders	6	5.7	116	6.9	122	6.8
Uncertain	6	5.7	107	6.4	113	6.3
Total	106	100.0	1683	100.0	1789	100.0

Table 7.43   Race/Ethnicity and Level of School Board Emphasis on Superintendent Role Conceptualizations

Role/level of emphasis	Minority		Nonminority		All	
	f	%	f	%	f	%
Instructional leader (n = 1822)						
Substantial	79	72.5	1011	59.0	1090	59.8
Moderate	24	22.0	609	35.6	633	34.7
Low	6	5.5	83	4.8	89	4.9
None	0	0.0	10	0.6	10	0.6
Total	109	100.0	1713	100.0	1822	100.0
Manager (n = 1822)						
Substantial	90	82.6	1340	78.2	1430	78.5
Moderate	17	15.6	347	20.3	364	20.0
Low	2	1.8	23	1.3	25	1.4
None	0	0.0	3	0.2	3	0.1
Total	109	100.0	1713	100.0	1822	100.0
Statesman/political leader (n = 1800)						
Substantial	63	59.4	938	55.4	1001	55.6
Moderate	28	26.5	599	35.4	627	34.8
Low	13	12.2	143	8.4	156	8.7
None	2	1.9	14	0.8	16	0.9
Total	106	100.0	1694	100.0	1800	100.0
Applied social scientist (n = 1815)						
Substantial	29	26.6	259	15.2	288	15.9
Moderate	36	33.0	708	41.5	744	41.0
Low	33	30.3	601	35.2	634	34.9
None	11	10.1	138	8.1	149	8.2
Total	109	100.0	1706	100.0	1815	100.0
Effective communicator (n = 1819)						
Substantial	97	89.0	1454	85.0	1551	85.3
Moderate	12	11.0	241	14.1	253	13.9
Low	0	0.0	13	0.8	13	0.7
None	0	0.0	2	0.1	2	0.1
Total	109	100.0	1710	100.0	1819	100.0

meaning that they did not perceive any factors to be restricting access (46.8% compared to 29.6% for *Minority* group members). All responses regarding this question are in Table 7.51.

The high level of job satisfaction discussed previously in relation to gender also held true for comparisons based on race/ethnicity. If given an opportunity to refashion their careers, 86.3% of the *Minority* group and 88.6% of the *Nonminority* group said they *definitely* or *probably* would again be a superintendent. This question was posed differently in the 2000 study; however, in that research, only 65.9% of the *Nonminority* group and 67.0% of the *Minority* group responded that they would again choose a career as a superintendent (Glass, Björk, & Brunner, 2000). Data comparing the answers for the two groups on this issue are in Table 7.52.

Professional Preparation and Affiliation

Responses from *Minority* and *Nonminority* respondents, as groups, regarding the quality of their academic preparation for the superintendency were nearly identical. Overall, 78% of the *Minority* group and 77.7% of the *Nonminority* group rated their academic preparation as either *excellent* or *good*. Table 7.53 includes these data.

Ratings for the credibility of former professors were very high; 79.4% of the *Minority* group and 81.1% of the *Nonminority* group rated their credibility as either *excellent* or *good*. These response data are in Table 7.54

Respondents in both groups were highly involved in professional associations. An identical 84.4% in both groups answered that their involvement was either *considerable* or *moderate*. Response data comparing the two groups on level of involvement in professional associations are in Table 7.55.

Table 7.44   Race/Ethnicity and Level of Community Involvement

Level of involvement	Minority		Nonminority		All	
	f	%	*f*	%	*f*	%
Considerable	44	40.4	661	38.5	705	38.6
Moderate	45	41.3	675	39.3	720	39.4
Limited	18	16.5	367	21.3	385	21.0
None	2	1.8	16	0.9	18	1.0
Total	109	100.0	1719	100.0	1828	100.0

Table 7.45   Race/Ethnicity and Teaching Experience

Years of teaching experience	Minority		Nonminority		All	
	f	%	*f*	%	*f*	%
0	1	0.9	14	0.9	15	0.9
1–5	31	28.7	379	23.3	410	23.6
6–10	41	38.0	623	38.3	664	38.3
11–15	14	13.0	338	20.8	352	20.3
16–20	9	8.3	169	10.4	178	10.2
21–25	4	3.7	61	3.7	65	3.8
26+	8	7.4	43	2.6	51	2.9
Total	108	100.0	1627	100.0	1735	100.0

Table 7.46   Race/Ethnicity and First Administrative Position

First administrative position	Minority		Nonminority		All	
	f	%	f	%	f	%
Elementary school assistant principal	11	10.1	120	7.0	131	7.2
Elementary school principal	11	10.1	235	13.7	246	13.5
Dean of students	3	2.8	47	2.8	50	2.7
Junior high or middle school assistant principal	17	15.6	196	11.4	213	11.7
Junior high or middle school principal	3	2.8	88	5.1	91	5.0
High school assistant principal	17	15.6	330	19.2	347	19.0
High school principal	9	8.2	248	14.5	257	14.1
Athletic director	3	2.8	59	3.4	62	3.4
District level director/coordinator	24	22.0	248	14.5	272	14.9
Assistant/associate/deputy superintendent	2	1.8	13	0.8	15	0.8
State education department administrator	0	0.0	12	0.7	12	0.6
School business official or chief financial officer	1	0.9	14	0.8	15	0.8
School district treasurer	0	0.0	3	0.2	3	0.2
Superintendent of schools	6	5.5	59	3.4	65	3.6
Other	2	1.8	43	2.5	45	2.5
Total	109	100.0	1715	100.0	1824	100.0

Minority group respondents were slightly more likely to belong to AASA (80.8% compared to 78.5% of the *Nonminority* group) but slightly less likely to belong to a state superintendent's association (84.6% compared to 91.9% of the *Nonminority* group). In the 2000 study, 73.7% of the superintendents of color were AASA members (Glass, Björk, & Brunner, 2000).

Future Plans

Respondents were asked to identify their intended career status in 2015. Among *Minority* group respondents, 59.8% planned to remain a superintendent (either in their current place of employment or in another school district); among the *Nonminority* group, 50.3% planned to do the same. Response data comparing the two groups are in Table 7.56.

Table 7.47 Race/Ethnicity and Age as a Novice Superintendent

Age as a novice superintendent	Minority		Nonminority		All	
	f	*%*	*f*	*%*	*f*	*%*
Less than 36	10	9.2	232	13.6	242	13.3
36–40	14	12.8	290	17.0	304	16.8
41–45	15	13.8	336	19.8	351	19.4
46–50	36	33.0	412	24.2	448	24.7
51–55	22	20.2	308	18.1	330	18.2
56–60	8	7.3	108	6.3	116	6.4
61 or more	4	3.7	17	1.0	21	1.2
Total	109	100.0	1703	100.0	1812	100.0

Table 7.48 Race/Ethnicity and Experience as a Superintendent

Years as a superintendent	Minority		Nonminority		All	
	f	*%*	*f*	*%*	*f*	*%*
1	6	5.5	100	5.8	106	5.8
2–4	40	36.7	451	26.3	491	26.9
5–8	34	31.2	466	27.2	500	27.4
9–12	14	12.8	258	15.0	272	14.9
13 or more	15	13.8	441	25.7	456	25.0
Total	109	100.0	1716	100.0	1825	100.0

Summary

This chapter included response comparisons based on gender and race/ethnicity for selected survey questions. The following are among the most notable outcomes of this chapter:

- The percentage of female superintendents increased considerably since the 2000 study. The current representation, 24.1%, is the highest ever reported and substantially higher than the 13.2% reported in 2000.
- Female superintendents, on average, were older and had more teaching experience than their male peers. They were twice as likely to have had more than 20 years of teaching experience before becoming an administrator.

Table 7.49   Race/Ethnicity and Time Elapsed between First Applying for and Being Employed in the Superintendency

Years between initial application and employment	Minority		Nonminority		All	
	f	%	f	%	f	%
0*	5	4.6	97	5.7	102	5.7
Less than 1	71	65.7	1138	67.5	1209	67.3
1	11	10.2	176	10.4	187	10.4
2	12	11.1	151	9.0	163	9.1
3	6	5.6	58	3.4	64	3.6
4	0	0.0	29	1.7	29	1.6
5 or more	3	2.8	38	2.3	41	2.3
Total	108	100.0	1687	100.0	1795	100.0

*These respondents were appointed to the position without having been an applicant.

Table 7.50   Race/Ethnicity and Encountering Discrimination

Discrimination encountered	Minority		Nonminority		All	
	f	%	f	%	f	%
Yes	48	44.9	328	19.1	376	20.6
No	52	48.6	1322	76.9	1374	75.2
Uncertain	7	6.5	69	4.0	76	4.2
Total	107	100.0	1719	100.0	1826	100.0

- While males and females both reported the same top three reasons for being selected to their current position (*personal characteristics, potential to be a change agent,* and *ability to be an instructional leader*), the most important among females was *to be an instructional leader*, whereas among males it was *personal characteristics.*
- Superintendents often mentored colleagues aspiring to be administrators and especially those aspiring to be superintendents. About 83% of all respondents reported that they have mentored, and percentages for males and females serving in this role were essentially identical.
- Males, on average, became novice superintendents at an earlier age than did their female peers. More than half (56.3%) of males reached the position by the age of 45, and they were four times as likely as women to be a novice superintendent before the age of 36.
- Superintendents, regardless of race or gender, expressed a high level of job satisfaction: 97% of all respondents indicated that they were *very satisfied* or *moderately satisfied* with their position. Similarly, superintendents reported a high probability they would choose the same career path

Table 7.51   Race/Ethnicity and Perceptions of Factors Restricting Access to the Superintendency for Persons of Color

Perceived restrictions	Minority (n = 108)		Nonminority (n = 1645)	
	f	%	f	%
Absence of mentors who are district or school administrators	42	38.9	435	26.4
Absence of mentors who are professors of school administration	24	22.2	191	11.6
Prejudice (i.e., hostile feelings, opinions, or attitudes of a racial, religious, or national group)	44	40.1	334	20.3
Racial/ethnic discrimination (i.e., treatment of a person based on race/ethnicity rather than on individual merit)	51	47.2	339	20.6
Limited role models (people of color who are superintendents)	45	41.7	558	33.9
None	32	29.6	770	46.8
Other	3	2.8	90	5.5

Note: Respondents were able to select all response options that applied; percentages are based on the frequency of responses for each possible answer divided by the number in each group responding to the survey question relevant to these data.

Table 7.52   Race/Ethnicity and Willingness to Re-select the Superintendency

Would again be a superintendent	Minority		Nonminority		All	
	f	%	f	%	f	%
Definitely yes	77	70.6	1053	62.6	1130	63.1
Probably yes	17	15.7	438	26.0	455	25.4
Unsure	8	7.3	115	6.9	123	6.9
Probably no	7	6.4	71	4.2	78	4.3
Definitely no	0	0.0	5	0.3	5	0.3
Total	109	100.0	1682	100.0	1791	100.0

all over again if given the chance: 88.6% of the males and 87.7% of the females answered *definitely yes* or *probably yes*. Likewise, 86.3% of the *Minority* group and 88.6% of the *Nonminority* group answered *definitely yes* or *probably yes*.
- *Minority* group respondents were considerably more likely to view community diversity as an asset than were members of the *Nonminority* group. Slightly more than half of the former (52.3%)

Table 7.53   Race/Ethnicity and Evaluation of Academic Preparation to be a Superintendent

Rating	Minority		Nonminority		All	
	f	%	f	%	f	%
Excellent	28	25.7	415	24.6	443	24.7
Good	57	52.3	894	53.1	951	53.1
Fair	18	16.5	300	17.8	318	17.7
Poor	4	3.7	59	3.5	63	3.5
None*	2	1.8	16	1.0	18	1.0
Total	109	100.0	1684	100.0	1793	100.0

*Did not complete an academic preparation program.

Table 7.54   Race/Ethnicity and Perceived Credibility of Former Professors

Level of perceived credibility	Minority		Nonminority		All	
	f	%	f	%	f	%
Excellent	32	29.9	571	33.7	603	33.4
Good	53	49.5	804	47.4	857	47.5
Fair	20	18.7	279	16.4	299	16.6
Poor	2	1.9	43	2.5	45	2.5
Total	107	100.0	1697	100.0	1804	100.0

Table 7.55   Race/Ethnicity and Level of Involvement in Professional Organizations

Level of involvement	Minority		Nonminority		All	
	f	%	f	%	f	%
Considerable	42	41.2	604	35.5	646	35.8
Moderate	44	43.2	830	48.9	874	48.4
Limited	17	16.7	257	15.1	274	15.2
None	3	2.9	9	0.5	12	0.6
Total	106	100.0	1700	100.0	1806	100.0

Table 7.56   Race/Ethnicity and Career Plan for 2015

Career plan	Minority		Nonminority		All	
	f	%	*f*	%	*f*	%
Remain in my current position	30	28.0	550	32.1	580	31.8
Remain a superintendent but in a different district	34	31.8	312	18.2	346	19.0
Be a district or school administrator other than a superintendent	1	0.9	24	1.4	25	1.4
Be a college or university professor	5	4.7	51	3.0	56	3.1
Be a college or university administrator	0	0.0	6	0.4	6	0.3
Be an elementary or secondary school teacher	0	0.0	1	0.1	1	0.1
Be a full-time education consultant	9	8.4	8	0.5	17	0.9
Be a full-time employee in a field outside education	1	0.9	17	1.0	18	1.0
Be retired but continuing to work in some capacity on a part-time basis	20	18.7	562	32.7	582	32.0
Be retired and not employed in any capacity	7	6.6	182	10.6	189	10.4
Total	107	100.0	1713	100.0	1820	100.0

indicated that community diversity was a *major* or *minor asset*, whereas slightly less than one-third of the *Nonminority* group (31.4%) expressed the same opinions.

- Only slight differences existed between *Minority* and *Nonminority* respondents with respect to teaching experience. The modal response in both groups was 6 to 10 years.
- *Nonminority* group respondents more often entered the superintendency before the age of 46 than did their peers in the *Minority* group.
- *Nonminority* group respondents were twice as likely as their peers in the *Minority* group to have had more than 12 years of experience as a superintendent at the time of this study.
- *Minority* group respondents were more than twice as likely as their peers in the *Nonminority* group to report that they had encountered discrimination in their pursuit of the superintendency.

8

Professional Preparation

In the last 20 years, American schools have seen extraordinary political, societal, economic, and demographic changes that have played a significant role in reshaping public education. Moreover, the widespread adoption and implementation of standards-based reform have dramatically altered the definition of successful educational leadership (Usdan, 2002). As politicians, business leaders, and the media thrash out publicly the level of accountability to be assumed by school leaders, they also have focused on university-based administrator preparation programs. Although rhetoric frequently outstrips reality, scathing national reports critical of university programs (e.g., Hale & Moorman, 2003; Hess, 2003; Levine, 2005) have contributed to waning public trust and confidence that once was enjoyed by professors delivering traditional academic preparation.

Skepticism about the efficacy of preservice academic preparation has been especially prevalent in relation to university-based preparation programs for superintendents (Orr, 2006; Young, 2005). For example, some critics (e.g., Broad Foundation & Thomas B. Fordham Institute, 2003) contend that administration preparation is basically irrelevant or ineffective, thus making both it and state licensing unnecessary requirements. Moreover, they argue that such criteria only serve to prevent competent noneducators from being superintendents. Yet, their policy position is void of empirical evidence supporting their contentions that many prominent noneducators could and would serve effectively as superintendents if spared the indignity of having to complete a preservice preparation program in a college of education (Kowalski, 2004).

Traditionally, novice superintendents have entered practice after successfully completing an academic degree or licensing program qualifying them for state licensure. Requirements for academic preparation for both teachers and administrators have been largely or entirely driven by state licensing criteria (Wise, 1992, 1994). Because each state sets licensing policy independently, variation exists across states in areas such as the required degrees, required credit hours, and years of required experience in both teaching and school-level administration (Kowalski, 2006, 2008a). In some states, like Connecticut, Illinois, Missouri, Oklahoma, and Texas, applicants must also pass a state examination (National Conference of State Legislatures, 2010).

Several states are considering or have enacted alternative ways to certify administrators whose backgrounds are in areas other than education (Fusarelli, 2005). While 45 states have alternative programs for recruiting and training teachers, this practice has been less common for school-level administrators because virtually all states require aspiring principals to be experienced, fully certified teachers (Feistritzer, 2003). With regard to superintendents, many states allow districts to apply for a certification or licensing waiver for persons assumed to have the requisite management skills (National Conference of State Legislatures, 2010).

Research reveals that most superintendent preparation programs offer similar courses in school administration, including finance, personnel administration, organizational theory, school law, and school-community relations (Glass, Björk, & Brunner, 2000). Some programs, though not all, also require a field experience such as an internship (Young, 2005). To date, there is no national curriculum for superintendent preparation. Arguably, the absence of such a curriculum attenuates efforts to develop national licensing criteria (Petersen, Fusarelli, & Kowalski, 2008).

The content in this chapter is divided into two major parts. The first addresses issues primarily related to preservice academic preparation; the second addresses issues primarily related to continuing education.

Preservice Academic Preparation and Licensing

According to Glass, Björk, and Brunner (2000), all of the previous 10-year studies of the American superintendency, going back to 1923, have explored the issue of academic preparation. Such data also were collected and analyzed in this study.

Overall Rating of Academic Preparation

Asked to rate their academic preparation, almost 8 out of 10 respondents said that it was either *good* or *excellent*. Data showing a summary of ratings are in Table 8.1. Ratings reported here parallel those reported in the 2000 study; 74% of the respondents in that research expressed the same opinion (Glass, Björk, & Brunner, 2000). Ratings of academic preparation since 1982 are compared in Table 8.2. Even reports critical of traditional preparation, such as Levine's *Educating School Leaders* (2005), have found that about two-thirds of administrators rated their preparation courses as having been *valuable*, while 56% viewed them to have been *high quality* experiences.

Data in Table 8.3 reveal superintendent ratings based on years of experience as a superintendent. Though respondents with only 1 year of experience rated their preparation slightly higher than more experienced peers (85.9% rated their preparation as *excellent* or *good*), high ratings held true across the experience categories. High ratings provided by novice superintendents are especially noteworthy given the likelihood that they are employed in small-enrollment districts where they have little or no district-level support staff (Glass, Björk, & Brunner, 2000; Kowalski, Petersen & Fusarelli, 2009). In this study, 68.3% were employed in districts with fewer than 3,000 students.

Table 8.1   Overall Evaluation of Academic Preparation for the Superintendency

Response options	District enrollment									
	Fewer than 300		300 to 2,999		3,000 to 24,999		25,000 or more		All	
	f	%	f	%	f	%	f	%	f	%
Excellent	45	26.6	248	23.6	138	27.0	11	20.4	442	24.8
Good	82	48.6	573	54.5	275	53.8	32	59.3	962	53.9
Fair	35	20.7	192	18.3	80	15.7	10	18.5	317	17.8
Poor	7	4.1	38	3.6	18	3.5	1	1.8	64	3.5
Total	169	100.0	1051	100.0	511	100.0	54	100.0	1785	100.0

Table 8.2   Overall Evaluation of Academic Preparation for the Superintendency: 1982 to 2010

Response options	1982	1992	2000	2010
Excellent	26.8%	26.8%	26.2%	24.8%
Good	47.4%	47.4%	47.4%	53.9%
Fair	NA	22.0%	22.2%	17.8%
Poor	NA	4.6%	4.6%	3.5%

Table 8.3   Overall Evaluation of Academic Preparation, Analyzed by Years of Experience as a Superintendent

Overall evaluation	Years of experience as a superintendent											
	1		2–4		5–8		9–12		13 or more		All	
	f	%	f	%	f	%	f	%	f	%	f	%
Excellent	33	31.1	131	26.7	125	25.4	58	21.6	101	22.4	448	24.8
Good	58	54.8	252	51.4	261	53.1	148	55.0	252	56.0	971	53.7
Fair	10	9.4	90	18.4	94	19.1	49	18.2	80	17.8	323	17.9
Poor	5	4.7	17	3.5	12	2.4	14	5.2	17	3.8	65	3.6
Total	106	100.0	490	100.0	492	100.0	269	100.0	450	100.0	1807	100.0

State Licensing

Over the past decade, several critics (e.g., Hess, 2003) have urged state policymakers to rescind or at least modify state licensing policy so that noneducators could serve in administrative positions. Nine states have either stopped issuing a superintendent's license or have made such a license voluntary; among the remaining states, half have provisions allowing either alternative paths to licensure or the issuance of emergency/temporary licenses (Feistritzer, 2003; National Conference of State Legislatures, 2010). Consequently, licensure is a pivotal policy issue for the education profession generally and for superintendents specifically. Among respondents in this study, 94.7% held a superintendent's license or endorsement. Data concerning this issue are in Table 8.4.

In several states, superintendents can acquire a superintendent's license without having completed a separate and defined superintendent preparation program. As data in Table 8.5 reveal, however, 84.9% of the respondents in this study had completed such a program. Response data concerning completion of a preparation program are in Table 8.5.

Possessing an Earned Doctorate

As defined in this study, an earned doctorate excluded honorary degrees but included both PhD and EdD degrees and doctorates awarded outside of education (e.g., the JD degree). Though no state re-quires a doctorate for initial state licensing of superintendents, the percentage of practitioners in the position possessing this level of education increased substantially from 1971 to 2000 (Glass, Björk, &

Brunner, 2000). The increasing prominence of superintendents with doctorates prompted several authors to examine the relevance (e.g., Grogan & Andrews, 2002) and necessity (e.g., Levine, 2005) of this level of education for superintendents. Such interrogations, however, neither produced major reforms nor eliminated weak and ineffective programs. In fact, the number of programs awarding doctoral degrees in education increased by 48% between 1993 and 2003, and according to Baker, Orr, and Young (2007), much of this growth was attributable to doctoral programs for district and school administrators. Most of the recently created programs are at regional comprehensive colleges and universities, and the doctor of education degree (EdD) was the first doctoral degree to be awarded at many of these institutions (Townsend, 2002).

In this study, 45.3% of the superintendents reported having a doctoral degree—a figure that is identical to the finding reported in 2000 by Glass, Björk, and Brunner. All response data concerning doctorates are in Table 8.6.

The fact that the percentage of superintendents with a doctoral degree did not increase in the last 10 years is especially noteworthy when considered in relation to the trend prominent in the 3 previous decades. From 1971 to 2000, the percentage of superintendents with a doctorate increased from 29.2% to 45.3% (Glass, Björk, & Brunner, 2000). Comparison data for doctorates since 1971 are provided in Table 8.7.

Opinions of Former Professors

Critics, such as Levine (2005) have portrayed most school administration programs as having weak faculty, some of whom even lack experience as practitioners. Authors (e.g., Clark, 1999; Grogan & Andrews, 2002;

Table 8.4   Holding a Valid State Superintendent License or Endorsement

Response options	Fewer than 300		300 to 2,999		3,000 to 24,999		25,000 or more		All	
	f	%	f	%	f	%	f	%	f	%
Yes	165	94.8	1019	95.0	496	95.0	50	86.2	1730	94.7
No	9	5.2	54	5.0	26	5.0	8	13.8	97	5.3
Total	174	100.0	1073	100.0	522	100.0	58	100.0	1827	100.0

Table 8.5   Completion of Accredited University Preparation Program for Superintendent Licensure

Response options	Fewer than 300		300 to 2,999		3,000 to 24,999		25,000 or more		All	
	f	%	f	%	f	%	f	%	f	%
Yes	155	89.1	942	87.5	417	80.0	39	67.2	1553	84.9
No	19	10.9	135	12.5	104	20.0	19	32.8	277	15.1
Total	174	100.0	1077	100.0	521	100.0	58	100.0	1830	100.0

Table 8.6　Having an Earned Doctoral Degree from an Accredited University

Response options	District enrollment									
	Fewer than 300		300 to 2,999		3,000 to 24,999		25,000 or more		All	
	f	%	f	%	f	%	f	%	f	%
Yes, EdD in educational admin/leadership	24	13.9	263	24.3	223	42.3	31	52.5	541	29.4
Yes, EdD in another area of education	2	1.2	22	2.0	23	4.4	3	5.1	50	2.7
Yes, PhD in educational admin/leadership	9	5.2	74	6.8	95	18.0	6	10.2	184	10.0
Yes, PhD in another area of education	0	0.0	15	1.3	21	4.0	1	1.7	37	2.0
Yes, PhD in another discipline	0	0.0	5	0.5	5	0.9	0	0.0	10	0.5
Yes, a doctoral degree other than a PhD or EdD	1	0.6	6	0.6	4	0.8	1	1.7	12	0.7
No	137	79.1	699	64.5	156	29.6	17	28.8	1009	54.7
Total	173	100.0	1084	100.0	527	100.0	59	100.0	1843	100.0

Table 8.7　Data for Earned Doctoral Degrees: 1971 to 2010

	1971	1982	1992	2000	2010
Percent with an earned doctoral degree	29.2%	39.5%	36.0%	45.3%	45.3%

Table 8.8　Perceptions of Professor Credibility

Response options	District enrollment									
	Fewer than 300		300 to 2,999		3,000 to 24,999		25,000 or more		All	
	f	%	f	%	f	%	f	%	f	%
Excellent	72	42.1	350	32.8	167	32.1	17	31.0	606	33.4
Good	71	41.5	521	48.9	248	47.6	24	43.6	864	47.7
Fair	25	14.6	173	16.2	85	16.3	13	23.6	296	16.3
Poor	3	1.8	22	2.1	21	4.0	1	1.8	47	2.6
Total	171	100.0	1066	100.0	521	100.0	55	100.0	1813	100.0

Van Meter, 1999; Young, Petersen, & Short, 2002) analyzing university-based preparation and other alternatives, however, contend that university professors are arguably in the best position to provide productive environments and experiences that help students become reflective and competent practitioners.

In this study, 81.1% of the respondents rated the credibility of their former professors as *good* or *excellent*. Perhaps equally noteworthy, only 65.9% of the superintendents participating in the 2000 study did likewise (Glass, Björk, & Brunner, 2000). Response data for this issue based on district enrollment are in Table 8.8. Responses were also examined in relation to the years of experience in the superintendency. Generally, experience in the position did not appear to have a discernible effect on ratings; however, novice superintendents rated the credibility of their former professors slightly higher than did their more experienced peers. Response data for professor credibility based on experience in the superintendency are in Table 8.9.

Importance of Specific Courses

Respondents in this study were asked to identify the importance of courses commonly included in administrator preparation. Because the superintendents only responded for courses they had completed, the number of responses for each varies. The courses are listed in Table 8.10, and the data reveal the three courses perceived to be of greatest importance were *school law*, *school finance*, and *school public relations*. Response data for course importance are in Table 8.10

Superintendent Continuing Education

Superintendents commonly engage in continuing education, and these experiences are offered by a variety of sources, such as professional organizations, state departments of education, regional service centers, and universities. The importance of lifelong learning is now widely recognized across professions, and in the case of superintendents, it is often a required experience linked to license renewal (Kowalski, 2008a).

Providers

Participants in this study were asked to identify the professional organizations that have sponsored in-service or staff development programs that they had completed since becoming a superintendent.

Table 8.9   Perceptions of Professor Credibility by Years of Experience

Response options	Years of Superintendent Experience											
	1		2–4		5–8		9–12		13 or more		All	
	f	*%*	*f*	*%*	*f*	*%*	*f*	*%*	*f*	*%*	*f*	*%*
Excellent	49	45.0	181	37.2	175	34.7	84	30.4	125	27.2	614	33.4
Good	43	39.5	229	47.0	243	48.1	128	46.4	230	50.0	873	47.5
Fair	15	13.7	68	14.0	77	15.2	50	18.1	93	20.2	303	16.5
Poor	2	1.8	9	1.8	10	2.0	14	5.1	12	2.6	47	2.6
Total	109	100.0	487	100.0	505	100.0	276	100.0	460	100.0	1837	100.0

Table 8.10   Perceived Importance of Academic Courses in Superintendent Preparation

Courses	Levels of Perceived Importance							
	Extremely important		Moderately important		Unimportant		Did not take course	
	f	%	f	%	f	%	f	%
School law (n = 1863)	1354	72.7	456	24.5	37	1.9	16	0.9
School finance (n = 1862)	1184	63.6	544	29.2	96	5.2	38	2.0
School public relations (n = 1858)	933	50.2	723	38.9	91	4.9	111	6.0
Human resource management (n = 1857)	930	50.1	768	41.4	75	4.0	84	4.5
Curriculum (n = 1860)	782	42.0	940	50.6	115	6.2	23	1.2
Decision making (n = 1859)	719	38.7	828	44.5	174	9.4	138	7.4
District administration (n = 1859)	607	32.7	948	51.0	179	9.6	125	6.7
Instructional methods, pedagogy (n = 1858)	585	31.5	1010	54.4	222	11.9	41	2.2
Politics of education (n = 1855)	519	28.0	849	45.8	249	13.4	238	12.8
School facility planning/management (n = 1854)	504	27.2	926	49.9	197	10.7	227	12.2
Program evaluation (n = 1851)	500	27.0	988	53.4	200	10.8	163	8.8
Organizational theory (n = 1861)	491	26.4	1014	54.5	304	16.3	52	2.8
Tests and measurements (n = 1855)	427	23.0	1052	56.7	276	14.9	100	5.4
Research (n = 1854)	402	21.7	1033	55.7	373	20.1	46	2.5
Diversity (n = 1849)	261	14.1	840	45.4	408	22.1	340	18.4

Findings reported in district enrollment categories are in Table 8.11, and they reveal that regardless of district enrollment, the three most attended programs were offered by the *state superintendent associations*, followed by *state government* and the *American Association of School Administrators (AASA)*. Table 8.12 includes response data for the same subject reported by levels of experience in the superintendency. As might be expected, novice superintendents reported attending fewer programs because they had been in office 1 year or less at the time of this study. Findings reported for 2010 are very similar to those reported by Glass, Björk, and Brunner in 2000.

Usefulness of Continuing Education Programs

Respondents were asked to rate their continuing education experiences based on their usefulness for superintendents. The outcomes reported by district enrollment categories are in Table 8.13. They

Table 8.11   Organizations that Provided In-Service/Staff Development by Superintendents

Response options	District enrollment							
	Fewer than 300		300 to 2,999		3,000 to 24,999		25,000 or more	
	f	%	f	%	f	%	f	%
State superintendent association (n = 1603)	136	8.5	967	60.3	450	28.1	50	3.1
State government (e.g., state dept. of education) (n = 1216)	111	9.1	760	62.5	314	25.8	31	2.6
AASA (n = 987)	79	8.0	525	53.2	341	34.6	42	4.2
ASCD (n = 778)	51	6.6	429	55.1	268	34.4	30	3.9
NSBA (n = 572)	38	6.6	281	49.1	218	38.1	35	6.2
ASBO (n = 389)	32	8.2	251	64.5	98	25.2	8	2.1
Federal government (e.g.. Dept. of Education) (n = 366)	44	12.0	200	54.6	109	29.8	13	3.6
School study councils (n = 291)	16	5.5	161	55.3	110	37.8	4	1.4
NASSP (n = 220)	20	9.0	124	56.4	71	32.3	5	2.3
NAESP (n = 98)	9	9.2	54	55.1	31	31.6	4	4.1
Other (n = 253)	20	7.9	140	55.4	80	31.6	13	5.1

AASA: American Association of School Administrators
ASCD: Association for Supervision and Curriculum Development
ASBO: Association of School Business Officials
NSBA: National School Boards Association
NASSP: National Association of Secondary School Principals
NAESP: National Association for Elementary School Principals

reveal that 83.3% of all respondents found professional development opportunities to have been *useful* or *very useful*. Table 8.14 includes response data reported by levels of experience in the superintendency.

In 2000, 28.9% of the participating superintendents rated their continuing education experiences *very useful*, and 24.7% rated them as *useful*. Thus, the usefulness ratings in this study were considerably higher.

Valued Topics

Respondents were asked if they considered common continuing education topics relevant. The topics and responses are listed in Table 8.15. The three topics identified as being most relevant were

Table 8.12 Organizations that Provided In-Service/Staff Development Completed by Superintendents by Years of Experience

Response options	Years of Superintendent Experience									
	1		2–4		5–8		9–12		13 or more	
	f	%	f	%	f	%	f	%	f	%
State superintendent association (n = 1625)	83	5.1	421	26.0	458	28.2	248	15.2	415	25.5
State government (e.g., state dept. of education) (n = 1234)	58	4.7	308	25.0	358	29.0	198	16.0	312	25.3
AASA (n = 1000)	41	4.1	194	19.4	265	26.5	160	16.0	340	34.0
ASCD (n = 794)	31	3.9	199	25.0	203	25.6	127	16.0	234	29.5
NSBA (n = 581)	24	4.1	141	24.3	154	26.5	81	13.9	181	31.2
ASBO (n = 398)	16	4.0	107	26.9	122	30.7	61	15.3	92	23.1
Federal government (e.g., dept. of education) (n = 374)	16	4.3	90	24.1	91	24.3	60	16.0	117	31.3
School study councils (n = 295)	6	2.0	66	22.4	84	28.5	35	11.9	104	35.2
NASSP (n = 221)	5	2.3	50	22.6	66	29.9	33	14.9	67	30.3
NAESP (n = 98)	0	0.0	30	30.6	28	28.6	15	15.3	25	25.5
Other (n = 254)	13	5.1	74	29.1	63	24.8	40	15.8	64	25.2

AASA: American Association of School Administrators
ASCD: Association for Supervision and Curriculum Development
ASBO: Association of School Business Officials
NSBA: National School Boards Association
NASSP: National Association of Secondary School Principals
NAESP: National Association for Elementary School Principals

law/legal issues, finance, and *personnel management.* This finding, coupled with the finding related to the importance of specific academic courses (see Table 8.10), reveals the extent to which superintendents face legal and fiscal problems, even in a political climate where reform and accountability occupy center stage.

Both research and practice make it clear that the key to enhancing the leadership capacity of district superintendents is through ongoing professional development. The importance of career staged, collaboratively designed learning opportunities is acknowledged as effective and meaningful forms of professional development (Petersen, 2010). Topics identified by superintendents in this and previous studies are generally technical in nature and lend themselves to the day-to-day demands and responsibilities.

Table 8.13   Usefulness of Continuing Education Programs for Superintendents

Response options	District enrollment									
	Fewer than 300		300 to 2,999		3,000 to 24,999		25,000 or more		All	
	f	%	f	%	f	%	f	%	f	%
Very useful	69	41.1	490	46.0	222	43.2	15	27.9	796	44.1
Useful	69	41.1	409	38.3	203	39.5	26	48.1	707	39.2
Somewhat useful	28	16.7	155	14.5	80	15.6	12	22.2	275	15.3
Not useful	2	1.1	13	1.2	9	1.7	1	1.8	25	1.4
Total	168	100.0	1067	100.0	514	100.0	54	100.0	1803	100.0

Table 8.14   Usefulness of Continuing Education Programs for Superintendents by Years of Experience

Response options	Years of Superintendent Experience											
	1		2–4		5–8		9–12		13 or more		All	
	f	%	f	%	f	%	f	%	f	%	f	%
Very useful	53	48.6	204	41.8	229	45.5	128	47.2	193	42.4	807	44.2
Useful	41	37.6	206	42.2	194	38.6	95	35.1	177	38.9	713	39.0
Somewhat useful	15	13.8	71	14.6	74	14.7	44	16.2	77	16.9	281	15.4
Not useful	0	0.0	7	1.4	6	1.2	4	1.5	8	1.8	25	1.4
Total	109	100.0	488	100.0	503	100.0	271	100.0	455	100.0	1826	100.0

Summary

Content in this chapter is intended to describe and enrich understanding of how superintendents rate their formal professional learning experiences. Such experiences include those completed prior to licensing and continuing education occurring post licensure. The following are the most noteworthy findings reported in this chapter:

- Just over three-fourths of the superintendents (78.7%) rated their preservice academic preparation as *good* or *excellent*.
- The vast majority of superintendents (94.7%) held a valid state license or endorsement for their position. Further, 85% had completed an accredited university designed to prepare superintendents.
- Slightly less than half (45.3%) of all the responding superintendents possessed an earned doctoral degree. This percentage is identical to the finding reported in 2000. Thus, the trend

Table 8.15   Topics Considered Relevant for Professional Development

Topics identified as relevant	District enrollment							
	Fewer than 300		300 to 2,999		3,000 to 24,999		25,000 or more	
	f	%	f	%	f	%	f	%
Law/legal issues (n = 1467)	141	9.6	900	61.3	390	26.6	36	2.5
Finance (n = 1353)	138	10.2	845	62.5	342	25.2	28	2.1
Personnel management (e.g., collective bargaining) (n = 1061)	90	8.5	678	63.9	270	25.4	23	2.2
School reform/improvement (n = 956)	76	7.9	517	54.1	322	33.7	41	4.3
Superintendent-board relations (n = 952)	93	9.8	528	55.4	298	31.3	33	3.5
School-community relations (n = 701)	66	9.4	393	56.1	213	30.4	29	4.1
Facility planning/ management (n = 609)	58	9.5	388	63.7	152	25.0	11	1.8
School safety/crisis management (n = 606)	64	10.6	373	61.6	149	24.5	20	3.3
Conflict management (n = 601)	68	11.3	324	53.9	190	31.6	19	3.2
Policy development/ management (n = 555)	51	9.2	331	59.6	154	27.8	19	3.4
Student discipline (n = 221)	43	19.5	124	56.1	51	23.1	3	1.3
Other (n = 61)	4	6.6	24	39.3	27	44.3	6	9.8

toward an increasing percentage of superintendents having doctoral degrees reported between 1971 and 2000 was not sustained in this study. Superintendents in districts with 3,000 or more students, however, were much more likely to possess a doctorate than their peers in smaller districts. Just over 70% of the superintendents in these larger districts had a doctorate.

- Most superintendents (81.1%) rated the credibility of their former professors as *good* or *excellent*.
- The four academic courses rated as having the highest levels of importance were *school law, school finance, school community relations,* and *human resource management.*
- Superintendents were most likely to have attended continuing education provided by *state superintendent associations, state government,* and *AASA.*

- Most superintendents (83.3%) rated their continuing education experiences as *useful* or *very useful*.
- Potential continuing education topics identified as having the greatest value were *law/legal issues, finance, personnel management, school reform/improvement, superintendent-board relations,* and *school-community relations.*

9

Politics, Mandates, Standards, and Government Relations

This chapter presents benchmark data designed to trace the evolving political frame of the superintendency. The topic has received only superficial attention in preceding national studies of district superintendents.

Bolman and Deal describe the political frame of organizations as consisting of five propositions: (1) coalitions, (2) enduring differences, (3) scarce resources, (4) differences that give rise to conflict, making power the most important resource, and (5) bargaining, negotiating, and jockeying for position (1997, p. 163). These propositions are all too familiar to school superintendents, and they have elevated the importance of political leadership in recent years (Hoy & Miskel, 2008; Kowalski, 2011). Some describe political leadership as a struggle (Bell, 1988; Guthrie & Schuermann, 2010), while others see this responsibility in a democratic frame, that is, as an opportunity to embrace a wider community in decision making (Marshall & Gerstl-Pepin, 2005). Focusing on protracted efforts to achieve school reform, Björk and Lindle noted that "school superintendents cannot deny the role that politics and interest groups play in the core of their professional work" (2001, p. 87).

In the 1982 AASA superintendency study, the authors, Cunningham and Hentges, focused on a series of issues then considered significant. Specifically, they traced the changes in 18 issues from 1971 to 1982. The 1971 listing contained items such as greater visibility of the superintendent; school staff relations, strikes, or other forms of teacher militancy; growth of federal involvement in education; assessment of educational outcomes; caliber of responsibilities assigned to or removed from school boards; social/cultural issues, such as race relations, integration, or segregation; and increasing attacks upon the superintendent. A decade later, the authors reported on many of the same items but expanded the list to include planning and goal setting, accountability and credibility, administrator-board relations, and compliance with state and federal record-keeping requirements (Cunningham & Hentges, 1982, p. 38). Under the authorship of Glass, Björk, and Brunner, the 2000 study addressed accountability/credibility, strategic planning and mission statements, administrator/board relations, assessing and testing learner outcomes, community involvement in decision making, legislative and local efforts to implement choice programs, and school-based decision making.

This study looked more extensively at political pressures superintendents experienced. While political influence manifests itself in many ways, the overt demonstration of political influence in the form of petitions or shows of force at a board meeting tend to dominate one's image of political pressures superintendents face.

This chapter is divided into three parts. The first includes findings pertaining to experiencing political action; the second includes superintendent opinions on a variety of issues that have political implications; the third relates to opinions about federal, state, and local government support and involvement.

Experiences with Political Action

Encountering Political Action

School board meetings and public forums remain among the few settings in which citizens, individually or collectively, are still able to pursue their interest through democratic discourse and political action. Table 9.1 includes the frequency with which overt political action took place in school districts, disaggregated by district enrollment. While overt political influence was reported to occur only *occasionally* (27.2%) or *rarely* (59.6%) across all sizes of districts, the incidence of overt political influence was greater in larger districts than in smaller districts. Almost two-thirds of the superintendents in the largest districts, for example, indicated that overt political influence had been employed *occasionally* or *often*. Fewer than one in five of their counterparts from the smallest districts reported having the same experiences. Although overt political action occurred less frequently in small communities, Lamkin reminds us that superintendents in rural settings must maneuver around relationships that are "close-knit" and "life-long" and "have a prevalence of emotional responses to considerations for change in those communities" (2006, p. 19).

Issues Generating Political Action

This study also examined specific incidents that generated district-level political action in the recent past. As data in Table 9.2 reveal, reported levels of political pressures increased as district size increased; issues were cited more frequently by superintendents in larger districts. With the exception of *extracurricular activities*, superintendents in larger districts identified issues more frequently than did their peers. This dissimilar outcome for *extracurricular activities* is probably explained by the fact that superintendents in very large districts typically were less involved in such programs. Because their districts have multiple secondary schools, superintendents are more likely to have ultimate responsibility for dealing with conflict emanating from these programs.

Activities Commonly Involving Stakeholders

While data in Table 9.2 relate to issues, data in Table 9.3 pertain to community involvement in various activities and functions. District size again appears to have been a factor influencing stakeholder

Table 9.1 Frequency of Overt Political Action

Response options	District enrollment									
	Fewer than 300		300 to 2,999		3,000-24,999		25,000 or more		All	
	f	%	f	%	f	%	f	%	f	%
Often	6	3.6	31	3.0	37	7.4	10	18.5	84	4.8
Occasionally	28	16.5	271	26.1	155	31.1	25	46.3	479	27.2
Rarely	108	63.9	642	61.9	281	56.3	18	33.3	1049	59.6
Never	27	16.0	93	9.0	26	5.2	1	1.9	147	8.4
Total	169	100.0	1037	100.0	499	100.0	54	100.0	1759	100.0

Table 9.2   Issues that Generated District-Level Political Action during the Past Three Years

Issues	District enrollment									
	Fewer than 300		300 to 2,999		3,000 to 24,999		25,000 or more		All	
	f	%	f	%	f	%	f	%	f	%
Curriculum (e.g., sex education, teaching evolution)	23	14.3	142	13.8	103	20.3	18	31.0	286	16.3
Requests for additional funding (e.g., tax referenda)	57	35.4	450	43.7	282	55.5	32	55.2	821	46.7
Instructional approaches (e.g., cooperative learning, online courses)	20	12.4	115	11.2	69	13.6	14	24.1	218	12.4
Government mandates	34	21.1	173	16.8	133	26.2	22	37.9	362	20.6
Locally-initiated reform proposals	9	5.6	97	9.4	90	17.7	11	19.0	207	11.8
School facility development	43	26.7	499	48.4	271	53.3	28	48.3	841	47.9
Redrawing school boundaries	2	1.2	58	5.6	166	32.7	37	63.8	263	15.0
Extracurricular activities (including athletics)	90	55.9	564	54.8	179	35.2	15	25.9	848	48.3
Racial tensions	2	1.2	37	3.6	49	9.6	12	20.7	100	5.7
Special education	25	15.5	166	16.1	117	23.0	23	39.7	331	18.8
Proposal to consolidate either districts or schools	36	22.4	180	17.5	85	16.7	18	31.0	319	18.2
Employment decisions (e.g., reduction in force)	48	29.8	407	39.5	173	34.1	24	41.4	652	37.1
Other	17	10.6	129	12.5	66	13.0	13	22.4	225	12.8

Note: Respondents were able to select all response options that applied.

involvement. As an example, citizens were more likely to be involved in *extracurricular activities* in smaller districts. The three issues identified as having the most frequent citizen involvement were *long-range planning*, *constructing a district or school vision*, and *facility planning*. In fact, stakeholders were twice as likely to be involved in these three activities as they were in all other activities.

Table 9.3   Activities in Which Community Stakeholders Commonly Have Been Involved

Activities	District enrollment									
	Fewer than 300		300 to 2,999		3,000 to 24,999		25,000 or more		All	
	f	*%*	*f*	*%*	*f*	*%*	*f*	*%*	*f*	*%*
Constructing district or school vision	79	47.0	661	63.0	364	71.2	42	72.4	1146	64.2
Long-range or strategic planning	89	53.0	713	68.0	402	78.7	44	75.9	1248	69.9
Curriculum revisions (e.g., adopting/re-vamping sex education)	38	22.6	277	26.4	228	44.6	32	55.2	575	32.2
Recommending policy and rules for cocurricular and extracurricular activities planning/ management	73	43.5	318	30.3	148	29.0	15	25.9	554	31.0
Recommending policy and rules for student conduct and discipline	65	38.7	334	31.8	184	36.0	21	36.2	604	33.8
Fiscal planning and management	33	19.6	286	27.3	203	39.7	34	58.6	556	31.1
Program evaluation	34	20.2	209	19.9	121	23.7	14	24.1	378	21.2
Facility planning	65	38.7	645	61.5	334	65.4	37	63.8	1081	60.5
Student transportation	28	16.7	126	12.0	66	12.9	13	22.4	233	13.1
Other	8	4.8	51	4.9	27	5.3	3	5.2	89	5.0

Note: Respondents were able to select all response options that applied.

Superintendent Opinions

Respondents were asked to identify if selected variables were perceived to be assets or liabilities for their districts. All of the variables have both educational and political implications.

Visioning and Planning

Respondents were asked to state their opinions on a number of issues that have political implications. The first was the value of visioning and planning. Scholars uniformly posit that broad citizen involvement is essential for these core strategic planning activities. At the same time, however, such involvement often spawns political activity. Asked if visioning and planning were an asset or liability, 87.1% responded that it was either a *major* or *minor asset*. Essential to understanding this question is the inherent need that superintendents have to gain broad stakeholder participation in creating a vision for the district and conducting the associated planning. Both are subject to the political ebb and flow of the community and its constituents (Björk & Lindle, 2001). Response data for opinions on the value of visioning and planning are in Table 9.4.

District Climate

Myriad authors (e.g., Fullan, 2001; Sarason, 1996) have pointed out that institutional climate, and especially culture, is a highly influential variable in relation to organizational effectiveness. Just a fraction under 85% of the respondents viewed district culture as either a *major* or *minor asset*. While inexact at best, the topics of district climate and culture suggest a proxy for determining public acceptance of the work of the superintendent and district. Opinion data regarding the value of district climate are in Table 9.5.

School Facilities

School facilities not only are important with respect to accommodating education services and to ensuring student safety, but also they have symbolic significance. They directly or indirectly convey

Table 9.4   Visioning and Planning: Perceived Value to Schools

Opinions	District enrollment									
	Fewer than 300		300–2,999		3,000–24,999		25,000 or more		All	
	f	*%*	*f*	*%*	*f*	*%*	*f*	*%*	*f*	*%*
Major asset	41	23.6	420	39.0	326	62.5	36	62.1	823	44.9
Minor asset	98	56.3	494	45.8	164	31.4	17	29.3	773	42.2
Neither an asset nor a liability	24	13.8	124	11.5	18	3.5	3	5.2	169	9.2
Minor liability	7	4.0	35	3.3	11	2.1	2	3.4	55	3.0
Major liability	4	2.3	5	0.4	3	0.5	0	0.0	12	0.7
Total	174	100.0	1078	100.0	522	100.0	58	100.0	1832	100.0

messages about the community philosophy and willingness to support education. In many states, the renovation and construction of school facilities is a major political issue because taxpayers must approve increased tax rates for debt service. Opinion data regarding the value of school facilities are in Table 9.6; the data were reported on the perceptions of superintendents regarding the facilities of their districts. Superintendents in larger districts were more inclined to see facilities as an asset than were their peers in smaller districts. As examples, 71.9% and 82.5% of the superintendents from the two largest categories of districts indicated that they perceived facilities as a *major* or *minor asset*, whereas 60.9% and 68.2% of their peers from the two smallest enrollment categories expressed the same sentiments.

Table 9.5   District Climate, Including Culture: Perceived Value to Schools

Opinions	District enrollment									
	Fewer than 300		300–2,999		3,000–24,999		25,000 or more		All	
	f	*%*	*f*	*%*	*f*	*%*	*f*	*%*	*f*	*%*
Major asset	75	43.1	492	45.6	282	53.9	34	58.6	883	48.1
Minor asset	64	36.8	403	37.3	183	35.0	16	27.6	666	36.3
Neither an asset nor a liability	15	8.6	87	8.1	23	4.4	3	5.2	128	7.0
Minor liability	17	9.8	86	8.0	32	6.1	4	6.9	139	7.6
Major liability	3	1.7	12	1.0	3	0.6	1	1.7	19	1.0
Total	174	100.0	1080	100.0	523	100.0	58	100.0	1835	100.0

Table 9.6   District Facilities: Perceived Value to Schools

Opinions	District enrollment									
	Fewer than 300		300–2,999		3,000–24,999		25,000 or more		All	
	f	*%*	*f*	*%*	*f*	*%*	*f*	*%*	*f*	*%*
Major asset	50	28.7	414	38.5	243	46.6	31	54.4	738	40.4
Minor asset	56	32.2	320	29.7	132	25.3	16	28.1	524	28.7
Neither an asset nor a liability	19	10.9	78	7.3	29	5.6	2	3.5	128	7.0
Minor liability	32	18.4	172	16.0	80	15.4	3	5.3	287	15.7
Major liability	17	9.8	92	8.5	37	7.1	5	8.7	151	8.2
Total	174	100.0	1076	100.0	521	100.0	57	100.0	1828	100.0

Competition from Charter Schools and Private Schools

Charter schools are hybrid institutions. Legally, they are public schools and funded as such; operationally, however, they function more like private schools (Kowalski, 2010). Advocates argue that these institutions, by virtue of providing additional competition to traditional public schools, are a catalyst for school reform across all types of elementary and secondary schools. Although few superintendents viewed charters as an asset, only about 20% viewed them as a liability. Among all respondents, 78.5% opined that they were *neither an asset nor a liability*. Opinion data regarding the value of charter schools are in Table 9.7.

Private schools always have constituted a form of parental choice. Superintendent opinions about the value of these institutions were slightly more negative than they were for charter schools; however, a majority (68.6%) still viewed them as *neither an asset nor a liability*. Opinion data regarding the value of private schools are in Table 9.8.

Table 9.7 Competition from Charter Schools: Perceived Value to Schools

Opinions	District enrollment									
	Fewer than 300		300–2,999		3,000–24,999		25,000 or more		All	
	f	%	f	%	f	%	f	%	f	%
Major asset	2	1.2	8	0.8	4	0.8	0	0.0	14	0.7
Minor asset	2	1.2	11	1.0	14	2.7	3	5.2	30	1.7
Neither an asset nor a liability	156	91.8	864	81.4	363	70.4	34	58.6	1417	78.5
Minor liability	5	2.9	139	13.1	100	19.4	20	34.5	264	14.6
Major liability	5	2.9	40	3.7	35	6.7	1	1.7	81	4.5
Total	170	100.0	1062	100.0	516	100.0	58	100.0	1806	100.0

Table 9.8 Competition from Private, Including Parochial Schools: Perceived Value to Schools

Opinions	District enrollment									
	Fewer than 300		300–2,999		3,000–24,999		25,000 or more		All	
	f	%	f	%	f	%	f	%	f	%
Major asset	0	0.0	10	0.9	9	1.7	0	0.0	19	1.0
Minor asset	3	1.8	25	2.3	15	2.9	7	12.1	50	2.7
Neither an asset nor a liability	140	81.9	754	70.0	325	62.6	32	55.2	1251	68.6
Minor liability	23	13.5	257	23.9	149	28.7	16	27.6	445	24.4
Major liability	5	2.8	31	2.9	21	4.1	3	5.2	60	3.3
Total	171	100.0	1077	100.0	519	100.0	58	100.0	1825	100.0

Community Diversity

Given the fact that racial/ethnic diversity in America is increasing annually, superintendents' dispositions toward community diversity are clearly a relevant professional and political issue. Overall, 11.7% of the respondents saw community racial/ethnic diversity as either a *minor* or *major liability*. Once again, however, the modal response was that community diversity was *neither an asset nor a liability*. Opinion data regarding the value of community diversity are in Table 9.9.

Media Coverage

Historically, administrators have been ambivalent toward journalists, believing that many of them were only interested in negative news. In the present information-based society, however, enlightened superintendents realize that the media can perform some valued services, such as keeping the public informed of existing and emerging education needs (Kowalski, 2011). Regardless of community size, Fowler reminds us that because "the media must screen, select, explain, and recontextualize information, they inevitably play a major role in the policy process" (2000, p. 156).

Respondent feelings toward media coverage were mixed, but overall, they were more positive than negative. Respondents were more than twice as likely to view media coverage as either a *major* or *minor asset* (52.6%) than they were to view it as either a *major* or *minor liability* (19.9%). Also notable, respondents from larger districts were more inclined to view media coverage as an asset, perhaps because they are subjected to more coverage. Opinion data regarding the value of media coverage are in Table 9.10.

Employee Unions

Although employee unions are now common in school districts, the conflict they often generate remains a political concern for many superintendents. Respondents in this study were almost three times as likely to view employee unions as a *major* or *minor liability* (41.1%) than they were to view them as a *major* or *minor asset* (14.2%). Opinion data regarding the value of employee unions are in Table 9.11.

Table 9.9   Racial/Ethnic Diversity in the Community: Perceived Value to Schools

Opinions	District enrollment									
	Fewer than 300		300–2,999		3,000–24,999		25,000 or more		All	
	f	%	f	%	f	%	f	%	f	%
Major asset	16	9.2	126	11.7	161	30.8	28	48.3	331	18.1
Minor asset	13	7.5	143	13.3	97	18.6	14	24.1	267	14.6
Neither an asset nor a liability	126	72.4	674	62.6	203	38.9	15	25.9	1018	55.6
Minor liability	17	9.8	115	10.7	49	9.4	1	1.7	182	9.9
Major liability	2	1.1	18	1.7	12	2.3	0	0.0	32	1.8
Total	174	100.0	1076	100.0	522	100.0	58	100.0	1830	100.0

Community Involvement

In a democratic society, administrators, and especially superintendents, are expected to provide professional leadership while remaining subservient to the will of the people (Wirt & Kirst, 2009). Specifically, superintendents are advised to encourage community involvement in the public schools. Expectedly, the vast majority of respondents (78.7%) opined that community involvement was either a *major* or *minor* *asset*. Opinion data regarding the value of community involvement are in Table 9.12.

Student, Employee, and Board Member Behavior

Superintendents were asked to state their opinions regarding the behavior of three in-district groups: students, employees, and school board members. Responses show that a substantial majority viewed

Table 9.10   Media Coverage: Perceived Value to Schools

Perceived value	*District enrollment*									
	Fewer than 300		*300–2,999*		*3,000–24,999*		*25,000 or more*		*All*	
	f	*%*	*f*	*%*	*f*	*%*	*f*	*%*	*f*	*%*
Major asset	17	9.8	186	17.4	101	19.4	13	22.4	317	17.5
Minor asset	46	26.6	397	37.2	172	33.1	24	41.4	639	35.1
Neither an asset nor a liability	79	45.7	305	28.6	109	21.0	8	13.8	501	27.5
Minor liability	27	15.6	139	13.0	94	18.1	8	13.8	268	14.7
Major liability	4	2.3	41	3.8	44	8.4	5	8.6	94	5.2
Total	173	100.0	1068	100.0	520	100.0	58	100.0	1819	100.0

Table 9.11   Employee Unions: Perceived Value to Schools

Opinions	*District enrollment*									
	Fewer than 300		*300–2,999*		*3,000–24,999*		*25,000 or more*		*All*	
	f	*%*	*f*	*%*	*f*	*%*	*f*	*%*	*f*	*%*
Major asset	2	1.2	32	3.0	27	5.2	4	7.0	65	3.6
Minor asset	10	5.8	96	9.0	78	15.0	9	15.8	193	10.6
Neither an asset nor a liability	122	70.5	467	43.6	201	38.7	23	40.4	813	44.7
Minor liability	26	15.0	285	26.6	110	21.1	11	19.3	432	23.7
Major liability	13	7.5	190	17.8	104	20.0	10	17.5	317	17.4
Total	173	100.0	1070	100.0	520	100.0	57	100.0	1820	100.0

behavior in all three groups either as a *major* or *minor asset*. Response data for these opinions are in Tables 9.13, 9.14, and 9.15.

Administrators, Teachers, and Support Staff

Superintendents typically depend on district-level and school-level administrators to assist them in providing essential leadership and management. Overwhelmingly, respondents in this study viewed their administrative staff as either a *major* or *minor asset*. Opinion data regarding the value of administrative staff are in Table 9.16.

Likewise, the quality of a district's teaching staff and nonprofessional support staff influences institutional effectiveness. Almost identical to their views about the value of administrators, the substantial

Table 9.12   Community Involvement: Perceived Value to Schools

Opinions	District enrollment									
	Fewer than 300		300–2,999		3,000–24,999		25,000 or more		All	
	f	%	f	%	f	%	f	%	f	%
Major asset	62	35.8	437	40.7	268	51.2	36	62.1	803	43.9
Minor asset	59	34.1	384	35.8	178	34.0	16	27.6	637	34.8
Neither an asset nor a liability	30	17.3	159	14.8	39	7.5	2	3.5	230	12.6
Minor liability	17	9.9	80	7.5	33	6.3	4	6.9	134	7.3
Major liability	5	2.9	14	1.2	5	1.0	0	0.0	24	1.4
Total	173	100.0	1074	100.0	523	100.0	58	100.0	1828	100.0

Table 9.13   Student Behavior: Perceived Value to Schools

Opinions	District enrollment									
	Fewer than 300		300–2,999		3,000–24,999		25,000 or more		All	
	f	%	f	%	f	%	f	%	f	%
Major asset	81	46.6	487	45.1	236	45.3	25	43.1	829	46.3
Minor asset	41	23.6	311	28.8	135	25.9	15	25.9	502	27.4
Neither an asset nor a liability	30	17.2	194	18.0	92	17.7	11	19.0	327	17.8
Minor liability	18	10.3	83	7.7	53	10.1	7	12.1	161	8.8
Major liability	4	2.3	4	0.4	5	1.0	0	0.0	13	0.7
Total	174	100.0	1079	100.0	521	100.0	58	100.0	1832	100.0

Table 9.14   Employee Behavior: Perceived Value to Schools

Opinions	District enrollment									
	Fewer than 300		300–2,999		3,000–24,999		25,000 or more		All	
	f	%	f	%	f	%	f	%	f	%
Major asset	85	48.9	417	38.8	228	43.6	32	55.2	762	41.7
Minor asset	38	21.8	330	30.7	157	30.0	16	27.6	541	29.6
Neither an asset nor a liability	28	16.1	190	17.7	84	16.1	6	10.3	308	16.8
Minor liability	21	12.1	120	11.2	48	9.2	4	6.9	193	10.5
Major liability	2	1.1	17	1.6	6	1.1	0	0.0	25	1.4
Total	174	100.0	1074	100.0	523	100.0	58	100.0	1829	100.0

Table 9.15   School Board Member Behavior: Perceived Value to Schools

Opinions	District enrollment									
	Fewer than 300		300–2,999		3,000–24,999		25,000 or more		All	
	f	%	f	%	f	%	f	%	f	%
Major asset	74	42.8	495	45.9	248	47.9	32	55.2	849	46.4
Minor asset	43	24.9	279	25.9	123	23.8	9	15.5	454	24.8
Neither an asset nor a liability	27	15.6	139	12.9	50	9.7	5	8.6	221	12.1
Minor liability	19	11.0	116	10.8	59	11.4	8	13.8	202	11.1
Major liability	10	5.7	49	4.5	38	7.2	4	6.9	101	5.6
Total	173	100.0	1078	100.0	518	100.0	58	100.0	1827	100.0

majority of respondents indicated that the district's teaching staff (94.2%) and the district's nonprofessional support staff (90.2%) were either *major* or *minor assets*. Opinion data regarding the value of teachers and nonprofessional employees are in Tables 9.17 and 9.18 respectively.

Parental/Family Support for Students

Extant literature is replete with studies demonstrating that parental/family support is a critical factor in student success. Just over three-fourths of the respondents (78.5%) indicated that this variable was either a *major* or *minor asset* in their districts. Opinion data regarding the value of parental/family support for students are in Table 9.19.

Table 9.16   Administrative Staff: Perceived Value to Schools

Opinions	District enrollment									
	Fewer than 300		300–2,999		3,000–24,999		25,000 or more		All	
	f	%	f	%	f	%	f	%	f	%
Major asset	98	56.7	733	68.3	416	79.5	40	70.2	1287	70.4
Minor asset	38	22.0	279	26.0	87	16.6	12	21.1	416	22.7
Neither an asset nor a liability	30	17.3	45	4.2	12	2.3	4	7.0	91	5.0
Minor liability	7	4.0	16	1.4	6	1.2	1	1.7	30	1.6
Major liability	0	0.0	1	0.1	2	0.4	0	0.0	3	0.2
Total	173	100.0	1074	100.0	523	100.0	57	100.0	1827	100.0

Table 9.17   Teaching Staff: Perceived Value to Schools

Opinions	District enrollment									
	Fewer than 300		300–2,999		3,000–24,999		25,000 or more		All	
	f	%	f	%	f	%	f	%	f	%
Major asset	109	63.7	694	64.5	385	74.5	41	70.7	1229	67.5
Minor asset	41	24.0	323	30.0	109	21.1	13	22.4	486	26.7
Neither an asset nor a liability	14	8.2	36	3.4	11	2.1	3	5.2	64	3.5
Minor liability	6	3.5	21	2.0	9	1.7	1	1.7	37	2.0
Major liability	1	0.6	2	0.2	3	0.6	0	0.0	6	0.3
Total	171	100.0	1076	100.0	517	100.0	58	100.0	1822	100.0

Table 9.18   Nonprofessional Support Staff: Perceived Value to Schools

Opinions	District enrollment									
	Fewer than 300		300–2,999		3,000–24,999		25,000 or more		All	
	f	%	f	%	f	%	f	%	f	%
Major asset	96	55.8	584	54.1	323	62.1	37	63.8	1040	56.7
Minor asset	46	26.7	395	36.6	155	29.8	16	27.6	612	33.5
Neither an asset nor a liability	19	11.1	61	5.7	29	5.6	4	6.9	113	6.3
Minor liability	10	5.8	35	3.2	12	2.3	1	1.7	58	3.2
Major liability	1	0.6	4	0.4	1	0.2	0	0.0	6	0.3
Total	172	100.0	1079	100.0	520	100.0	58	100.0	1829	100.0

Athletic Programs

Although athletic programs provide opportunities for learning and personal development outside the classroom, they often are the source of political tensions. Disgruntled groups may seek to influence the funding, personnel, and eligibility decisions. Nevertheless, a substantial majority of respondents in this study (84.7%) said that athletics were either a *major* or *minor asset*. Opinion data regarding the value of athletic programs are in Table 9.20.

Federal, State, and Local Funding, Mandates, and Standards

Federal Government

The superintendents were asked to state their opinions regarding three aspects of federal involvement in public elementary and secondary education: federal funding, federal mandates and accountability

Table 9.19   Parental/Family Support: Perceived Value to Schools

Opinions	District enrollment									
	Fewer than 300		300–2,999		3,000–24,999		25,000 or more		All	
	f	%	f	%	f	%	f	%	f	%
Major asset	68	39.1	401	37.4	231	44.4	29	50.0	729	39.9
Minor asset	65	37.4	428	39.9	195	37.5	17	29.3	705	38.6
Neither an asset nor a liability	13	7.5	99	9.2	34	6.5	2	3.5	148	8.1
Minor liability	19	10.9	122	11.4	43	8.3	9	15.5	193	10.6
Major liability	9	5.2	22	2.1	17	3.3	1	1.7	49	2.8
Total	174	100.0	1072	100.0	520	100.0	58	100.0	1824	100.0

Table 9.20   Athletic Programs: Perceived Value to Schools

Opinions	District enrollment									
	Fewer than 300		300–2,999		3,000–24,999		25,000 or more		All	
	f	%	f	%	f	%	f	%	f	%
Major asset	60	34.5	439	40.9	246	47.5	30	51.7	775	42.5
Minor asset	71	40.8	470	43.8	210	40.5	19	32.8	770	42.2
Neither an asset nor a liability	28	16.1	118	11.0	45	8.7	9	15.5	200	11.0
Minor liability	10	5.8	38	3.5	14	2.7	0	0.0	62	3.4
Major liability	5	2.8	8	0.8	3	0.6	0	0.0	16	0.9
Total	174	100.0	1073	100.0	518	100.0	58	100.0	1823	100.0

standards, and the No Child Left Behind Act (NCLB). Historically, the erosion of local autonomy felt by many superintendents has been well documented (e.g., Björk & Gurley, 2005; Faber, 1991; Fuhrman, Clune, & Elmore, 1991), and these concerns relate to both the federal and state involvement. Further, responses on funding need to be considered in light of prevailing economic conditions. A recent study by McCord and Ellerson (2009), for example, reported that 75% of the superintendents said that dwindling resources had required them to make significant budget cuts, to sacrifice essential programs and services. Collectively, superintendents responding in this study reported eliminating more than 17,500 jobs.

Substantially more superintendents viewed federal funding as either a *major* or *minor liability* (55.3%) than those who viewed it as a *major* or *minor asset* (35.8%). Opinion data regarding federal funding are in Table 9.21.

Opinions regarding the value of federal mandates and accountability standards were even more negative. Only 14.9% thought they were either a *major* or *minor asset*, whereas 74.5% thought they were a *major* or *minor liability*. Opinion data regarding federal mandates and accountability standards are in Table 9.22.

Table 9.21   Federal Funding: Perceived Value to Schools

Opinions	District enrollment									
	Fewer than 300		*300–2,999*		*3,000–24,999*		*25,000 or more*		*All*	
	f	*%*	*f*	*%*	*f*	*%*	*f*	*%*	*f*	*%*
Major asset	31	17.9	132	12.2	66	12.6	15	25.9	244	13.3
Minor asset	34	19.7	248	23.0	118	22.6	12	20.7	412	22.5
Neither an asset nor a liability	16	9.3	92	8.5	50	9.6	6	10.3	164	8.9
Minor liability	45	26.0	272	25.2	135	25.9	14	24.1	466	25.5
Major liability	47	27.1	334	31.1	153	29.3	11	19.0	545	29.8
Total	173	100.0	1078	100.0	522	100.0	58	100.0	1831	100.0

Table 9.22   Federal Mandates and Accountability Standards: Perceived Value to Schools

Opinions	District enrollment									
	Fewer than 300		*300–2,999*		*3,000–24,999*		*25,000 or more*		*All*	
	f	*%*	*f*	*%*	*f*	*%*	*f*	*%*	*f*	*%*
Major asset	3	1.7	26	2.4	18	3.6	3	5.2	50	2.7
Minor asset	16	9.2	118	11.0	76	14.6	12	20.7	222	12.2
Neither an asset nor a liability	26	14.9	104	9.7	57	11.0	6	10.3	193	10.6
Minor liability	46	26.4	368	34.3	168	32.3	19	32.8	601	32.9
Major liability	83	47.6	457	42.6	201	38.7	18	31.0	759	41.6
Total	174	100.0	1073	100.0	520	100.0	58	100.0	1825	100.0

Opinions about NCLB were quite negative. Nearly two-thirds of the superintendents (64.4%) said that the detriments associated with this law have been *far greater* or *slightly greater* than the benefits. Opinion data regarding the benefits of NCLB are in Table 9.23.

State Government

Respondents were asked to state their opinions regarding state funding and state mandates and accountability standards. Approximately two-thirds said that state funding was a liability with 55.2% indicating that it was a *major liability*. Conversely, 25% said that state funding was either a *major* or *minor asset*. Opinion data regarding state funding are in Table 9.24.

Opinions expressed about state mandates and accountability standards were similar to those expressed for state funding. About one-fourth of the respondents (24.2%) viewed the mandates and standards as either a *major* or *minor asset*, whereas 62.8% viewed them as a *major* or *minor liability*. Opinion data regarding state mandates and accountability standards are in Table 9.25.

Local Funding

Despite litigation and subsequent reform legislation, many school districts continue to receive a substantial portion of their revenues from local taxes, primarily the ad valorem property tax. Respondents were asked to state their opinion on the value of local funding. The results were mixed. Half (50.9%) considered local funding to be either a *major* or *minor asset*, whereas 35.8% considered it to be a *major* or *minor liability*. Dissimilarities among state funding formulas and dissimilarities in state aid within individual states obviously temper opinions on this matter. Opinion data on the value of local funding are in Table 9.26.

Table 9.23   No Child Left Behind Act: Perceived Value to Schools

Opinions	District enrollment									
	Fewer than 300		*300–2,999*		*3,000–24,999*		*25,000 or more*		*All*	
	f	*%*	*f*	*%*	*f*	*%*	*f*	*%*	*f*	*%*
Detriments have been far greater than benefits	63	36.8	385	35.8	179	34.7	16	28.6	643	35.4
Detriments have been slightly greater than benefits	50	29.2	301	28.0	161	31.3	15	26.8	527	29.0
Benefits have been slightly greater than detriments	50	29.2	329	30.6	135	26.2	18	32.1	532	29.3
Benefits have been far greater than the detriments	8	4.8	60	5.6	40	7.8	7	12.5	115	6.3
Total	171	100.0	1075	100.0	515	100.0	56	100.0	1817	100.0

Table 9.24   State Funding: Perceived Value to Schools

Opinions	District enrollment									
	Fewer than 300		300–2,999		3,000–24,999		25,000 or more		All	
	f	%	f	%	f	%	f	%	f	%
Major asset	34	19.7	174	16.2	66	12.6	16	27.6	290	15.8
Minor asset	17	9.8	107	9.9	42	8.1	2	3.5	168	9.2
Neither an asset nor a liability	13	7.5	40	3.7	18	3.5	1	1.7	72	4.0
Minor liability	30	17.3	166	15.4	85	16.3	8	13.8	289	15.8
Major liability	79	45.7	589	54.7	311	59.6	31	53.5	1010	55.2
Total	173	100.0	1076	100.0	522	100.0	58	100.0	1829	100.0

Table 9.25   State Mandates and Accountability Standards: Perceived Value to Schools

Opinions	District enrollment									
	Fewer than 300		300–2,999		3,000–24,999		25,000 or more		All	
	f	%	f	%	f	%	f	%	f	%
Major asset	4	2.3	56	5.3	39	7.6	3	5.2	102	5.7
Minor asset	27	15.8	168	16.0	118	23.1	18	31.6	331	18.5
Neither an asset nor a liability	23	13.5	141	13.4	60	11.7	9	15.8	233	13.0
Minor liability	62	36.3	362	34.5	141	27.6	14	24.6	576	32.3
Major liability	55	32.1	323	30.8	153	30.0	13	22.8	544	30.5
Total	171	100.0	1050	100.0	511	100.0	57	100.0	1789	100.0

Table 9.26   Local Funding: Perceived Value to Schools

Opinions	District enrollment									
	Fewer than 300		300–2,999		3,000–24,999		25,000 or more		All	
	f	%	f	%	f	%	f	%	f	%
Major asset	57	33.3	343	32.0	165	32.0	17	29.3	582	32.0
Minor asset	34	19.9	204	19.1	94	18.3	11	19.0	343	18.9
Neither an asset nor a liability	33	19.3	147	13.7	55	10.7	7	12.1	242	13.3
Minor liability	18	10.5	171	16.0	87	16.9	5	8.6	281	15.5
Major liability	29	17.0	206	19.2	114	22.1	18	31.0	367	20.3
Total	171	100.0	1071	100.0	515	100.0	58	100.0	1815	100.0

Legal Interventions

Especially during the last half of the previous century, the courts became a political force in setting education policy. Superintendents were asked to state their opinion about the value of legal interventions. More than half (56.8%) said it was *neither an asset nor a liability*; only 9.4% indicated that it was either a *major* or *minor asset*. Opinion data on the value of legal interventions are in Table 9.27.

Legislative Position Taken by AASA

As an advocate for public education and superintendents, AASA takes positions on important legislative matters. Respondents were asked to state their opinions about these positions. Just over half (52.6%) felt that the positions were politically balanced. A small percentage thought the positions were *too conservative* (5%), and a small percentage (6.4%) thought they were *too liberal*. Opinion data on the value of ASSA's legislative positions are in Table 9.28.

Summary

As one ponders the changing role of superintendents, whether it is framed by the five propositions of Bolman and Deal (1997) or by a more nuanced definition of the emerging political leadership role of superintendents, the data presented in this chapter help build a clear image of where that role is headed. Several summary statements appear to be supported by the survey data:

- Superintendents saw the reform movement, including standards and assessment, as empowering increasing numbers of individuals; organized political action for matters related to curriculum, instruction, and reform, however, was reported generating comparatively less organized political action.
- Superintendents willingly worked with politically empowered individuals. They were less likely to consider coalitions of like-minded, empowered individuals (e.g., unions) as an asset.
- Superintendents recognized that the intensity of political action was associated with district size (enrollment); though political action occurred across all districts, it was reported more often by superintendents of large districts.

Table 9.27   Legal Interventions: Perceived Value to Schools

Opinions	District enrollment									
	Fewer than 300		300–2,999		3,000–24,999		25,000 or more		All	
	f	%	f	%	f	%	f	%	f	%
Major asset	1	0.6	13	1.2	17	3.3	0	0.0	31	1.7
Minor asset	14	8.1	85	7.9	39	7.5	4	6.9	142	7.7
Neither an asset nor a liability	124	72.1	632	58.7	254	48.6	29	50.0	1039	56.8
Minor liability	27	15.7	276	25.6	157	30.0	21	36.2	481	26.2
Major liability	6	3.5	71	6.6	56	10.6	4	6.9	137	7.6
Total	172	100.0	1077	100.0	523	100.0	58	100.0	1830	100.0

Table 9.28   Legislative Positions Taken by AASA: Perceived Value to Schools

Opinions	District enrollment									
	Fewer than 300		300–2,999		3,000–24,999		25,000 or more		All	
	f	%	f	%	f	%	f	%	f	%
Too conservative	5	2.9	57	5.3	26	5.0	4	6.9	92	5.0
Too liberal	9	5.2	78	7.3	30	5.8	0	0.0	117	6.4
Balanced politically	68	39.1	529	49.3	324	62.2	39	67.2	960	52.6
Unaware of the positions taken	54	31.0	243	22.6	81	15.5	9	15.5	387	21.2
Aware of the positions taken but have no opinion	38	21.8	167	15.5	60	11.5	6	10.4	271	14.8
Total	174	100.0	1074	100.0	521	100.0	58	100.0	1827	100.0

- Superintendents considered community involvement and parent/family support as essential in relation to forging district missions and visions.
- Superintendents, regardless of the size of the student enrollment, viewed employee groups as assets for building a productive district culture.
- Superintendents generally did not view competition from charter and private schools as a liability for their districts.
- Superintendents, particularly in large districts, viewed diversity as an asset, but at the same time, they acknowledged the negative impact of racial tensions.
- Superintendents perceived the loss of local autonomy caused by state and federal standards and assessments and court interventions to be more of a liability than an asset.
- Superintendents saw inadequate funding as a major problem.
- Superintendents viewed the legislative positions taken by AASA generally as representing a balanced political view and meeting their needs.

References

Achilles, C. M., & Lintz, M. N. (1983). *Public confidence in public education: A growing concern in the 80s.* Paper presented at the annual meeting of the Mid-South Educational Research Association, Nashville, TN.

Anyon, J. (2005). What "counts" as educational policy? Notes toward a new paradigm. *Harvard Educational Review, 75*(1), 65–88.

Baker, B., Orr, M. T., & Young, M. D. (2007). Academic drift, institutional production, and professional distribution of graduate degrees in educational leadership. *Educational Administration Quarterly, 43*(3), 279–318.

Bauman, P. C. (1996). *Governing education: Public sector reform or privatization.* Boston: Allyn & Bacon.

Bell, T. H. (1988). *The thirteenth man.* New York: Free Press.

Berliner, D. C. (2006). Our impoverished view of educational research. *Teachers College Record, 108*(6), 949–995.

Beverage, L. H. (2003). *Inhibiting factors to effectiveness and the adaptability of new superintendents in Virginia.* PhD diss., University of Virginia, Charlottesville.

Björk, L. G. (2001). Institutional barriers to educational reform: A superintendent's role in district decentralization. In C. C. Brunner & L. G. Björk (Eds.), *The new superintendency* (pp. 205–228). New York: JAI.

Björk, L. G., & Gurley, D. K. (2005). Superintendent as educational statesman and political strategist. In L. G. Björk & T. J. Kowalski (Eds.), *The contemporary superintendent: Preparation, practice, and development* (pp. 163–185). Thousand Oaks, CA: Corwin.

Björk, L. G., & Keedy, J. (2001). Politics and the superintendency in the U.S.A.: Restructuring in-service education. *Journal of In-Service Education, 27*(2), 275–302.

Björk, L. G., Kowalski, T. J., & Browne-Ferrigno, T. (2005). Learning theory and research: A framework for changing superintendent preparation and development. In L. G. Björk & T. J. Kowalski (Eds.), *The contemporary superintendent: Preparation, practice, and development* (pp. 71–106). Thousand Oaks, CA: Corwin.

Björk, L. G., Kowalski, T. J., & Young, M. (2005). National education reform reports: Implications for professional preparation and development. In L. G. Björk & T. J. Kowalski (Eds.), *The contemporary superintendent: Preparation, practice, and development* (pp. 45–70). Thousand Oaks, CA: Corwin.

Björk, L., & Lindle, J. C. (2001). Superintendent and interest groups. *Educational Policy, 15*(1), 76–91.

Blase, J., & Anderson, G. (1995). *The micropolitics of educational leadership: From control to empowerment.* New York: Teachers College Press.

Blount, J. (1998). *Destined to rule the schools: Women and the superintendency, 1873–1995.* Albany: State University of New York Press.

Blumberg, A. (1985). *The school superintendent: Living with conflict.* New York: Teachers College Press.

Bolman, L. G., & Deal, T. E. (1997). *Reframing organizations: Artistry, choice, and leadership.* San Francisco: Jossey-Bass.

Boyd, W. L. (1976). The public, the professionals, and educational policy: Who governs? *Teachers College Record, 77*(4), 539–578.

Broad Foundation & Thomas B. Fordham Institute. (2003). *Better leaders for America's schools: A manifesto.* Los Angeles: Author.

Brunner, C. C. (1999). *Sacred dreams: Women and the superintendency.* Albany: State University of New York Press.

Brunner, C. C. (2003). Invisible, limited, and emerging discourse: Research practices that restrict and/or increase access for women and people of color to the superintendency. *Journal of School Leadership, 13*(4), 428–450.

Brunner, C. C., & Grogan, M. (2007). *Women leading school systems: Uncommon roads to fulfillment.* Lanham, MD: Rowman & Littlefield Education.

Brunner, C. C., Grogan, M., & Björk, L. (2002). Shifts in the discourse defining the superintendency: Historical and current foundations of the position. In J. Murphy (Ed.), *The educational leadership challenge: Redefining leadership for the 21st century* (pp. 211–238). Chicago: University of Chicago Press.

Burgoon, J. K., & Hale, J. L. (1984). The fundamental topoi of relational communication. *Communication Monographs, 51,* 193–214.

Burroughs, W. A. (1974). *Cities and schools in the gilded age.* Port Washington, NY: Kennikat.

Callahan, R. E. (1962). *Education and the cult of efficiency: A study of the social forces that have shaped the administration of public schools.* Chicago: University of Chicago Press.

Callahan, R. E. (1966). *The superintendent of schools: A historical analysis.* (ERIC Document Reproduction Service No. ED 010 410)

Canales, M. T., Tejeda-Delgado, C., & Slate, J. R. (2010). Superintendents/principals in small rural school districts: A qualitative study. *International Journal of Educational Leadership Preparation, 5*(1). Retrieved from http://cnx .org/content/m33853/latest

Carlson, R. (1969). *Career and place bound superintendents: Some psychological differences.* (ERIC Document Reproduction Service No. ED 031 781)

Carter, G. R., & Cunningham, W. G. (1997). *The American school superintendent: Leading in an age of pressures.* San Francisco: Jossey-Bass.

Chen, Chen-Su. (2009). *Numbers and types of public elementary and secondary local education agencies from the common core of data: School year 2007–08.* NCES 2010-306. Washington, DC: National Center for Education Statistics, Institute of Education Sciences, U.S. Department of Education. Retrieved from http://nces.ed.gov/ pubs2010/2010306/findings.asp

Clampitt, P. G. (1991). *Communicating for managerial effectiveness.* Newbury Park, CA: Sage.

Clark, D. L. (1989). Time to say enough! *Agenda, 1*(1), 1, 4.

Clark, D. L. (1999). Searching for authentic educational leadership in university graduate programs and with public school colleagues. In J. Murphy & P. B. Forsyth (Eds.), *Educational administration: A decade of reform* (pp. 228–236). Thousand Oaks, CA: Corwin.

Coleman, D. G., & Brockmeier, J. (1997). A mission possible: Relevant mission statements. *School Administrator, 54*(5), 36–37.

Collier, V. (1987). *Identification of skills perceived by Texas superintendents as necessary for successful job performance.* PhD diss., University of Texas, Austin.

Conley, D. T. (2003). *Who governs our schools? Changing roles and responsibilities.* New York: Teachers College Press.

Connelly, V., & Rosenberg, M. S. (2003). *The development of teaching as a profession: Comparison with careers that achieve full professional standing.* Gainesville: Center on Personnel Studies in Special Education, University of Florida.

Cooper, B. S., & Boyd, W. L. (1987). The evolution of training for school administrators. In J. Murphy & P. Hallinger (Eds.), *Approaches to administrative training in education* (pp. 3–27). Albany: State University of New York Press.

Cooper, B. S., Fusarelli, L. D., Jackson, B. L., & Poster, J. (2002). Is "superintendent preparation" an oxymoron? Analyzing changes in programs, certification, and control. *Leadership and Policy in Schools, 1*(3), 242–255.

Cooper, B. S., Fusarelli, L. D., & Randall, F. V. (2004). *Better policies, better schools: Theories and applications.* Boston: Allyn & Bacon.

Council of the Great City Schools. (2008–2009). Urban school superintendents: Characteristics, tenure, and salary. *Urban Indicator, 10*(Winter), 1–11.

Cox, E. P. (2006). Pay for performance contract provisions for school superintendents. *AASA Journal of Scholarship and Practice, 2*(4), 31–38.

Cuban, L. (1976). *The urban school superintendent: A century and a half of change.* Bloomington, IN: Phi Delta Kappa Educational Foundation.

Cuban, L. (1988). How schools change reforms: Redefining reform success and failure. *Teachers College Record, 99*(3), 453–477.

Cubberley, E. P. (1924). *Public school administration.* Boston: Houghton Mifflin.

Cunningham, L., & Hentges, J. (1982). *The American school superintendency 1982: A summary report.* Arlington, VA: American Association of School Administrators.

Cunningham, W. G., & Cordeiro, P. A. (2006). *Educational leadership: A problem based approach* (3rd ed.). Columbus, OH: Pearson.

Currall, S. C., Towler, A. J., Judge, T. A., & Kohn, L. (2005). Pay satisfaction and organizational outcomes. *Personnel Psychology, 58*, 613–640.

Dana, J. A., & Bourisaw, D. M. (2006). Overlooked leaders. *American School Board Journal, 193*(6), 27–30.

Danzberger, J. P., Kirst, M. W., & Usdan, M. D. (1992). *Governing public schools: New times, new requirements.* Washington, DC: Institute for Educational Leadership.

Davis, S. H. (1998). Why do principals get fired? *Principal, 28*(2), 34–39.

Derrington, M. L., & Sharratt, G. C. (2009). Self-imposed barriers. *School Administrator, 66*(8), 18, 21.

DeYoung, A. J. (1986). Excellence in education: The opportunity for school superintendents to become ambitious? *Educational Administration Quarterly, 22*(2), 91–113.

DiPaola, M. (2007). Revisiting superintendent evaluation: Do you and your school board members view it as an event or a continuous process? *The School Administrator, 6*, 64. Retrieved from www.aasa.org/SchoolAdministratorArticle.aspx?id=6672

Drucker, P. F. (1999). *Management challenges for the 21st century.* New York: HarperCollins.

Eaton, W. E. (1990). The vulnerability of school superintendents: The thesis reconsidered. In W. E. Eaton (Ed.), *Shaping the superintendency: A reexamination of Callahan and the cult of efficiency* (pp. 11–35). New York: Teachers College Press.

Elmore, R. F. (2007). Education: A "profession" in search of practice. *Teaching in Educational Administration, 15*(1), 1–4.

Faber, C. F. (1991). Is local control of the schools still a viable option? *Harvard Journal of Law and Public Policy, 14*(1), 447–482.

Feistritzer, C. E. (2003). *Certification of public-school administrators.* Washington, DC: National Center for Education Information.

Fix, M., & Passel, J. S. (2003). *U.S. immigration: Trends and implications for schools.* Presentation at the National Association for Bilingual Education NCLB Implementation Institute, New Orleans, LA.

Foskett, N., Lumby, J., & Fidler, B. (2005). Evolution or extinction? Reflections on the future of research in educational leadership and management. *Educational Management, Administration, and Leadership, 33*(2), 245–253.

Fowler, F. C. (2000). *Policy studies for educational leaders: An introduction.* Upper Saddle River, NJ: Prentice Hall.

Fuhrman, S., Clune, W., & Elmore, R. (1991). Research on education reform: Lessons on the implementation of policy. In A. Odden (Ed.), *Education policy implementation* (pp. 197–218). Albany: State University of New York Press.

Fullan, M. (1994). *Change forces: Probing the depths of educational reform.* Philadelphia: Falmer.

Fullan, M. (2001). *Leading in a culture of change.* San Francisco: Jossey-Bass.

Fusarelli, B. C. (2005). When generals or colonels become superintendents. In G. J. Petersen & L. D. Fusarelli (Eds.), *The politics of leadership: Superintendents and school boards in changing times* (pp. 117–134). Greenwich, CT: Information Age.

Fusarelli, B. C., & Cooper, B. S. (2009). *The rising state: How state power is transforming our nation's schools.* Albany: State University of New York Press.

Fusarelli, B. C., & Fusarelli, L. D. (2005). Reconceptualizing the superintendency: Superintendents as applied social scientists and social activists. In L. G. Björk & T. J. Kowalski (Eds.), *The contemporary superintendent: Preparation, practice, and development* (pp. 187–206). Thousand Oaks, CA: Corwin.

Gee, E. G., & Daniel, P. T. K. (2009). *Law and public education: Cases and materials* (4th ed.). Newark, NJ: LexisNexis Matthew Bender.

Gideon, B. H. (2002). Structuring schools for teacher collaboration. *Education Digest, 68*(2), 30–34.

Gilland, T. M. (1935). *The origins and development of the powers and duties of city-school superintendents.* Chicago: University of Chicago Press.

Glass, T. E. (1992). *The study of the American superintendency: America's education leaders at a time of reform.* Arlington, VA: American Association of School Administrators.

Glass, T. E., Björk, L., & Brunner, C. C. (2000). *The study of the American school superintendency, 2000: A look at the superintendent of education in the new millennium.* Arlington, VA: American Association of School Administrators.

Glass, T. E., & Franceschini, L. A. (2007). *The state of the American school superintendency: A mid-decade study.* Lanham, MD: Rowman & Littlefield Education.

Goodman, G., & Young, I. P. (2006). The value of extracurricular support in increased student achievement. *Educational Research Quarterly, 30*(1), 3–13.

Grady, M., Ourada-Sieb, T., & Wesson, L. (1994). Women's perceptions of the superintendency. *Journal of School Leadership, 4*(2), 156–170.

Grogan, M. (1996). *Voices of women aspiring to the superintendency.* Albany: State University of New York Press.

Grogan, M. (2008). The short tenure of a woman superintendent: A clash of gender and politics. *Journal of School Leadership, 18*(6), 634–660.

Grogan, M., & Andrews, R. (2002). Defining preparation and professional development for the future. *Educational Administration Quarterly, 38*(2), 233–256.

Grunig, J. E. (1989). Symmetrical presuppositions as a framework for public relations theory. In C. H. Botan (Ed.), *Public relations theory* (pp. 17–44). Hillsdale, NJ: Lawrence Erlbaum Associates.

Guthrie, J. W., & Sanders, T. (2001, January 7). Who will lead the public schools? *New York Times.*

Guthrie, J. W., & Schuermann, P. J. (2010). *Successful school leadership: Planning, politics, performance, and power.* Boston: Allyn & Bacon.

Gutmann, A. (1987). *Democratic education.* Princeton, NJ: Princeton University Press.

Guzley, R. (1992). Organizational climate and communication climate: Predictors of commitment to the organization. *Management Communication Quarterly, 5*(4), 379–402.

Hale, E. L., & Moorman, H. N. (2003). *Preparing school principals: A national perspective on policy and program innovations.* Washington, DC: Institute for Educational Leadership.

Hawley, W. D. (1988). Missing pieces in the educational reform agenda: Or, why the first and second waves may miss the boat. *Educational Administration Quarterly, 24*(4), 416–437.

Heck, R. H., & Hallinger, P. (2005). The study of educational leadership and management: Where does the field stand today? *Educational Management, Administration, and Leadership, 33*(2), 229–244.

Heneman, H. G., & Judge, T. A. (2006). *Staffing organizations* (6th ed.). Middleton, WI: Mendota.

Hess, F. M. (2003). *A license to lead: A new leadership agenda for America's schools.* Washington, DC: Progressive Policy Institute.

Hodgkinson, H., & Montenegro, X. (1999). *The U.S. school superintendent: The invisible CEO.* Washington, DC: Institute for Educational Leadership.

Howlett, P. (1993). The politics of school leaders, past and future. *Education Digest, 58*(9), 18–21.

Hoy, W. K. (1996). Science and theory in the practice of educational administration: A pragmatic perspective. *Educational Administration Quarterly, 32*(3), 366–378.

Hoy, W. K., & Miskel, C. G. (2008). *Educational administration: Theory, research, and practice* (8th ed.). New York: McGraw-Hill.

Johnson, J. A., Collins, H. W., Dupuis, V. L., & Johnson, J. H. (1988). *Introduction to the foundations of American education* (7th ed.). Boston: Allyn & Bacon.

Johnson, S. M., & Papay, J. P. (2010). Expecting too much of performance pay? *The School Administrator, 67*(3), 22–27.

Jones, E., & Montenegro, X. (1990). *Women and minorities in school administration.* Arlington, VA: American Association of School Administrators.

Joyce, B., & Murphy, C. (1990). Epilogue: The curious complexities of cultural change. In B. Joyce (Ed.), *Changing school culture through staff development* (pp. 243–250). Alexandria, VA: Association for Supervision and Curriculum Development.

Kalbus, J. C. (2000). Path to the superintendency. *Urban Education, 35*(5), 549–556.

Katz, M. (1971). *Class, bureaucracy, and schools: The illusion of educational change in America.* New York: Praeger.

Keedy, J. L., & Björk, L. G. (2002). Superintendents and local boards and the potential for community polarization: The call for use of political strategist skills. In B. Cooper and L. Fusarelli (Eds.), *The promises and perils facing today's school superintendent* (pp. 103–128). Lanham, MD: Scarecrow.

Kellogg Foundation. (1961). *Toward improved school administration: A decade of professional effort to heighten administrative understanding and skills.* Battle Creek, MI: Author.

Kirst, M. W. (1988). Recent state education reform in the United States: Looking backward and forward. *Educational Administration Quarterly, 24*(3), 319–328.

Kowalski, T. J. (1995). *Keepers of the flame: Contemporary urban superintendents.* Thousand Oaks, CA: Corwin.

Kowalski, T. J. (2001). The future of local school governance: Implications for board members and superintendents. In C. Brunner & L. Björk (Eds.), *The new superintendency* (pp. 183–201). Oxford: JAI, Elsevier Science.

Kowalski, T. J. (2004). The ongoing war for the soul of school administration. In T. J. Lasley (Ed.), *Better leaders for America's schools: Perspectives on the manifesto* (pp. 92–114). Columbia, MO: University Council for Educational Administration.

Kowalski, T. J. (2005). Evolution of the school superintendent as communicator. *Communication Education, 54*(2), 101–117.

Kowalski, T. J. (2006). *The school superintendent: Theory, practice, and cases* (2nd ed.). Thousand Oaks, CA: Sage.

Kowalski, T. J. (2008a). Preparing and licensing superintendents in three contiguous states. *Planning and Changing, 39,* 240–260.

Kowalski, T. J. (2008b). *Public relations in schools* (4th ed.). Boston: Allyn & Bacon.

Kowalski, T. J. (2009). Need to address evidence-based practice in educational administration. *Educational Administration Quarterly, 45,* 375–423.

Kowalski, T. J. (2010). *The school principal: Visionary leadership and competent management.* New York: Routledge.

Kowalski, T. J. (2011). *Public relations in schools* (5th ed.). Boston: Allyn & Bacon.

Kowalski, T. J., & Brunner, C. C. (2005). The school superintendent: Roles, challenges, and issues. In F. English (Ed.), *Handbook of educational leadership* (pp. 142–167). Thousand Oaks, CA: Sage.

Kowalski, T. J., Petersen, G. J., & Fusarelli, L. D. (2007). *Effective communication for school administrators: A necessity in an information age.* Lanham, MD: Rowman & Littlefield.

Kowalski, T. J., Petersen, G. J., & Fusarelli, L. D. (2009). Novice superintendents and the efficacy of professional preparation. *AASA Journal of Scholarship and Practice, 5*(4), 16–26.

Kowalski, T. J., Petersen, G. J., & Fusarelli, L. D. (In press). Promoting civic "public" engagement in education through distributive leadership and deliberative democracy. *Leadership and Policy in Schools.*

Kowalski, T. J., Place, A. W., Edmister, J., & Zigler, T. (2009). Need for practice-based research in school administration. *Mid-Western Educational Researcher, 22*(4), 2–8.

Kowalski, T. J., & Sweetland, S. R. (2002). Unrestricted reemployment of retired administrators: Effective policy or cause for concern? In G. Perreault (Ed.), *The 10th annual yearbook of the National Council of Professors of Educational Administration* (pp. 312–324). Lanham, MD: Rowman & Littlefield.

Kowalski, T. J., & Sweetland, S. R. (2005). Retire-rehire policy in state pension programs for school administrators. *Planning and Changing, 36*(1 & 2), 3–22.

Kreider, R. (2008). *Current population reports: Living arrangements of children, 2004.* U.S. Census Bureau. www.census .gov/prod/2008pubs/p70-114.pdf

Lamkin, M. L. (2006). Challenges and changes faced by rural superintendents. *The Rural Educator, 48*(2), 17–25.

Larson, M. S. (1977). *The rise of professionalism: A sociological analysis.* Berkeley, CA: University of California Press.

Lawler, E. E. (1994). *Motivation in work organizations.* San Francisco: Jossey-Bass.

Leithwood, K. (1994). Leadership for school restructuring. *Educational Administration Quarterly, 30*(4), 498–518.

Levin, H. M. (1987). Education as a public and private good. *Journal of Policy Analysis and Management, 6,* 628–641.

Levin, H. M. (1999). The public-private nexus in education. *American Behavioral Scientist, 43*(1), 124–137.

Levine, A. (2005). *Educating school leaders.* Washington, DC: Education Schools Project.

Littlejohn, S. W. (1992). *Theories of human communication* (4th ed.). Belmont, CA: Wadsworth.

Loder, T. L. (2005). Women administrators negotiate work-family conflicts in changing times: An intergenerational perspective. *Educational Administration Quarterly, 41*(5), 741–776.

Luthans, F. (1981). *Organizational behavior* (3rd ed.). New York: McGraw-Hill.

Malen, B., & Cochran, M. V. (2008). Beyond pluralistic patterns of power: Research on the micropolitics of schools. In B. S. Cooper, J. G. Cibulka, & L. D. Fusarelli (Eds.), *Handbook of education politics and policy* (pp. 148–178). New York: Routledge.

Marshall, C., & Gerstl-Pepin, C. (2005). *Re-framing educational politics for social justice.* Boston: Pearson.

May, W. F. (2001). *Beleaguered rulers: The public obligation of the professional.* Louisville, KY: Westminster John Knox.

McCord, R. S., & Ellerson, N. M. (2009). *Looking back, looking forward: How the economic downturn continues to impact school districts.* Arlington, VA: American Association of School Administrators.

Melby, E. O. (1955). *Administering community education.* Englewood Cliffs, NJ: Prentice Hall.

Michener, H. A., DeLamater, J. D., & Myers, D. J. (2004). *Social psychology* (5th ed.). Belmont, CA: Wadsworth.

Morgan, C., & Petersen, G. J. (2002). The superintendent's role in leading academically effective school districts. In B. S. Cooper & L. D. Fusarelli (Eds.), *The promise and perils of the modern superintendency* (pp. 175–196). Lanham, MD: Scarecrow.

Murphy, J. (1994). The changing role of the superintendency in restructuring districts in Kentucky. *School Effectiveness and School Improvement, 5*(4), 349–375.

Murphy, J. (2002). Reculturing the profession of educational leadership: New blueprints. *Educational Administration Quarterly, 38*(2), 176–191.

Murphy, J. (2007). Questioning the core of university-based programs for preparing school leaders. *Phi Delta Kappan, 88*(8), 582–585.

National Commission on Excellence in Education. (1983). *A nation at risk: the imperative for educational reform*. Washington, DC: GPO.

National Conference of State Legislatures. (2010). *School leadership: Licensure and certification*. Retrieved April 20, 2010 from http://www.ncsl.org/default.aspx?tabid=12928

No Child Left Behind Act of 2001, Pub. L. No. 107-110, 115 Stat. 1425 (2002).

Norton, M. S., Webb, L. D., Dlugosh, L. L., & Sybouts, W. (1996). *The school superintendency: New responsibilities, new leadership*. Boston: Allyn & Bacon.

Opfer, V. D. (2005). Personalization of interest groups and the resulting policy nonsense. In G. J. Petersen & L. D. Fusarelli (Ed.), *The politics of leadership: Superintendents and school boards in changing times* (pp. 73–93). Greenwich, CT: Information Age.

Orr, M. T. (2006). Mapping innovation in leadership preparation in our nation's schools of education. *Phi Delta Kappan, 87*(7), 492–499.

Ortiz, F. I. (1982). *Career patterns in education: Women, men, and minorities in educational administration*. New York: Praeger.

Ortiz, F. I., & Ortiz, D. J. (1995). How gender and ethnicity interact in the practice of educational administration: The case of Hispanic female superintendents. In R. Donmoyer, M. Imber, & J. Scheurich (Eds.), *The knowledge base in educational administration: Multiple perspectives* (pp. 158–173). Albany: State University of New York Press.

Osterman, K. F. (1994). Communication skills: A key to collaboration and change. *Journal of School Leadership, 4*(4), 382–398.

Owings, W. A., & Kaplan, L. S. (2006). *American public school finance*. Belmont, CA: Thomson Wadsworth.

Petersen, G. J. (1999). Demonstrated actions of instructional leaders: A case study of five superintendents. *Education Policy Analysis Archives, 7*(18). Retrieved March 23, 2010, from http://epaa.asu.edu/ojs/article/view/553

Petersen, G. J. (2010). At the epicenter of educational change: Challenges and the role of professional development for executive leaders. In S. Conley & B. S. Cooper (Eds.), *Preparing tomorrow's school leaders: Growth and life cycle approaches* (pp. 171–195). Lanham, MD: Rowman & Littlefield Education.

Petersen, G. J., & Barnett, B. G. (2005). The superintendent as instructional leader: Current practice, future conceptualizations, and implications for preparation. In L. G. Björk & T. J. Kowalski (Eds.), *The contemporary superintendent: Preparation, practice, and development* (pp. 107–136). Thousand Oaks, CA: Corwin.

Petersen, G. J., & Fussarelli, L. D. (2001, November). *Changing times, changing relationships: An exploration of the relationships between superintendents and boards of education*. Paper presented at the annual meeting of the University Council for Educational Administration, Cincinnati, OH.

Petersen, G. J., Fusarelli, L. D., & Kowalski, T. J. (2008). Novice superintendent perceptions of preparation adequacy and problems of practice. *Journal of Research on Leadership Education, 3*(2), 1–16.

Petersen, G. J., & Short, P. M. (2002). An examination of the school board president's perception of the district superintendent's interpersonal communication competence and board decision making. *Journal of School Leadership, 12*(4), 411–436.

Petersen, G. J., & Williams, B. M. (2005). The board president and superintendent: An examination of influence through the eyes of the decision makers. In G. J. Petersen & L. D. Fusarelli (Eds.), *The politics of leadership: Superintendents and school boards in changing times* (pp. 23–49). Greenwich, CT: Information Age.

Peterson, M. R. (1999). *Superintendent competencies for continued employment as perceived by Louisiana public school superintendents and board presidents*. PhD diss., University of Southern Mississippi, Hattiesburg.

Planty, M., Hussar, W., Snyder, T., Provasnik, S., Kena, G., Dinkes, R., KewalRamani, A., & Kemp, J. (2008). *The condition of education, 2008* (NCES 2008-031). Washington, DC: National Center for Education Statistics, Institute of Education Sciences, U.S. Department of Education.

Renchler, R. (1992). Urban superintendent turnover: The need for stability. *Urban Superintendents' Sounding Board, 1*(1), 2–13.

Richmond, V. P., McCroskey, J. C., Davis, L. M., & Koontz, K. A. (1980). Perceived power as a mediator of management communication style and employee satisfaction: A preliminary investigation. *Communication Quarterly, 28*(4), 37–46.

Sarason, S. B. (1996). *Revisiting the culture of the school and the problem of change*. New York: Teachers College Press.

Scarpello, V., Huber, V., & Vandenberg, R. J. (1998). Compensation satisfaction: Its measurement and dimensionality. *Journal of Applied Psychology, 73*(2), 163–171.

Schein, E. H. (1996). Culture: The missing concept in organization studies. *Administrative Science Quarterly, 41*(2), 229–240.

Schneider, W. E. (1994). *The reengineering alternative: A plan for making your current culture work*. Burr Ridge, IL: Irwin Professional Publishing.

Scoolis, J. (1998). What is vision and how do you get one? *Thrust for Educational Leadership, 28*(2), 20–21.

Sergiovanni, T. J. (2006). *The principalship: A reflective practice perspective*. Boston: Pearson Education.

Sergiovanni, T. J., Burlingame, M., Coombs, F. S., & Thurston, P. W. (1999). *Educational governance and administration* (4th ed.). Boston: Allyn & Bacon.

Shakeshaft, C. (1989). *Women in educational administration* (Rev. ed.). Newbury Park, CA: Sage.

Shakeshaft, C. (1999). The struggle to create a more gender-inclusive profession. In J. Murphy & K. S. Louis (Eds.), *Handbook of research on educational administration* (pp. 98–118). Englewood Cliffs, NJ: Prentice Hall.

Sharp, W. L., & Walter, J. K. (2004). *The superintendent: The profession and the person* (2nd ed.). Lanham, MD: Scarecrow.

Simmons, J. C. (2005). Superintendents of color: Perspectives on racial and ethnic diversity and implications for professional preparation and practice. In L. G. Björk & T. J. Kowalski (Eds.), *The contemporary superintendent: Preparation, practice, and development* (pp. 251–282). Thousand Oaks, CA: Corwin.

Smoley, E. R., Jr. (1999). *Effective school boards: Strategies for improving board performance*. San Francisco: Jossey-Bass.

Snavely, W. B., & Walters, E. V. (1983). Differences in communication competence among administrative social styles. *Journal of Applied Communication Research, 11*(2), 120–135.

Snyder, T. D., Dillow, S. A., & Hoffman, C. M. (2009). *Digest of Education Statistics, 2008* (NCES 2009-020). Washington, DC: National Center for Education Statistics, Institute of Education Sciences, U.S. Department of Education.

Snyder, T. D., & Hoffman, C. M. (2003). *Digest of Education Statistics, 2002*. Washington, DC: National Center for Education Statistics, Institute of Education Sciences, U.S. Department of Education.

Spillane, R., & Regnier, P. (1998). *The superintendent of the future: Strategy and action for achieving academic excellence*. Gaithersburg, MD: Aspen.

Spring, J. (1990). *The American school: 1642–1990* (2nd ed.). New York: Longman.

Strizek, G. A., Pittsonberger, J. L., Riordan, K. E., Lyter, D. M., Orlofsky, G. F., & Gruber, K. (2006). *Characteristics of schools, districts, teachers, principals, and school libraries in the United States: 2003–04 schools and staffing survey* (NCES 2006-313 Revised). Washington, DC: National Center for Education Statistics, Institute of Education Sciences, U.S. Department of Education.

Sykes, G. (1991). In defense of teacher professionalism as a policy of choice. *Educational Policy, 5*(2), 137–149.

Thayer, L. O. (1961). *Administrative communication*. Homewood, IL: Richard D. Irwin.

Thomas, W. B., & Moran, K. J. (1992). Reconsidering the power of the superintendent in the progressive period. *American Educational Research Journal, 29*(1), 22–50.

Title VII of the Civil Rights Act of 1964. 42 U.S.C. § 1981-2000h-6.

Townsend, B. K. (2002). *Rethinking the Ed.D., or what's in a name?* Paper presented at the annual meeting of the Association for the Study of Higher Education, Sacramento, CA.

Trombetta, J. J., & Rogers, D. P. (1988). Communication climate, job satisfaction, and organizational commitment: The effects of information adequacy, communication openness, and decision participation. *Management Communication Quarterly, 1*(4), 494–514.

Tyack, D. (1972). The "One Best System": A historical analysis. In H. Walberg & A. Kopan (Eds.), *Rethinking urban education* (pp. 231–246). San Francisco: Jossey-Bass.

Tyack, D., & Hansot, E. (1982). *Managers of virtue: Public school leadership in America, 1820–1980*. New York: Basic Books.

Usdan, M. D. (2002). Reactions to articles commissioned by the National Commission for the Advancement of Educational Leadership Preparation. *Educational Administration Quarterly, 38*(2), 300–307.

U.S. Department of Education. (n.d.). *IDEA '97: The Individuals with Disabilities Education Act amendments of 1997*. Retrieved on April 14, 2010, from http://www2.ed.gov/offices/OSERS/Policy/IDEA/index.html

U.S. Department of Education, National Center for Education Statistics. (n.d.). *Percentage distribution of public elementary and secondary students, by race/ethnicity and locale: 2003–04*. Accessed at http://nces.ed.gov/pubs2007/ruraled/figures/fig1_3.asp

U.S. Department of Labor. *Title IX, education amendments of 1972*. Retrieved on April 14, 2010, from http://www.dol.gov/oasam/regs/statutes/titleix.htm

Vang, M. (2008). *Effects of student achievement on the job satisfaction of public elementary school principals: An empirical study*. PhD diss., California State University, Fresno, and University of California, Davis.

Van Meter, E. J. (1999). The persistent saga: Changing instruction and curriculum to better prepare school leaders. In J. Murphy & P. B. Forsyth (Eds.), *Educational administration: A decade of reform* (pp. 170–191). Thousand Oaks, CA: Corwin.

Van Til, W. (1971). Prologue: Is progressive education obsolete? In W. Van Til (Ed.), *Curriculum: Quest for relevance* (pp. 9–17). Boston: Houghton Mifflin.

Webb, L. D., & Norton, M. S. (2006). *Human resources administration: Personnel issues and needs in education* (4th ed.). Upper Saddle River, NJ: Merrill Prentice Hall.

Weiler, H. N. (1990). Comparative perspectives on educational decentralization: An exercise in contradiction? *Educational Evaluation and Policy Analysis, 12*(4), 433–448.

Williams, M. L., McDaniel, M. A., & Nguyen, N. T. (2006). A meta-analysis of the antecedents and consequences of pay satisfaction. *Journal of Applied Psychology, 91*(2), 392–413.

Wirt, F. M., & Kirst, M. W. (2009). *The political dynamics of American education* (4th ed.). Berkeley, CA: McCutchan.

Wise, A. (1992). The case for restructuring teacher preparation. In L. Darling-Hammond, G. A. Griffin, & A. Wise (Eds.), *Excellence in teacher education: Helping teachers develop learning-centered schools* (pp. 179–201). Washington, DC: National Education Association.

Wise, A. (1994). The coming revolution in teacher licensure: Redefining teacher preparation. *Action in Teacher Education, 16*(2), 1–13.

Young, I. P. (1997). Dimensions of employee compensation: Practical and theoretical implications for superintendents. *Educational Administration Quarterly, 33*(4), 506–525.

Young, I. P. (2003). The trouble with pay for performance. *American School Board Journal, 190*(11), 40–42.

Young, I. P. (2007). Salaries for new superintendents: A public relations concern for many school boards. *Journal of School Public Relations, 28*(2), 124–136.

Young, I. P. (2008). *The human resource function in educational administration* (9th ed.). Upper Saddle River, NJ: Prentice Hall.

Young, I. P., Reimer, D., & Young, K. H. (2010). What to pay: Effects of organizational characteristics and human capital endowments for initial salaries of female and male middle school principals. *International Journal of Educational Leadership Preparation, 5*(1).

Young, M. D. (2005). Building effective school system leadership: Rethinking preparation and policy. In G. J. Petersen & L. D. Fusarelli (Eds.), *The politics of leadership: Superintendents and school boards in changing times* (pp. 157–179). Greenwich, CT: Information Age.

Young, M. D., Petersen, G. J., & Short, P. M. (2002). The complexity of substantive reform: A call for interdependence among key stakeholders. *Educational Administration Quarterly, 38*(2), 137–175.

About the Authors

Theodore J. Kowalski is the Kuntz Family Endowed Chair and professor of educational administration at the University of Dayton. The author of 29 books and over 150 book chapters, monographs, and refereed journal articles, he is a former public school teacher, principal, superintendent, and college of education dean. Dr. Kowalski is editor of the *Journal of School Public Relations* and serves on the editorial boards of *Educational Administration Quarterly* and the *AASA Journal of Scholarship and Practice*. He has received numerous awards, including the Outstanding Faculty Research Award from Teachers College, Ball State University, the Outstanding Research Award from the School of Education and Allied Professions at the University of Dayton, and the Alumni Award for Scholarship from the University of Dayton.

Robert S. McCord is an associate professor in the Department of Educational Leadership at the University of Nevada, Las Vegas, where he codirects the Center for Education Policy Studies. His teaching and scholarship focus on education law and policy. Prior to joining the faculty of UNLV in 1999, Dr. McCord was employed for 30 years by the 300,000-student Clark County School District, where he began as a teacher and completed his service to the district as an assistant superintendent, directing school accountability and government relations. He is actively involved in professional organizations, including AASA, where he serves as professor-in-residence. In addition, he has served on the board of directors of WestEd for more than 15 years.

George J. Petersen is professor and dean of the School of Education at California Lutheran University. He is the author or coauthor of 2 books and over 100 book chapters, professional articles, research papers, monographs, and commissioned reports. Much of Dr. Petersen's scholarly work has focused on the executive leadership of district superintendents and their beliefs, roles, and work in the area of instructional leadership and policy. In recognition of his scholarship and service to the field, he was the winner of the University of California–Santa Barbara's Gevirtz School of Education Distinguished Alumni Award in 2008. Dr. Petersen's work has been widely published and internationally recognized.

I. Phillip Young is a professor of education at the University of California–Davis and is codirector of a joint doctoral program involving UC campuses and the California State University–Fresno. In the past, he has served as a professor at the University of Wisconsin–Madison and at the Ohio State University, where he held an endowed professorship in educational leadership. His areas of interest are selection/recruitment and compensation within the public school setting. Dr. Young is the author of *The Human Resource Function in Educational Administration*, he has developed compensation systems for over 60 public school districts, and his research has been published frequently in leading refereed journals.

Noelle Ellerson is the policy analyst for AASA, a position she has held since 2007. She conducts research and analysis supporting AASA's advocacy work for public education and AASA members. Additionally, she works on urban education issues for AASA membership and is responsible for AASA's survey and data programs. She regularly speaks on federal education policy to school leaders across the country. She graduated from Nazareth College of Rochester and completed a master's degree in public policy and education administration at the Rockefeller College at the University of Albany (SUNY). She recently completed the Institute for Educational Leadership Education Policy Fellowship Program.

Always Pearson Learning!

Pearson recognizes that each student has a unique path to learning and each teacher a distinctive way of reaching students. To ensure that today's students build practical, lifelong skills, we provide content, services, and technology that engage today's digital natives with assessment-driven, personalized learning, as well as professional development for new and seasoned teachers.

This commitment is demonstrated through innovative print and digital education materials for Pre-K through college, school improvement strategies, student information systems and learning management systems, career certification programs, and testing and assessment products that set the standard for the industry.

We share your goal of advancing academic achievement for all students and teachers with skills that matter in the classroom and in life.

PearsonSchool.com
800-848-9500

Copyright Pearson Education, Inc., or its affiliates. All rights reserved.

PEARSON

Breinigsville, PA USA
01 February 2011
254559BV00002B/1-168/P